Otherworldly Mothering

Otherworldly Mothering

The Maternal Grammar
of Black Women's Writing
1970–1990

MARIKA CESCHIA

LOUISIANA STATE UNIVERSITY PRESS

BATON ROUGE

Published by Louisiana State University Press
lsupress.org

Designer: Michelle A. Neustrom
Typefaces: Whitman, text; ITC Avant Garde Gothic Pro, display

Cover illustration courtesy Shutterstock/Deka Vision.

Portions of chapter 2 first appeared as "Willa's Maternal Ethics of Care in Gloria Naylor's
Linden Hills (1985)," in *USSO Studies*, March 3, 2022.

Library of Congress Cataloging-in-Publication Data

Names: Ceschia, Marika, author.
Title: Otherworldly mothering : the maternal grammar of Black women's
    writing, 1970–1990 / Marika Ceschia.
Description: Baton Rouge : Louisiana State University Press, 2024. |
    Includes bibliographical references and index.
Identifiers: LCCN 2024002002 (print) | LCCN 2024002003 (ebook) |
    ISBN 978-0-8071-8249-9 (cloth) | ISBN 978-0-8071-8295-6 (pdf) |
    ISBN 978-0-8071-8294-9 (epub)
Subjects: LCSH: American fiction—African American authors—History and
    criticism. American fiction—Women authors—History and criticism. |
    American fiction—20th century—History and criticism. | African
    American mothers in literature. | African Americans in literature. |
    Ontology in literature. | Racism in literature. | LCGFT: Literary criticism.
Classification: LCC PS153.B53 C47 2024 (print) | LCC PS153.B53 (ebook) |
    DDC 813/.54099287—dc23/eng/20240506
LC record available at https://lccn.loc.gov/2024002002
LC ebook record available at https://lccn.loc.gov/2024002003

In memory of my beloved grandparents

CONTENTS

ACKNOWLEDGMENTS

Many people have contributed to this project and helped make it better. First of all, I would like to thank Professor Andrew Warnes for his precious advice, much-needed encouragement, and patience. I send a massive "thank you" for believing in this project right from the start, offering guidance, and pushing me to pursue it.

I would like to thank Dr. Sam Durrant and Dr. Rachel Farebrother for their feedback and kind support. I thank the Quilting Points reading group at the University of Leeds, which has provided a friendly and stimulating arena for discussing some ideas related to this project. I thank all my students, my colleagues, my friends, and all the staff at the University of Leeds, who have made me feel part of a vibrant international community. Thanks for welcoming me with open arms and making me feel at home away from home.

Lastly, I would like to express my deepest gratitude to my family for their sacrifices and their unwavering love and support. I thank my father, Paolo. I know how much you care even if you do not always show it. Thanks to my brother, Matteo, for always being there and putting up with my numerous breakdowns. You have always been a lighthouse guiding me during my emotional storms. Thanks to my wonderful mother, Teresa, for having always made us your priority. I cannot fathom all the sacrifices you have made so that I could pursue my passion for literature. I owe you all much more than words can say.

Otherworldly Mothering

Introduction

In her essay "One Child of One's Own" (1983), Alice Walker notes how the white woman "fears knowing that Black women want the best for their children just as she does. But she also knows Black children are to have less in this world so that her children, white children, will have more (in some countries, all). Better then to deny that the Black woman has a vagina. Is capable of motherhood. Is a woman" (373–74). As Jennifer C. Nash has underlined, for Walker racial terror operates through a failure "to imagine Black women *as* mothers [. . .] as life-giving" (146, original italics): since its coherence depends upon such an erasure, racial terror's symbolic order sustains itself through the enforced denial of a Black maternal imaginary. But, as Nash suggests, what is denied is a specific type of maternal imaginary: one that connects the Black maternal to a life-giving power. Racial terror resignifies the Black maternal as a site of ontological annihilation, rendering it illegible as a praxis of insurgent Black social life.

Caribbean scholar Sylvia Wynter posits the existence of a similar lack of maternal imaginary in her "Afterword: Beyond Miranda's Meanings," where she interprets Shakespeare's *The Tempest* as reenacting the founding structure of the onto-epistemic order of 'Man.' While her afterword is usually discussed in relation to her theorization of "demonic ground," I want to draw attention to a pivotal, if undertheorized, aspect of her argument: maternal erasure. First published at the end of the 1980s, Wynter's essay is contemporaneous not only to Walker's but also to Hortense Spillers's "Mama's Baby, Papa's Maybe," which is similarly preoccupied with maternal erasure and displacement, a point to which I will return. While Spillers discusses it in relation to the historical context of slavery, Wynter traces the long durée of such a denial of the Black maternal, locating its origins in the 1492 arrival of Columbus in the New World.

Analyzing the function of the foundational "ontological absence" of the Black female subject position in the symbolic order of Man, Wynter not only discusses the co-optation of sexual desire. She also echoes Spillers's remarks about the displacement of the maternal; in Man's foundational ontology, Miranda remains "the only symbolically canonized potential genitrix" of "a superior mode of human life" (360–61). By contrast, "Caliban's woman" is assigned the place of the "ontologically absent potential genitrix [. . .] of another population of human" that will serve the function of the 'Other' to Man (360). With the advent of slavery, "Africans bought and sold as 'trade goods' were now made to fill the same slot" of Caliban, and Black women, that of "Caliban's woman" (363). In the dominant symbolic order of Man, the Black maternal cannot be recognized as a valid site of subject formation or as a source of what Wynter calls "symbolic life:" Man's system of meaning originated in such a violent denial and must perpetuate this erasure to sustain itself.

As we shall see, this erasure enables the tethering of the Black maternal to various forms of death-in-life, resulting in the violent ontological transformations that "reduce Caliban to a labor-machine as the new 'massa damnata'" (360). The maternal becomes co-opted for the ends of capital, engendering what I call, following Meina Yates-Richard, a mother-machine dynamic. Nowhere in this symbolic order, which forms the basis of "our present Western world system," does "Caliban's woman" appear "as an alternative source of an alternative system of meanings" (360), enforcing a semantic closure.

The well-known hospital scene in Ralph Ellison's novel *Invisible Man* (1952) provides an illuminating allegorical reenactment of this mother-machine dynamic that the erasure of the Black maternal enables. As it symbolically narrativizes the dynamics that both Wynter and Spillers have theorized, this scene underlines how, in an antiblack world, the Black maternal remains tethered to various forms of death-in-life, highlighting the issues this book addresses.

The inability of invisible man to transcend the semantic closure of Man's symbolic order becomes clear in the famous hospital scene. Awakening in a "factory hospital," the unnamed narrator realizes he is trapped in a machine-box that emits human-like sounds. Treating him "as though he were a child," the doctors seek to erase his identity and remake him into a different subject. Hearing strange sounds that recall the cries of a woman in labor, he is unable to answer the doctors' questions:

"WHO . . . ARE . . . YOU? [. . .] *Where were you born?*" and "WHO WAS YOUR MOTHER?" (232, original italics). This prompts invisible man to realize he has forgotten the maternal: "*Mother, who was my mother? Mother, the one who screams when you suffer—but who? This was stupid, you always knew your mother's name. Who was it that screamed? Mother? But the scream came from the machine. A machine my mother?*" (232, original italics). These questions are reminiscent of the episode in James Baldwin's *The Fire Next Time* (1963) where the church's pastor asks him: "Whose little boy are you?" which "was precisely the phrase used by pimps and racketeers on the Avenue" (39). Observing that "[p]erhaps part of the terror they had caused me to feel came from the fact that I unquestionably wanted to be *somebody's* little boy" (39, original italics), Baldwin expresses a longing absent in Ellison's text, where, by contrast, the narrator seems unconcerned by his maternal forgetting, having accepted the idea of a mother-machine.

Displacing the maternal, the machine enables the doctors to rebirth the nameless protagonist into a "new man," who is a motherless "non-man" without identity and background. In a surreal birthing scene, Ellison's narrator feels "a tug at my belly" and looks "down to see one of the physicians pull the cord which was attached to the stomach node" (230–31). One of the doctors with a "steady scientific gaze" even supplies invisible man with a name: "'What is your name? Oh here, I have it'" (237).

At the end of this procedure, while the protagonist is declared "cured," he feels so weak that he muses: "But how shall I live?" (238). He is then taken in by Mary Rambo, who is presented as a carer of stray children. She says to him, "*You better come on round and rest till you feel stronger* [. . .] *You take it easy, I'll take care of you like I done a heap of others*" (243, original italics). However, the text highlights her unsuitability as a maternal surrogate through invisible man's longing to leave: "She was a landlady, I was a tenant [. . .] I'd have to get away" (310–11). If he wants to find a job and "become a Harlem leader," he must abandon Mary. He asks himself, "Why should it be that the very job which might make it possible for me to do some of the things which she expected of me required that I leave her?" (304). Dramatizing a process of maternal forgetting and displacement, the novel cannot find an adequate replacement. Failing to (re)engage in maternal performance, the scene's foregrounding of a mother-machine dynamic from the dispossessed son's perspective forestalls the possibility of a creative re-embracement of the maternal. The Black maternal haunts Ellison's scene and the entire novel as an absent presence to which the narrator is unable to reattach himself, making it impossible to draw upon the creative possibilities inherent in a rewriting of maternal praxis as life-giving.

To counteract a mother-machine dynamic and its attendant ontological erasure, maternal relationality must be reclaimed. But, focusing on being the object rather than the subject of maternal praxis, Ellison's scene forecloses such a possibility and cannot reimagine maternal praxis as life-giving. Described from the perspective of the disinherited son, the scene offers a useful counterpoint to the texts analyzed in this book, which, by contrast, highlight a maternal perspective and render possible the disruption of such a mother-machine dynamic, breaching Man's foundational semantic closure through a creative reimagination of maternal praxis.

Otherworldly Mothering traces how Black women's writing strives to disrupt Man's symbolic order and its semantic closure through the rewriting of maternal praxis as a source of "an alternative system of meanings" in which the Black maternal has a radically transformative life-giving power that can enable the rewriting of the human beyond Man's limited order of meaning. Entering into dialogue with a long-standing tradition of Black feminist theorizations of the maternal and the human, this book interrogates the meaning of maternal praxis in selected canonical works of African American women's literature published in the 1970s and 1980s. I consider how this tradition of writing performs a reclamation of the maternal so as to untether it from Man's narrow and provincial definition of the human and its attendant erasure of the Black maternal as a source of life. I argue that, against a context of racial terror enabled via a maternal erasure and subsequent displacement, these texts engage in a rewriting of an ancestral archive of maternal praxis that can untether the maternal from the (re)production of various forms of death-in-life and reimagine it as an alternate praxis of being. As they reveal the liberatory possibilities that lay in a reclamation of maternal practice, these texts provide another angle from which to tackle the imposed ontological erasure of Black being through what I will term, in conversation with Spillers, a *maternal* grammar.

A maternal displacement or mother-machine dynamic similar to that described in Ellison's novel is the subject of her essay "Mama's Baby." While critics often tend to focus on Spillers's theorization of concepts such as "flesh," "hieroglyphs of the flesh," or "pornotroping," here I want to expand on and clarify her use of the term "grammar" and how it relates to the dynamics of the process of enslavement. Looking at North American slave codes, advertisements, and other historical records documenting the Middle Passage, whose anonymous portrayals of the enslaved "throw no face into view," Spillers traces the dominant symbolic order that she terms an American grammar, which promotes a hierarchical view of human beings (72–73). This brutal American grammar of description constitutes the basis of the enslavers' onto-epistemic scheme. It enables them to relegate enslaved people to the status of what Patterson has called "social death." But how does this violent grammar generate the categories of human and nonhuman, self and other, or selected and deselected life?

It is via an imposition of enforced kinlessness that this brutal American grammar performs the ontological annihilation of Black being: in the prevailing symbolic order of the enslaver there is no place for the recognition of kinship relations because "if 'kinship' were possible the property relations would be undermined, since 'offspring' would then 'belong' to a mother and a father" (Spillers, "Mama's" 75). Kin, much like gender formation, must have "no decisive legal or social efficacy: [. . .] kinship loses meaning, *since it can be invaded at any moment by the property relations*" (74–78). While enslaved people do not lack kinship relations, these ties become meaningless in the enslaver's system of meanings: as Douglass has observed, "My poor mother, like many other slave-women, had *many children* but NO FAMILY!" (*My Bondage* 149, original emphasis). While both the female and the male are robbed of the parental right and function, it is the maternal that becomes the primary locus for enforcing and perpetuating this kinlessness and its correlative erasure of Black being.

In an earlier essay, Spillers argues that the Black woman becomes "the route by which the dominant modes decided the distinction between humanity and 'other'" ("Interstices" 155). However, as she observes in "Mama's Baby," it is specifically the Black woman *in her role as mother* that symbolizes this "principal point of passage between the human and non-human world" (155). Slavery's erasure and co-optation of the maternal for the ends of capital enables its "dehumanizing, ungendering, and defacing project" ("Mama's" 72). Via *partus sequitur ventrem*, the process of enslavement entrenches this enforced kinlessness as heritable through birth, creating what enslavers regard as an "endless supply" of socially dead nonpersons who could be exploited for their own economic interests. In the onto-epistemic scheme of enslavers, generated and sustained by this American grammar, the lexis of "'reproduction,' [and] 'motherhood' [. . .] are thrown into unrelieved crisis" (75–76). While, as historian Tiya Miles and others have shown, slavery's violence does not preclude the formation of meaningful and long-lasting maternal bonds among the enslaved, it results in a distortion and misnaming of the maternal, re-signifying it as a death-bound realm outside symbolic life.

This onto-epistemic scheme makes it impossible to regard the Black maternal as a life-giving locus or as a legitimate site of subject formation; in Man's order, the Black maternal can only become discernible as representative of symbolic death. While viewing white mothers as "reproducers of freedom," enslavers construct Black mothers as reproducers of "a marketable and money-returning commodity" that can be owned and sold for their own economic interests. This maternal erasure enables the enslaver to transfigure maternal praxis and repurpose it towards capital accumulation rather than nurture, tethering Black mothering to the reproduction of "hereditary slavery" (Sublette 72). In the dominant order of the enslaver, motherhood is harnessed to the production of death rather than life so that enslaved children are born into "social death" and regarded as "quantities." Enslavers transfigure the Black maternal as an economic praxis of capital accumulation that results in an ontological erasure. Since enslaved women have no rights to their children and, in American society, matriarchy "is not a legitimate procedure of cultural inheritance" (Spillers, "Mama's" 80), this brutal American grammar enforces a double erasure of the maternal. Mothering becomes transfigured as an experience whose intelligibility as life-giving lies outside Man's dominant order of meaning.

Analyzing the dynamics that enable the ontological transmogrifications of slavery, Spillers's essay suggests a kind of foundational maternal erasure that chimes in with the one that, as we have seen, Wynter discussed in relation to Man's symbolic order. Even as their essays deploy distinct theoretical and historical frameworks, what Wynter and Spillers share is their understanding that the dominant order's denial of the Black maternal constitutes the very condition of possibility for that symbolic order to create and sustain its attendant construction of subjectivities.

Contending that history seems to show no movement, Spillers observes that the enslavers' brutal American grammar of description, "grounded in the originating metaphors of captivity and mutilation," continues to be "the ruling episteme that releases the dynamics of naming and valuation" ("Mama's" 68). But she also hints at the possibility of bringing into being "a new semantic order" that can disrupt this grammar, understanding this process as a "narrative" one. For her, this is the "narrative ambition" that can be found in canonical works of African American literature: "1) to break apart, to rupture violently the laws of American behavior that make such syntax possible; 2) to introduce a new semantic field/fold" (79). African American writers have long been engaged in a reimagination and rewriting of this antiblack world, attempting to provide different "dynamics of naming and valuation" that push against the enslavers' dominant order and its creation of a death-world for African Americans. Despite the racial violence of the American grammar she is tracing, Spillers concedes the possibility of rupturing this symbolic order or "ruling episteme" to rewrite a different cultural narrative for the human.

In her view, the problematizing of gender leaves the female "*out* of the traditional symbolics of female gender" and thus requires us "to make a place for this different social subject" ("Mama's" 80). She recasts this nonrecognition as an "*insurgent* ground" from which to "rewrite [. . .] a radically different text" of the human (67–80). But what will this text look like? If what must be conveyed is a different mode of enactment for the human, what alternative representational grammar would this require? To further explore Spillers's "radically different text for a female empowerment" (80), one capable of releasing different dynamics of naming and valuation, and arrive at a better understanding of these dynamics and their relation to the maternal, this study examines African American women's writings that engage with maternal performativity.

This book argues that narratives by African American women published during the post-Civil Rights era often seek a reappraisal of the maternal praxis warped by racial terror in an effort to (re)imagine Black subjectivities that, while affected by, are not completely determined by racial terror. Through the maternal, these texts provide access to an alternative symbolic order that pushes against the dominant one, challenging its tethering of Black mothering to death. If "chattel slavery forcibly instated disabled maternity as the primary mode of familial engagement for the blacks in the Americas" (Yates-Richard 494), we must focus on the ways that African American writing has sought to (re)enable the maternal through its insistent creative performance, drawing on a longstanding tradition of resistance to racial terror. If the enslavers' onto-epistemic scheme sought to violently undo Black subjectivities through a brutal denial of the maternal, enslaved people, drawing from non-Western knowledges, devised imaginative ways to keep maternal ties alive and in the process, created alternate worlds and ways of being in the world. The texts analyzed here reclaim this tradition, rewriting Western onto-epistemologies through a reappraisal of maternal praxis.

As we have seen, Ellison's and Baldwin's texts, written from the point of view of the disinherited son, tend to focus mainly on being the *object* of maternal practice; their narratives foreground the results of racial terror's warping of maternal praxis, i.e., a stunted development of subjectivity and a correlated search for maternal replacements. By contrast, written from a maternal perspective, the works analyzed here probe the meaning of being the *subject* of maternal praxis, directly engaging in its performance. Shifting the attention to being the performer, rather than the recipient, of maternal practice, these works not only move the maternal from periphery to center. They also posit humanity as their object of knowledge, treating subjectivity not as a *fait accompli* but as a continuous process of becoming and scrutinizing the techniques through which the human is made and unmade. As they produce knowledge about the human, they also rupture its onto-epistemic terrain. By divergent means, Toni Morrison's *Song of Solomon* (1977), Gloria Naylor's *Linden Hills* (1985), Paule Marshall's *Praisesong for the Widow* (1983), Audre Lorde's *Zami* (1982), and Toni Cade Bambara's *The Salt Eaters* (1980) all foreground the creative (re)production and performance of the maternal, revealing it as a primary site where the figure of the human can be made and unmade through a continual reinvention of subjectivities. Drawing attention to longstanding erasures and disruptions of the maternal that they link back to the violent onto-epistemic imaginary of slavery, their writings rewrite an ancestral archive of mothering to resist and critique the ascendancy of a neoliberal mode of reason. These texts suggest that, against the hierarchical and divisive processes of neoliberalism and its concomitant racialized and gendered ordering of being, maternal practice can offer a means through which to foster relational modes of subjectivities that emphasize a processual understanding of the human. They creatively respond to racial terror's undoing of Black being by generating a maternal praxis of being, not only unveiling but also rupturing the violent onto-epistemic foundations of the current hegemonic model of the human. Foregrounding maternal praxis as a way to remake Black being, these texts do not simply reiterate liberal humanist discourses. They denaturalize and reimagine the human, taking part in the long tradition of Black humanism, which, according to Wynter, "disenchants 'Man' as 'Man,'" and brings "into being different modes of the *human*" ("Disenchanting Discourse" 466, original emphasis).

Creating fictional microcosms where the maternal is warped by racial terror, these writings expose the relations that exist between the neoliberal order of reason and the conceptual edifice that Alys Eve Weinbaum has called "the slave episteme," which transfigures "wombs as founts of fungible and alienable commodities" (12). Foregrounding the maternal displacement at the basis of both, despite their contemporaneous setting, these narratives remain informed by the past as they highlight its echoes in the present. But, as these texts underscore how legacies of enslavement continue to haunt the present, they not only narrate a "counter-history" of neoliberal America as inhabiting "the time of slavery" (Hartman 759). They also envision an alternative symbolic order that aims to rewrite a "ruling episteme" based upon property relations or what Spillers has termed an American grammar. As this book will demonstrate, shifting the focus from being the object to being the subject of mothering and reimagining maternal praxis, these narratives draw on what I call a maternal grammar. Rooted in non-Western epistemologies, this maternal grammar allows these texts to create alternate literary spaces where embodied and relational modes of subjectivities escape and unsettle the provincial understanding of the human as Man. Co-opting the maternal and spurring neoliberal forms of racial terror, neoliberalism's normative order of reason can only apprehend Black being as ontological aporia and construct the Black maternal as the space for such ontological annihilation. But, through a reclamation of the maternal, these writings manage to construct alternate imaginative spaces or what I will term *other-worlds*, where liberatory onto-epistemic possibilities can emerge.

While none of the texts analyzed here are works of science fiction, in conjuring up otherworlds that engender onto-epistemic shifts, my discussion positions them in dialogue with Afrofuturism: like Afrofuturistic art, these texts engage in the creation of an "imaginative space for thinking" that unsettles Western humanism (Samatar 178, Womack 9). Rethinking identities and redefining "culture and notions of blackness for today and the future," Afrofuturists re-envision the past and speculate about the future (Womack 9). Taking part in an Afrofuturistic mode of storytelling while exploring the possibilities inherent in a reclamation of the maternal, these texts enable a creative reimagination of the human beyond the narrow constraints of Western modernity. In so doing, they engage in a reappraisal of Black humanism that can envision "a future for Black people" through the creation of maternal otherworlds that function as narrative spaces to unthink Western humanism and the brutal forms of racial violence upon which it is based.

However, while these texts' otherworlds attempt to eschew racial terror, they are never completely free from it: their very existence as coping mechanisms is a response to forms of racial violence. As we shall see, being narrative rewritings of what African American historian Stephanie H. Camp has called enslaved people's "rival geographies," their literary otherworlds draw upon Harriet Jacobs's narrative recreation of her garret or otherworldly "loophole of retreat," which I posit as a maternal Ur trope. Both real and unreal places, imaginary yet firmly grounded in the material circumstances of the present, they allow for the coexistence of contradictions and the negotiation of racial terror's maternal displacements. As these narratives will demonstrate, any place can potentially be transformed into an otherworld through maternal praxis: not just the Caribbean but New York as well. These literary otherworlds allow onto-epistemic shifts: they do not correspond to a particular geographical place but rather refer to its imaginative transformation, which both enables and sustains a creative remaking of subjectivities, underlining the complex interconnections between the production of space and being while foregrounding the central role of the maternal.

I develop my conception of otherworlds in conversation with Katherine McKittrick's pathbreaking study of Black feminist geographies and her emphasis on the "alterability of space and place" (xii). Building upon Wynter's work, in *Demonic Grounds* (2006), McKittrick traces how "Black women's geographies (such as their knowledges, negotiations, and experiences)" interact with "geographies of domination (such as transatlantic slavery and racial-sexual displacement)" (x). Emphasizing the ways in which geographies are socially produced, she notes how even the slave ship is "not stable and unchanging" (xii). While "ideologically enclosing Black subjects," at the same time, the ship generates "an oppositional geography: the ship as a location of Black subjectivity and human terror, Black resistance, and [. . .] Black possession" (xi). If, as McKittrick contends, "more humanly workable geographies can be and are imagined" (xiii), these texts' maternal otherworlds also enable the envisioning of 'more humanly workable' modes of being and inhabiting those geographies, emphasizing the link between maternal praxis and a reimagination of space and subjectivity.

Informed by the long-standing tradition of Black feminist theoretical and sociohistorical analyses of mothering and slavery, this book will focus on the processes through which such narrative otherworlds can be conjured up. I aim to show that these texts manage to create them not so much through an idealization of a lost mother figure or "a quest to contact lost, enslaved foremothers," as Caroline Rody's study suggests, but through a literary rearticulation of an archive of maternal praxis that goes back to the period of slavery. While many studies of the maternal in African American literature have often tended to center on maternal iconography or the mother-daughter relation, the main emphasis of this book will be on the narrative (re)production and performance of maternal practices that originated as maternal support systems during slavery and are then reimagined by these twentieth-century texts as a response to racial violence.

Unlike the works of Venetria K. Patton, Caroline Rody, Geneva Cobb Moore, and Marianne Hirsch, among others, this book will not focus on mothers or other maternal characters per se but on African American literary representations of maternal praxis to argue that they rewrite not only history but the human itself. What Patton's, Cobb-Moore's, and Rody's studies share in their distinct analyses of Black women's texts is a focus on maternal iconography and a tendency to interpret such narratives as revisionary Black feminist rewritings of history. This project builds upon their reading of Black women's texts as disrupting the linear time of history to write "a counter-narrative" against America's historical amnesia (Rody 7, Patton 3). However, focusing upon a discussion of maternal praxis, it aims to push the implications of their analyses of Black women's texts beyond questions of gender towards such matters as the construction of neoliberal subjectivities and the meanings of being human. As this book argues, centering the maternal, these writings provide a "counter-narrative" not only of history but of the human as Man; while they rewrite a maternal history, they also establish a maternal grammar with which to reimage the human against the brutal American grammar Spillers has traced.

Drawing on the philosophical work of Adrienne Rich and Sara Ruddick, Andrea O'Reilly's *Toni Morrison and Motherhood: A Politics of the Heart* (2004) has focused on what she terms "motherwork" (28). In O'Reilly's analysis, she often tends to assume the existence of "an authentic and true self." This authenticity of self is, according to her, "specifically the selfhood made possible through the preservation, nurturance, and cultural bearing of motherwork" (40). Building upon the works of Spillers and Wynter, this book departs from this view, arguing that African American women's writing shows how the very concept of an "authentic" or "true" self is what maternal praxis challenges: through it, human subjectivity is continuously made and unmade. As these texts question the stability of human ontology, fixed identities become untenable.

As my project advances a reading rooted neither in maternal iconography nor in assumptions of stable identities, it probes how and why a reassessment of maternal praxis is a necessary step toward a reconceptualization of what it means to be human. By focusing on maternal praxis, I want to untie the maternal from notions of gender and foreground instead the performative nature of mothering, which, as these texts show, is a communal practice that anybody can engage in to reimagine the human. In these texts, not only the maternal but the human itself is treated as a praxis that can and should be creatively and communally reimagined. Against a brutal context of racial terror, maternal practice enables a rethinking of the human; these texts share a sense that being human is a specifically *maternal* praxis. In so doing, they reveal the close connections between performances of the human and the maternal; shaped by specific onto-epistemologies, normative ways of mothering are constructed to uphold normative ways of being human.

Across Western cultures, the normative model of motherhood focuses on the biological mother as mainly, if not solely, responsible for her offspring and focuses on the child as needing almost exclusively the attention of one primary caregiver. In this "biocentric theory of motherhood" (Park 6), mothers who do not or cannot fulfill these romantic expectations are deemed "unfit," "unnatural," or "unworthy." Claims about who is entitled to assume the social and legal status of *mother*, "frequently racialized and class coded," are meant to control those who deviate from pre-established norms (Park 4). This normative understanding of motherhood cannot account for alternative ways of mothering that arise from different sociohistorical circumstances, especially among working-class women and women of color, which have been shut out from the cult of domesticity: "[b]ecause of varying historical experiences, these communities have constructed mothering in ways that diverge from the dominant model" (Glenn 5).

As a result of specific socioeconomic and cultural factors, the interchange-ability of roles and the broadening of kinship ties that have tended to characterize Black families have allowed an expansion of who can mother, reframing the meaning of the maternal in collective terms and untethering it from notions of biological essentialism. Black feminist scholar Patricia Hill Collins has foregrounded the central role of communal mothering or "othermothering" in Black diasporic communities.[1] Derived from West African traditions and then adapted to the New World during slavery, this cooperative nature of childcare endured throughout the twentieth century. The persistence of these woman-centered networks of childcare support have helped Black women resist oppression and "may have greater theoretical importance than currently recognized" (180). Collins argues that African American women who engage in othermothering endorse different values and "challenge prevailing capitalist property relations" and the related assumption underlying the Western ideal of the family, i.e., that children are "private property" (182).

By focusing on these texts' rewriting of maternal praxes informed by this tradition, my study builds upon Collins's work to show how these othermothering practices, endorsing a distinct set of values, can bring about maternal otherworlds that push beyond the dominant construction of the human and its related onto-epistemic imaginary. As the texts analyzed here demonstrate, alternative maternal practices underscore praxes of being that do not align with a liberal humanist understanding of subjectivity, unsettling the reification of the human as Man while highlighting its performative nature. Debates around who does and does not perform "appropriate" mothering are thus, first and foremost, questions about who can and cannot inhabit the spaces of normative subjectivity or "symbolic life."

Much like conceptions of who counts as a "mother" or what constitutes "acceptable" mothering are sociohistorically specific, normative ideas around the "human" and the praxis of being human are fluid and ever-changing. Black feminist theorists like Spillers and Wynter posit "differing modes of the *human*" that emphasize "the historicity and mutability of the 'human' itself, gesturing toward different, catachrestic conceptualizations of this category" (*Habeas Viscus* 264, original emphasis). In her numerous essays and interviews, Wynter has repeatedly underlined the performative nature of the human. Drawing on Judith Butler, she observes, "The enactments of such gender roles are always a function of the enacting of a specific genre of being hybridly human [. . .] Why not then the performative enactment of all our roles, of all our role allocations [. . .] all as praxes, therefore, rather than nouns" (263).

According to Wynter, narratives play a central role in this "performative enactment" (34). Regarding myths, cosmogonies, and other origin narratives as "technologies [. . .] by which we prescribe our own roles," she calls the human as Man a "narrativization" (27). Expanding upon her insights, McKittrick locates one such narrative or "origin story" in the "mathematics of the unliving" constituted by what Spillers has described as a brutal American grammar of description, i.e., the list, the breathless numbers, the absolutely economic ("Mathematics" 17). As my discussion has shown, Man's origin story and its related abjection of Blackness is engendered and sustained by an erasure of the Black maternal as a valid site of subject formation: normative constructions of the human are linked to constructions not only of their respective Others but also of normative mothering.

This "non genetically chartered" myth, and its attendant semantic closure, is then "*neurochemically* implement[ed]" through biological genetic codes; this is the hybrid "*bios/mythoi*" processual dynamic of "our present ethnoclass (i.e., Western bourgeois) conception of the human" as Man and its "archipelago of Human Otherness" (26–27). Through this hybrid inscription of Man's maternal erasure, Black subjects emerge in a context which relegates them to an abject status, engendering the experience of what W.E.B. Du Bois has called "double consciousness" or the paradoxical sensation of both "being; and *désêtre*—a term used by Aimé Césaire to describe 'dysbeing'—or nonbeing," i.e., "*symbolic death as out of place with respect to being human*" (Wynter and McKittrick 60).

This is the origin story crafted by *Man's* dominant order of meaning according to *their* brutal grammar and semantic closure. In Man's narrativization of this story, Blackness becomes tethered to a "mathematics of the unliving" via a manipulation of the maternal. But can such an inscription be disrupted and the human (re)imagined? Chiming in with Spillers's understanding of the potentiality of Black women's "*insurgent* ground," Wynter theorizes the possibility of a silenced "demonic ground," located "outside our present mode of being/feeling/knowing," which constitutes a locus of liminality where other ways of being can be imagined. But how can such an unsettling terrain be accessed? The texts analyzed here, I argue, suggest that a rethinking of maternal praxis can offer a means to access such a demonic ground in order to rewrite a maternal origin story of the human upon which to base an otherworld that depends upon maternal relationality rather than erasure, reimagining Black being as other than ontological aporia.

This book reads African American women's literary narratives against the processual technologies that the system of slavery employed to remake humans into units of labor. In so doing, it enters into dialogue with Wynter's and Spillers's theorizations of the dynamics of liberal humanist subjectivities, which rest on the ontological negation of Black life performed through an erasure of the maternal, to argue that these texts suggest a link between the performative reenactment of an ancestral archive of maternal praxis and a creative rewriting of the human. Positing maternal praxis as a means to implement alternative discursive codes pertaining to what it means to be human, these narratives offer origin stories other than those of 'Man' and its "mathematics of the unliving," denaturalizing and unsettling their hegemony. Through their maternal grammar, these texts suggest a way to unthink the ethno-specific genre of the human based upon a brutal American grammar linked to slavery's economic co-optation of the maternal. The writing of these texts itself becomes a form of maternal praxis, which engages in an artistic remaking of the human through a maternal grammar, highlighting how Black women's maternal praxes continually engage in the performance of alternate forms of being human.

While both fatherhood and motherhood are denied under slavery, Spillers hints at the possibilities inherent in a maternal reclamation. Analyzing passages from Douglass's *Narrative* and Malcolm X's *Autobiography of Malcolm X*, Spillers concludes that the loss of the maternal has a destructive outcome, opening the offspring "to social ambiguity and chaos" ("Mama's" 76). As a result, "it is the heritage of the *mother* that the African American male must regain as an aspect of his own personhood" (80, original emphasis). Drawing on Douglass's narrative and Malcolm X's autobiography, Spillers focuses mainly on the experience of Black male subjectivity. However, her remarks have a more general validity and call to mind the observations of the British pediatrician Donald W. Winnicott: "If the child's humanity is mirrored initially in the eyes of its mother, or the maternal function, then we might be able to guess that the social subject grasps the whole dynamic of resemblance and kinship by way of the same source" (76). Maternal nurturance, in Spillers's account, is regarded as the *sine qua non* condition for the cultivation of both a psychological bond and a feeling of kinship. These, for Spillers, do not come about naturally but need to be generated through the performance of the maternal (70). Since kinlessness and maternal erasure, in her analysis, are what sustains a conception of human beings as property, then maternal practice, producing and enacting a feeling of kinship that undoes property relations, acquires the potential to rewrite this brutal American grammar. However, while she focuses on the autobiographical works of Harriet Jacobs/Linda Brent, Frederick Douglass, and Malcolm X, Spillers never fully develops her project of uncovering "a radically different text for a female empowerment" (79).

By contrast, the literary narratives of her near contemporaries, the subject of this book, participate in this "project of liberation," rupturing "the laws of American behavior that make such syntax possible" (80) through a reclamation of the maternal. They disrupt the brutal American grammar of description that, based upon the ongoing abjection of Blackness and the maternal, dictates the performative rules of the human as Man. Seeking to undo the profitable transformation of "*personality* into *property*," as Spillers puts it, these texts envision a new symbolic order based upon the maternal. Harking back to Douglass's and Jacobs's narratives, they attempt to disrupt the brutal American grammar of representation that makes racial terror possible with their own maternal grammar as they seek to reimagine the processes through which African American subjectivities are performed. But, as they draw upon a maternal heritage, rather than idealizing a lost mother figure, they narratively reimagine an archive of ancestral maternal practices that goes back to slavery.

Participating in a project of maternal recuperation, these texts emphasize the possibilities that a reenacting of the maternal can bring to African American subjectivities as they arise from textual representations. Throughout these narratives, the maternal emerges as a praxis with a transformative potential that seeks to provide an alternative to the brutal grammar that sustains our "genre-specific and auto-instituting mode of being human" rooted in a conception of Man as a bio-economic subject whose salvation is postulated in economic terms (Wynter 271). While Robert B. Stepto is right when he points out, in his seminal study of African American narrative *From Behind the Veil* (1979), that "the Afro-American quest for freedom has been more precisely a quest for freedom *and* literacy" (196, original italics), a close analysis of African American women's writing suggests that parallel to this quest runs one for the maternal, an Ur trope in African American women's writing. As evidenced in the texts analyzed here, maternal praxis becomes the vehicle for a reimagination of Black subjectivities that seeks to free those subjects from the brutal abjection imposed upon them by racial violence.

This project of maternal reclamation against the brutal American grammar Spillers has traced predates the twentieth century and acquires even more significance if analyzed against the maternal disruptions caused by slavery, which are narrativized in slave narratives. The violent separation of mother and child described in numerous slave autobiographies often prompts, especially in women's narratives, a sense that the retrieval of the maternal is interchangeable with the gaining of freedom. Emerging out of and in response to slavery, these texts frequently portray maternal disconnection as a brutal imposition with deleterious effects: maternal separation as the symbol for the undoing of the self and the making of a slave is often a feature of these texts. As a result, these works, especially those written by women, engage in a narrative attempt to recuperate the maternal bonds severed by slavery. If "the enslaved had been forced to *forget mother*" (Hartman 38, original italics), for Jacobs the journey towards freedom is also a journey back to the maternal, which is enabled through a narrative reinvention of maternal praxis, a point to which I will come back in my discussion of her loophole of retreat as an Ur trope for these texts' maternal otherworlds.

In Douglass's 1845 autobiography, *Narrative of the Life of Frederick Douglass*, the whipping of Aunt Hester at the hands of the slaveholder removes a maternal shield, constituting for the narrator (and Douglass's narrative persona) a threshold moment or "the blood-stained gate, the entrance to the hell of slavery" (319): her "heart-rending shrieks" (18), which call to mind the scream in Ellison's hospital scene, "open the way into the knowledge of slavery" (Moten 23). His "entrance to the hell of slavery" coincides with the withdrawal of the maternal shielding provided by his grandmother: "I had never seen anything like it before. I had always lived with my grandmother on the outskirts of the plantation [. . .] I had therefore been, until now, out of the way of the bloody scenes that often occurred on the plantation" (319–20). It is because of this maternal removal that Douglass retreats into a closet, attempting to recreate and reinhabit a womblike space where he can find the maternal shield of which slavery deprived him. Reminiscent of the womb-machine in Ellison's novel, the closet displaces the maternal and rebirths Douglass into nonbeing: this scene parallels Ellison's protagonist's rebirth through an artificial womb, accompanied by a scream and facilitated by white doctors. As Yates-Richard has observed, placing an artificial barrier between Douglass and Hester, the closet's displacement of the womb signals Douglass's first step toward maternal detachment (488). In Douglass's autobiography, to be a slave means to be deprived of motherly protection: while by law he is officially a slave from the moment he is born, it is when he enters a motherless state that he is made into a slave and unmade as a person at the psychological level. Chiming in with Spillers's theoretical insights, Douglass's *Narrative* establishes maternal separation as foundational to slavery's undoing of the self.

This focus on motherlessness as the hallmark of slavery is not unique to Douglass's text but characterizes other slave narratives. Harriet Jacobs begins her slave narrative, *Incidents in the Life of a Slave Girl* (1861), reflecting on the maternal protection that enabled her textual alter ego, Linda Brent, to enjoy a "happy childhood." It is only when her mother dies that Linda becomes aware of her condition as a slave: "When I was six years old, my mother died; and then, for the first time, I learned, by the talk around me, that I was a slave" (415). As is the case in Douglass's narrative, the initiation into racial terror corresponds to the loss of maternal protection since Jacobs's text identifies a state of motherlessness as the distinctive feature of slavery.

In both Douglass's and Jacobs's narratives, to be enslaved means to be left in a motherless state. From this similar point of departure, their texts then offer different conceptions of the meaning of freedom. As both Douglass and Jacobs try to rewrite a different subjectivity for themselves in order to challenge slavery's annihilation of personhood, they find remarkably different ways to do so. While in Douglass's narrative the quest for freedom remains anchored to his parallel quest for manhood and literacy, which require maternal detachment, in Jacobs's text it is the quest for the maternal that allows Linda to reach liberation for herself and her children.

For Douglass, freedom ultimately remains linked to the attainment of a public persona and independence, which necessitates a detachment from the maternal, recalling the dynamic of Ellison's novel. His battle with Mr. Covey is characterized as a rebirth into manhood that frees him from the psychological, if not physical, chains of slavery: "It was a glorious resurrection, from the tomb of slavery, to the heaven of freedom [. . .] however long I might remain a slave in form, the day had passed forever when I could be a slave in fact" (366). But his rebirth is represented as motherless; the narrator rebirths himself unaided, embracing the self-sufficiency of the American myth of the self-made man founded upon a liberal humanist mode of subjectivity. Douglass's text relates freedom to a sense of masculinist power and autonomy and a turning away from the maternal conceptualized as an obstacle to the attainment of a free subjectivity.

As David Leverenz has observed, "Douglass's preoccupation with manhood and power all but erases any self-representation linking him with women, family, and intimacy" (341): freedom is achieved through a reclamation of manhood and authority at the expense of the maternal. Douglass further erases his maternal links by changing his name. Even though this is done for the purpose of not being traced, in doing so, as Henry Louis Gates, Jr. has noted, he "self-consciously [. . .] abandons a strong matrilineal black heritage of five stable generations and embraces [. . .] a Scottish character named Douglass in Scott's *The Lady of the Lake*" (114). While he describes his yearning for freedom through maternal imagery, it is when he gives a speech in front of a white audience that he feels liberated (397). In Douglass's narrative, his final sense of individual achievement and autonomy dominates and takes over the tentative glimpses into maternal connections. In order to achieve a free subjectivity according to the ruling grammar of Man's onto-epistemic order, the narrator must leave behind the maternal.

Douglass's narrative loses sight of its initial awareness of slavery's forceful maternal displacement; the equation of "enslavement" with "mother," as a result of her perceived capacity to tether the child to a life of bondage, engenders further maternal disavowals in an attempt to gain the autonomy of the liberal humanist subject (Moten 25). Even though it does manifest maternal yearnings, Douglass's text, rather than rupturing the maternal abjection originating in slavery, ends up further severing such a link. This forecloses the possibilities that a maternal reclamation can generate for a remaking of Black subjectivities not tethered to white masculinist ideals.

In contrast to Douglass's focus on individual autonomy, Jacobs's narrative foregrounds a "vital, continuous sense of black community and family ties" (Leverenz 363). I argue that, in doing so, Jacobs's text also gives a different meaning to the word freedom, linking it to the maternal so that a reclamation of maternal praxis becomes the *sine qua non* condition of emancipation. While many slave narratives, Douglass's included, often tend to equate the quest for freedom with a quest for literacy, Jacobs's narrative suggests that freedom can be achieved through a reclamation of the maternal bonds that slavery violently severed. The motherless state into which the narrator is left by slavery prompts her to retrieve the maternal, rewriting it as a gateway to freedom. As Beth Maclay Doriani has argued, freedom for Linda involves interdependence (211). Whereas Douglass's work conceives of freedom as a repudiation of the maternal and the reclamation of an independent self, Jacobs's text equates freedom with a return to the mother. As Foreman has observed, in Jacobs's text, association with the Black mother results in "freedom rather than enslavement," overturning the doctrine of *partus sequitur ventrem* (502).

While in Douglass's narrative it is the fight with Mr. Covey that spurs the narrator's search for freedom, in Jacobs's text, it is Linda's determination to mother that drives her quest. Here the maternal becomes the Northern Star, guiding the heroine towards a long-awaited freedom: "I longed to be entirely free to act a mother's part towards my children" (169). Motherhood is presented, as Joanne M. Braxton has noted, as "a vehicle for the retrieval of lost self-respect," opening "the pathway to greater self-awareness" (33). Jacobs's narrative figures the maternal as the main impetus spurring Linda on her journey to attain freedom for herself and her children. Unlike Douglass's, her quest for freedom is a quest to retrieve, not to further break from, the maternal.

African American women's narratives published in the years after the Civil Rights movement are clearly very different from this canon. Unlike slave narratives, they are not written for a white audience; as such, they are free from the pressure to tell a progressive story, possessing a higher degree of creative and rhetorical freedom. As they emerge from a later historical period, they tend to manifest a distinct set of concerns and express those with remarkably different literary techniques. Yet, for all their formal and thematic differences, twentieth-century writing by African American women often carries significant echoes of this nineteenth-century archive. Grappling with slavery's resonance in the contemporary moment, these texts reveal that, while slavery might be officially "dead [. . .], the spirit which animated it still lives" (Harper 72). Much like the neo-slave narratives that have proliferated in the U.S. since the 1970s, they remain intellectually indebted to antebellum slave narratives, especially those authored by women. Comprising "residually oral, modern narratives of escape from bondage to freedom" (289), the neo-slave narrative genre highlights the centrality of slavery to the creation of America's national identity through the use of time-rupturing devices. In the texts discussed here, maternal praxis becomes one such time-breaching device as it allows them to explore the resonances of the past in the present while rewriting not only history but the human itself. Attempting to reinvent Black subjectivities against a context of ongoing racial violence, these texts often turn to the maternal to refashion it as a locus for an alternate praxis of being. Revisiting the link between the maternal and resistance against racial terror that was already evident in some slave narratives, these texts reframe maternal practice as a reclamation of the lives undone by racial terror's maternal co-optations.

These narratives' portrayals of maternal loss and displacement, and the subsequent subjective remaking into a motherless nonbeing, hint at those processes initiated by the Atlantic slave trade, and then perpetuated through the ongoing control and devaluation of Black motherhood. In some cases, as we will see, these narratives even evince awareness of the parallels between 1980s American society and the antebellum South in the persistence of distinct but related problematics of motherhood. Such is the case, for example, with Ruth's prolonged breastfeeding and Pilate's othermothering in *Song of Solomon*, with Willa's son's death and her ethics of care in *Linden Hills*, with Avey's and Jay's descent into *homo economicus*'s symbolic order and subsequent reclamation of a Pan-African semiotic in *Praisesong*, with the maternal abjection spurring a reunion in *Zami*, or with the erasure and retrieval of play as a form of maternal praxis in *The Salt Eaters*. These episodes, where the creative practices of various types of (other)mother figures rewrite the lives annihilated by neoliberal reason, vividly evoke the maternal that Douglass and Jacobs identified as a shield from slavery. In the neoliberal era, against an undoing of subjectivity redolent of the slave past, the maternal is once again looked upon as a way to (re)imagine it. Parallels between 1980s American society and the slaveholding South thus emerge from these narratives' shared emphasis on the capacity of the maternal to withstand the ongoing ontological erasure of Black being.

These narratives' portrayals of the maternal often emphasize moments when knowledge is derived from sources outside the neoliberal normative order of reason, such as those offered by the ancestral customs enslaved people managed to hold on to and reinvent in the New World. In so doing, they seek to imagine an alternative maternal grammar that stands in opposition to the one that sustains neoliberalism's economic logic. In response to its dehumanizing terrain, these texts invoke the maternal as a resilient praxis of being in order to resist the racial violence inflicted upon Black people. Seeking to perform an ontological erasure of Black being, racial terror co-opts the maternal, transmogrifying it into a space tethered to death. These texts unsettle this original displacement and reclaim the maternal as a valid site of subject formation, enabling a creative reimagination of the human beyond the narrow confines of Western modernity's episteme.

These writings shake the foundations of neoliberal reason through the conjuring up of narrative otherworlds based upon a maternal grammar. These alternative spaces can be thought of as literary reimaginations of the otherworldly loopholes enslaved women managed to negotiate, which are also narrativized in Jacobs's text. Echoing the dynamics of slavery, these texts contrast their representations of maternal practices with the maternal co-optation provoked by neoliberal forces and reclaim the maternal as a potential locus of onto-epistemic ruptures.

In the first section of this introduction, I trace how the violent co-optation of Black women's maternal praxes enabled onto-epistemic metamorphoses that relegated some people to the space of "living death," to use Jacobs's term. Drawing on the works of Black feminist historians such as Stephanie Jones-Rogers and Stephanie H. Camp, I will focus on the contradictions of slavery and the ways in which enslaved women found ways to contest the enslaver's power over their maternal space, time, and bodies. Highlighting slavery's co-optation of maternal practice as an engine of property development, I will discuss its relation to the processes by which enslaved people were reduced to what sociologist Orlando Patterson has called "social nonpersons," which formed the correlative Other to Man.

In the second section, I will illustrate what I term "otherworldly loopholes" from slavery. Starting from an analysis of Jacobs's description of her "loophole of retreat," which I employ as an Ur trope for the narratives analyzed here, I will explore how she, like other enslaved women, manages to conjure up an otherworld based upon an alternative symbolic order. After linking a state of orphanage to slavery, Linda Brent is determined to mother her children, but she must find a way to do so under the constraints imposed by slavery. As a result, she construes her own "loophole of retreat" where she can receive maternal care and mother in absentia. From there, she is able to watch over her children and evade the enslaver's control by inhabiting an otherworld where oppositions no longer hold. This otherworld forms a textual reinvention or literary translation of the one that enslaved women were able to inhabit as they challenged the plantation's foundational values with their rival epistemology.

In the third section, I will proceed to an overview of neoliberalism and its ascendancy in the period under consideration: the 1980s. Drawing on the work of Michel Foucault, Wendy Brown, and Sylvia Wynter, I will underline its re-making of the human into *homo economicus* according to a neoliberal mode of reason. This process is based upon dynamics that echo and extend the economic forms of maternal erasure and co-optation that were at the basis of the "slave episteme" or racial logic that regarded people as property and "wombs as founts of fungible commodities" (Weinbaum 83). This neoliberal mode of reason, while ostensibly preaching freedom, undermines Black lives via maternal erasure, ensuring that Black mothers still find themselves in an untenable position.

In the fourth section, I will conclude by reflecting on twentieth-century African American writing and how it has often drawn attention to the persistence of the problematics of mothering that characterized slavery. In the second half of the twentieth century African American women's writing, while retaining maternal ambivalence, has at the same time increasingly focused on strong maternal figures and their ability to withstand racial violence rather than on the impossibility of mothering in an antiblack world. The works of Gloria Naylor, Toni Morrison, Paule Marshall, Audre Lorde, and Toni Cade Bambara feature contemporary versions of the otherworldly loophole from slavery conjured up in Jacobs's narrative. These texts disrupt an American grammar of description that originated in slavery and is based on property relations, imagining what I term, following Spillers, a maternal grammar. Thus, their works must be understood in light of the historical context of slavery and the legacies of its unmaking of the human through maternal displacement.

Mothering During Slavery

As Alys Eve Weinbaum argues, "when we begin from an understanding of Atlantic slavery as an economic system that came over time to be based on (re) productive extraction and dispossession it becomes possible to see that contemporary (re)productive extraction and dispossession would be unthinkable—and thus unmaterializable—were it not for the creation and persistent recalibration of racialized ideas about wombs as founts of fungible and alienable commodities" (5). But, as this book argues, what also would be unthinkable without this process of commodification of the womb as a resource for the reproduction of "goods" that can be bought and sold are the violent onto-epistemological erasures that the process of enslavement entrenched and that neoliberalism continues to perpetuate, albeit in distinct, more covert, forms. It is this racialized economic transfiguration of wombs, or what Weinbaum calls "the slave episteme," and its foundational maternal erasure that becomes instrumental in slavery's transformation of "*personality* into *property*," materializing a "total objectification" of enslaved people (Spillers, "Mama's" 67).

An analysis of the process of enslavement, and the dynamics through which it engendered onto-epistemic transformations of the human via a maternal displacement, can contribute to a fuller understanding of the mechanisms through which the still globally hegemonic onto-epistemic order of Man was brought about and sustained via a co-optation of the maternal. As a result, an analysis of slavery as a terrain where the complex entanglements between the human and the maternal become prominent forms the backdrop of my exploration of African American women's narrative reclamation of maternal praxis against a context of racial and "maternal violence" (Jones-Rogers 120). It is to a discussion of the socio-historical context of slavery and its various forms of maternal erasure that I thus now turn.

In her book *They Were Her Property* (2019), historian Stephanie Jones-Rogers defines maternal violence as the violence that enslavers, including white mothers, committed against enslaved women in their maternal roles. This type of violence was rendered possible by the slave market's treatment of enslaved women, their labor, and the products of that labor as "goods" (120). She reframes the violent separation of enslaved women and children by sale and wet-nursing as specific types of maternal violence enabled by a process of commodification of the maternal. What I termed a mother-machine dynamic or the displacement of the maternal to a space of capital accumulation both engenders and sustains such commodification and the related forms of maternal violence that her study traces.

In the course of her discussion of the market that white women created for enslaved wet nurses and their role in slavery's market transactions, Jones-

Rogers reports that during a whipping of an enslaved woman the mistress asked the enslaver to punish her but to make sure not to injure the woman's breasts as she was breastfeeding: "she ordered him to whip the enslaved female thoroughly for her crime, but she asked that he 'spare her breasts, as she [was] giving suck to a very young child'" (117). While it is unclear whether the enslaved woman was nursing her own child or the white woman's, this episode is emblematic not only of the high economic value attached to enslaved women's breasts and milk, but also of the fraught status of Black women's mothering.

For enslaved women, breastfeeding was an important means to connect to their offspring and rebel against the regulation of their mothering. But through the care and nurturance they provided to enslaved children, Black women also paradoxically helped increase the enslaver's wealth by reproducing what was regarded as "chattel" or moveable property. As Shaw has remarked, "slave owners and enslaved women participated in the processes of mothering in ways that often, ironically, reinforced each others' interests" even though "their views were sometimes in opposition," confirming the claim that "[t]he history of antebellum slavery is fraught with paradoxes" (237–38). These paradoxes were engendered by the clashing of two distinct but overlapping symbolic orders that gave different meanings to the maternal: the enslavers' brutal American grammar and Black women's maternal grammar.

In the dominant onto-epistemic scheme, the maternal practice of African American women became brutally commodified with the result that the economic praxis and logic of capital was forced upon maternal practice, co-opting it: enslavers created "grading systems" that informed interested parties "about the quality of enslaved women's breast milk" and their reproductive capacities (Jones-Rogers 116). The dominant order transmogrified Black women's maternal care into an extractable commodity: this reduction of Black mothering to a mere economic function harnessed to capital accumulation enabled the process of the "thingification" (Césaire 42) of Black life represented by the systematic denial of personhood upon which chattel slavery was predicated. This mother-machine dynamic through which slavery disabled Black motherhood echoes the one we have seen at work in *Invisible Man*'s protagonist's rebirth: Black motherhood is disabled via a machine that functions as an artificially reconstructed womb, and then displaced as white male figures of authority step in to dictate the terms according to which the rebirth will take place.

Enslavers' appropriation and regulation of Black women's reproductive capacities were paramount for the development of slavery since it ensured the constant supply of "marketable goods" fit to labor: it is not by chance that en-slavers understood the category of "pregnant" as a work category. As well as the violent kidnapping and enslaving of people from Africa, slavery survived and prospered through this brutal exploitation of Black women's reproductive capacities: enslavers regarded Black women of childbearing age as "sound investments that would augment their wealth with little effort or additional expense" (Jones-Rogers 34; Weinbaum 9).

The institutionalization and legal entrenchment of slavery began as early as 1662, when "An Act Defining the Status of Mulatto Bastards" was promulgated in Virginia, ensuring *partus sequitur ventrem*: with this law, "the fertility of the enslaved woman became the basis for the increase of human property" (Solinger 262). As a result, the maternal became entrenched as a space of capital accumulation rather than nurture. For enslavers, "producing children was a cheap alternative to purchasing them at the market" (qtd. In Jones-Rogers 21), and when the slave trade was abolished in 1808, which many historians consider a "turning point" in American history (Sublette 38), the forced reproduction of enslaved people assumed an even more pivotal role in maintaining the "peculiar institution." Tethering the Black maternal to the reproduction of what was considered property, the racial and maternal violence of slavery's dominant order of meaning placed Black mothers in a painful and contradictory position; they were forced to mother against antiblack violence that constantly sought to make mothering as a nurturing practice almost unthinkable. Under the institution of slavery, their mothering decisions had contradictory outcomes and were never completely free from the interference of racial terror.

To maximize profit-making opportunities, enslavers forced enslaved mothers not only to take care of but also to breastfeed white children; co-opted for the ends of capital, Black women's bodies and milk were seen as saleable goods to be exploited. Recent historical research has shown that the wet nursing of white children by enslaved women was more widespread than previously thought (Jones-Rogers 102–5; West and Knight 38). White women created the demand for this type of invisible and intimate, but also skilled labor, and they sometimes planned their pregnancies according to those of their slaves: they "were crucial to the further commodification of enslaved women's reproductive bodies, through the appropriation of their breast milk and the nutritive and maternal care they provided to white children" (102). This demand transformed "the ability to suckle into a skilled form of labor" that, violently appropriated by enslavers, resulted in huge economic profits for them (102). As Jones-Rogers has documented, Black women's milk could increase their market value as lactating bondswomen were advertised to be hired or sold, and their financial worth assigned according to specific qualities such as the "freshness" of their milk (114–19). As the episode cited at the beginning of this section demonstrates, a high economic value was attached to Black women's breasts and milk, "a value which the slave market and the economy of slavery shaped profoundly" (Jones-Rogers 105). Not only Black women's bodies, but also their milk, was converted into capital: the mother-machine dynamic of slavery resulted in a world in which breastfeeding itself was co-opted for the needs of capital and transformed into a practice of property development rather than nurture.

As Black wet nurses were closely supervised by their white mistresses, their opportunities for resistance were quite limited. However, enslaved women still managed to exercise some form of agency, confirming that they were neither passive nor helpless dependents. Enslaved women formed networks of kinship, developing practices of mothering based on the communal care of children, regardless of whether or not they were biological mothers. Bondswomen often shared their breast milk with other babies, especially when enslaved mothers were forced to labor away from their children or when they passed away or were sold. These practices bear witness to another system of meaning that reclaims the maternal as a potentially life-giving space of nurture, untethering it from capital accumulation while rewriting the value of Black life.

Historians Emily West and Erin Shearer report that in order not to give birth to enslaved children, bondswomen tried to control their fertility or induce abortions, and sometimes they desperately resorted to infanticide. Enslaved women often chewed cotton roots as it was believed they had a contraceptive effect. They took calomel or turpentine in order to induce abortions, even though this posed serious health risks (1012). Archaeological findings attest to the use of other abortifacients, such as okra, senna, and castor oil, which were African plants with medicinal uses imported to the Americas (Wilkie 275). Since these acts have the potential to eschew an imposed economic co-optation, the dominant order reframes them as further legitimizations of that order's grammar. For example, a Georgia doctor, noticing that enslaved women had significantly more abortions than his white patients, commented about "the unnatural tendency in the African female to destroy her offspring" (quoted in Davis 44), highlighting her "unfitness" for the maternal role and attempting to reify the maternal erasure and ontological annihilation that sustain slavery.

As Angela Davis has observed though, this doctor never "considered how 'unnatural' it was to raise children under the slave system" (44). Black women aborted their children so as not to give birth to other "commodities." Theirs were desperate acts of maternal care that disrupted the enslavers' symbolic order and its tethering of the maternal to economic accumulation. Abortions and infanticides were their desperate attempts to rebel against the system of slavery, which depended upon the reproductive control of Black women. Performed in the interests of mothering, these acts were a powerful assertion of maternal agency: Black women's choices were "mothering decisions—decisions not to mother" (qtd. in Solinger 266–67). They were difficult and painful choices mothers sometimes desperately made in order to save their children from the brutal violence of chattel slavery and thus underscored the value of Black life beyond the onto-epistemic limitations of slavery. However, according to the enslavers' system of meanings, which constructed enslaved women "as chattel who reproduced a commodity [. . .] at the will of the owner" (Solinger 263), their children represented their sexual degradation and dehumanization. In this order of meaning, the Black maternal cannot become visible as a space of nurture and care. Thus, enslavers could only construe such acts as confirmations of their racist views of Black women as disconnected from the progeny of their wombs: as Morrison has argued, there is an assumption "that slave women are not mothers; they are 'natally dead,' with no obligation to their offspring" (21).

In the fraught and violent context of slavery, enslaved mothers found themselves "in a contradictory and irreconcilable position" (Gardner 207). Breastfeeding and lovingly caring for enslaved children could paradoxically aid the perpetuation of the "peculiar institution" since they involuntarily helped slaveholders increase their "human property" (Shaw 241). By contrast, desperate acts like infanticide disrupted the system of slavery: refusing to nurse enslaved children, as Ella does in *Beloved*, was for enslaved mothers one desperate way to protect them from slavery. However, as the white doctor's comments demonstrate, abortions and infanticide were also strategically used by slaveholders to corroborate their paternalistic claims about the "natural inferiority" and dependency of Blacks. While involuntarily helping to sustain the system, the nurturing and care enslaved women provided to enslaved children challenged these claims, underlining human sameness and interdependence. But in the case of infanticides, the dominant symbolic order could not register such acts without distorting them.

These contradictions highlight how, under the brutal system of slavery, the maternal labor of Black women was rendered highly visible and invisible at the same time. Enslavers were dependent upon the maternal labor of enslaved women to care for their "human property." Yet, at the same time, they refused to acknowledge the importance and even existence of such maternal labor as an act of love, claiming that Black women were "not 'civilized'—not really 'attached' to their children" (Bouson 133). To dehumanize enslaved people, enslavers needed to obliterate the very maternal practices that helped them sustain the system of slavery; erased by the violence of slavery and yet necessary to its sustenance, the maternal labor of Black women was not only heavily regulated but also brutally co-opted for enslavers' strictly economic ends. Harnessed to the reproduction of capital and disfigured into a purely economic practice, in the dominant symbolic order, maternal labor could only count in so far as it produced "human property" that enslavers could own and exploit for free labor.

Not interested in preserving family life, enslavers treated Black people "as individual units of labor rather than as members of family units" (Glenn 5), performing a "profitable atomizing of the captive body" (Weheliye 38). But we might ask how such atomizing and transformation from a member of a family to a unit of labor was enacted. Echoing Jacobs's observation that a negation of family ties reduces enslaved people to a "living death" status (59), Patterson identifies "natal alienation" and "social death" as the two main features of slavery: "[D]enied all claims on, and obligations to, his [sic] parents and living blood relations" as well as "on his more remote ancestors and on his descendants," the enslaved subject becomes "truly a genealogical isolate," losing "all ties of birth in both ascending and descending generations" (5–6). Under slavery, the Black subject becomes "a social nonperson." Violently uprooted and "[a]lienated from all 'rights' or claims of birth, he cease[s] to belong in his own right to any legitimate social order" (Patterson 5). Social death is the ultimate outcome of the loss of natality: the enslaved person is transformed into a socially dead "nonperson" inhabiting a liminal state. Desocialized and depersonalized, the enslaved is then introduced to the community of his or her enslaver as a "nonbeing" (Patterson 28–33).

Alongside Patterson, scholars like Achille Mbembe, Dennis Childs, Eduardo Grüner, Stephanie Smallwood, and Anthony Bogues have articulated a living death or "living corpse" status for the enslaved. According to Mbembe, "[s]lave-life is, in many ways, a form of death-in-life [. . .] Because the slave's life is like a 'thing,' possessed by another person, slave existence appears as the perfect figure of a shadow" (75). However, drawing on the work of Meillassoux, Patterson has also foregrounded the processual nature of slavery, understanding it as a ritual or "process involving several transitional phases" (29), the first one being that of social negation, and the second that of "the changing of the slave's name" (30).

Rather than a state of being, social death and living death might then be more productively understood as phases in the process of enslavement or onticidal "technologies" (Dillon 627) through which enslaved Africans are reduced, to use Sylvia Wynter's words, to "so many units of labour power" (335). Transformed into what Dillon terms, drawing upon Giorgio Agamben, "bare labour," "the dehumanized body of the enslaved African is *forced* to live in order to work without respite" (628). Observing that "[t]o lose your mother was to be denied your kin, country, and identity" (85), the scholar Saidiya Hartman has directly connected this transformation from human into bare labor via genealogical loss and social death with maternal erasure, which, echoing Spillers, she posits as the foundational process in the creation of the enslaved: "in the era of the trade the enslaved had been forced to *forget mother*" (38, original italics). Ushered in by this maternal abjection that enables the mother-machine dynamic discussed in this section, enslavement's process of "thingification" is a praxis that, based upon the technologies of natal alienation, social death, and living death, performs the transformation into "bare labour" and relies on maternal violence.

Might it be that reclaiming the maternal could disrupt the foundational dynamics of such brutal transformations, challenging Meillassoux's claim that "[t]he captive [. . .] can never be brought to life again as such since [. . .] the slave will remain forever an unborn being (non-né)" (qtd. in Patterson 30)? If the technologies of natal alienation and social death are aimed at the production of bare labor, can a reenactment of maternal praxis, through the elaboration of new modalities of relation, reanimate those who are reduced to "being tools for the master" (Patterson 10)?

Otherworldly Loopholes

As we have seen, in *Incidents*, Jacobs rewrites the maternal as a gateway to freedom. But what allows her to reimagine the maternal in such terms is her narrative construction of what I call her otherworldly loophole from slavery. After being forcefully separated from her children, her narrative alter ego is able to escape this maternal violence by transforming an attic into her otherworldly "loophole of retreat," where she is mothered while mothering. While sometimes she refers to it as her "prison" and "this dark hole," she acknowledges that it is there that her emancipation can begin: the narrator muses that "there was no place, where slavery existed, that could have afforded me so good a place of concealment" (528–29). This suggests that the attic is situated outside slavery, even though it is slavery's maternal violence that engendered its very condition of possibility. Jacobs's narrative highlights how hiding there constitutes for Linda "the only means of avoiding the cruelties the laws allowed him [the enslaver] to inflict upon me!" (532); among these cruelties is maternal violence.

Escaping the slaveholder's gaze, Linda manages to surreptitiously watch over her children by carving out a small "peeping-hole" from which she can observe her children grow. The narrator makes clear that she participates in their rearing by consulting with her grandmother and voicing her concerns. For example, when she hears her son talking back to the enslaver, she begs her "not to allow the children to be impertinent to the irascible old man" (528). Rather than temporarily abdicating or rejecting the role of mother, as some scholars have suggested, from her loophole Linda is able to retain it, albeit in absentia. Even though her children cannot see her, she can see and hear them, being absently present in their lives. She states, "How I longed to *tell* them I was there!" (527, original italics). Spying on her children, Linda can recuperate some form of mothering. After Mr. Sands, the father of her children, tells her daughter that they are "motherless" and that Linda is dead, she leaves her place of concealment, risking her life, to speak with her daughter and invalidate his claims. Against the invisibility to which Mr. Sands wants to relegate her, Linda is determined to assert her maternal presence, even if it might imperil her life.

While managing to mother her children, in the garret, Linda also receives the maternal support of her grandmother, who provides her with food, drinks, and bedclothes, as well as that of Aunt Nancy, her uncle, and brother (267). During the second winter she spends in the garret, Linda gets sick because of the cold and falls unconscious. She states, "My limbs were benumbed by inaction [. . .] even my face and tongue stiffened, and I lost the power of speech" (533), finding herself in a state between life and death. Her brother and grandmother worry she might be dying and constantly check on her "to inquire whether there were any signs of returning to life" (533). Describing how in the garret Linda is mothered while mothering, Jacobs's text constructs an otherworld, her loophole, "where day and night were all the same" (526) and where she can be both dead and alive.

As McKittrick has argued, "while in the garret, Brent accentuates what Gillian Rose calls "paradoxical space" [. . .] Brent is everywhere and nowhere, north and south [. . .] There is both a separation from and connection to the world outside the attic; she is both inside and outside, captive and free" (41–42). Building upon her insights, I want to suggest that her position in the attic also allows her to mother while not mothering. Here, assuming a ghostly presence, Linda is described as at the same time seen (by her grandmother and other relatives) and unseen (by her children and her enslaver), the subject and object of mothering, present and absent, dead and alive, mother and not mother, haunting the place. It is only there, in such an otherworldly loophole where oppositions no longer hold, that Linda can temporarily escape slavery's co-optation of the maternal and redeem her children in absentia. Her narrative suggests that mothering while not mothering is the result of racial terror's disruption of the maternal.

Based on her own mothering experience, this otherworldly loophole construed by Jacobs's narrative can be seen as a literary metaphor for the situation in which many enslaved women found themselves. As Spillers has noted, enslaved women were "both mother and mother dispossessed" as enslavement displaced maternity ("Mama's" 80). However, in the plantation economy, they sometimes were able to conjure up spaces of possibilities as they tried to withstand slavery's dehumanizing exploitation. Camp has documented not only the brutal restrictions that slaveholders violently imposed upon enslaved women or what she describes as their "geography of containment," but also the "alternative ways of knowing and using plantation and southern space" these women created, and the conflicts that arose as a consequence (13). This "rival geography," a term which she takes from Edward Said and adapts to the context of the plantation South, offered them chances not so much of complete autonomy but of creativity, play, and resistance to the slaveholders' control. Even though it "did not threaten to overthrow American slavery, nor did it provide slaves with autonomous space," it "did provide space for private and public creative expression, rest and recreation, alternative communication and, importantly, resistance to planters' domination of slaves' every move" (7). Enslaved mothers were sometimes able to reunite with their children during the night, traveling on foot as Douglass's mother did, and sometimes they managed to breastfeed their children outside the rigid schedule established by their enslavers. Within the plantation, the ability of slaveholders to control enslaved women's maternal space, time, and body coincided with the occasional ability of enslaved women to defy the enslaver's co-optation of mothering for economic ends.

The alternative geography Camp traces bears witness to different ways of knowing and being in the world that evidence alternate "origin stories" than those of the "mathematics of the unliving" (McKittrick 17). Enslaved women constructed their own otherworlds governed by a mode of reason that challenged the foundations of the enslaver's onto-epistemic scheme, conjuring up not only a rival geography but effectively endorsing a rival maternal onto-epistemology. This was based on African-derived practices of othermothering and communal support as well as the ancestral knowledge of conjure women who knew how to use herbs to poison the slaveholder or to abort. Out of what Achille Mbembe called the necropolitical space of slavery, alternative understandings of the world or what Wynter termed "counter-worlds" (qtd. in Erasmus 61), developed: "through new cultural practices," enslaved people reforged "communities of belonging" (61), mothering otherwise and shaping their own understanding of what it means to be human. These enabled them to inhabit their own loopholes of retreat, creatively reimagined in Jacobs's narrative reconstruction.

As we will see, the narratives upon which this book focuses rewrite Jacobs's otherworldly loophole as they reimagine an ancestral archive of Black women's maternal practices that allows them to inhabit liminal maternal spaces: they create what I have termed literary otherworlds that allow a reclamation of mothering despite racial violence. Showing how these are rendered necessary by the violent disruptions of the maternal engendered by racial terror, they foreground the possibility for a remaking of subjectivities that maternal praxis can generate: any place can potentially become an otherworld as a result of a maternal reimagination of the human in different terms than those established by Western modernity.

Neoliberal Reason

While the meanings that mothering acquires under neoliberal and antebellum America remain tied to each era's historical specificities and are thus not directly translatable, a closer scrutiny unveils troubling resonances. Revealing the afterlife of the mode of thought that Weinbaum has called the "slave episteme," the narratives upon which this study focuses suggest that, while antebellum and 1980s neoliberal America might seem unrelated historical periods, they share more similarities than might appear. Interrogating and placing side by side the distinct yet interrelated histories of maternal violence and disruption of each historical period can help us untangle the complex prehistory of the development of the onto-epistemic order of a culture based upon marketplace values and a related conception of the human as *homo economicus*. These texts' portrayals of maternal practices reveal that, while antebellum and neoliberal America are very distinct historical periods, the disruption of maternal praxis remains foundational for securing Man's onto-epistemic order. They highlight how many of the problematics of mothering during slavery persist in neoliberal America, if only under a different guise, establishing the maternal as a pivotal locus through which "master narratives of humanness" (McKittrick xxiv) are constructed but also disrupted.

Opposing the dehumanizing practices of neoliberalism and the various forms of racial terror on which it is based, these narratives challenge the orthodoxy of neoliberalism, underlining the existence of sinister historical continuities in the ways both neoliberal reason and slavery reconfigure the human under economic terms and legitimate the devaluation of Black lives through a maternal co-optation. While the so-called "Reagan Revolution" of the 1980s is often hailed as inaugurating a new era of prosperity in the United States, these texts refute the illusion of the "postracial" society promoted by Ronald Reagan's rhetoric. While neoliberalism might seem to have little in common with slavery, these narratives unveil the continuities that exist between the two. In doing so, they seek to reclaim the maternal and its possibilities for a reimagining of the subjectivities undone by racial terror.

As the dominant ideology of 1980s America preaching individual liberties, neoliberalism is often depicted as the antithesis of slavery: on the official website of Reagan's presidential library, Reaganomics is presented as the "Second American Revolution," linking it to the values of "equality and freedom," while he is described as a passionate defender of human rights who left a "freedom legacy." Reagan's America is thus staged as far removed from the antebellum slaveholding South. But what does "human" mean, and how is "human well-being" defined under neoliberalism? Who are those Americans who, in the words of Reagan, will "share in the bounty of a revived economy," and who are those whose existence, on the contrary, will need to be crushed to "make America great again?" Under the onto-epistemic order of neoliberalism, who can inhabit modes of "symbolic life," and who needs to be relegated to the status of "symbolic death?"

Rehashing dynamics that had been entrenched during slavery, neoliberal reason upholds a symbolic order that cannot register the Black maternal as a valid site of subject formation, reframing it as a deathbound space for the ontological annihilation of Black life. This enables a disruption of maternal practice, leaving Black mothers in an untenable position where they find themselves constantly under attack: African American mothers "have been positioned in the rhetoric [of neoliberalism] as manifestly unsuited for and incapable of assimilation into the market relations fostered by neoliberalism" (56). The racial violence that neoliberalism upholds and perpetuates relies upon an erasure and co-optation of the maternal, transforming it into a politically charged praxis where onto-epistemic negotiations occur.

As scholars such as Dorothy Roberts have shown, the 1970s and 1980s saw a revival of a longstanding castigation of Black single mothers. The "welfare queen" or "welfare mother" was one of the myths that made up what has been termed the "Reagan mythology." In his 1976 campaign, he repeatedly told the anecdote, playing on an established racist imaginary. Reminiscent of the "breeder" stereotype "that portrayed Black women as perpetual but indifferent mothers" (7) and that was popularized during slavery, the welfare queen myth constructs Black (and Brown) mothers as "irresponsibly procreating" an offspring that will become, much like them, a "burden to the state" and to taxpayers, recalling a similar dynamic at play during the campaign against so-called "crack mothers." While during slavery the Black maternal was disabled through its tethering to a status of non-being, the neoliberal symbolic order similarly invalidates the Black maternal by linking it to another form of death-in-life: the Black mother is seen as passing down to her progeny what is deemed a "culture of poverty," "nurturing it through her deviant mothering practices" (Gumbs 1) that do not conform to neoliberal values. In an antiblack world that perpetuates the devaluation of Black life, endorsing the "literal and social death of Black women and children" (Gumbs 2), the Black maternal continues to be delegitimized as a valid form of subject formation, i.e., a valid human-making site, and thus cannot be perceived as other than problematic and deviant, always in need of intervention.

Echoing the racist assumptions of enslavers, who regarded enslaved mothers as "indifferent" to their children, the negative stereotype of the welfare queen as a quintessentially "bad" mother draws upon a racist imaginary or what Collins has called a set of "controlling images" that characterize a dominant symbolic order that traces its roots to slavery. Daniel Patrick Moynihan's infamous 1965 report, "The Negro Family: The Case for National Action" popularized the related stereotype of the so-called "Black Matriarch" as a destroyer of family values. Much like the "welfare mother" is constructed as lazy and irresponsible and thus as the embodied antithesis of neoliberal values, what "family values" are the "Black Matriarch" supposedly menacing?

Moynihan is blamed African American single mothers for the widespread poverty in their communities in a rhetoric that, much like Reagan's, puts the emphasis on individual responsibilities. In the report, the African American family structure, traced back to slavery, is identified as "a tangle of pathology" that is "capable of reproducing itself without assistance from the white world" because of Black matriarchy: "the Negro community has been forced into a matriarchal structure which, because it is so far out of line with the rest of American society, seriously retards the progress of the group as a whole and imposes a crushing burden on the Negro male, and, in consequence, on a great many Negro women as well" (75). Pathologizing (and misnaming) the supposedly "matriarchal" structure of Black families, the report blamed Black women who allegedly emasculated Black men, precluding them from assuming the role of patriarch. Rather than considering Black mothers' experiences, the report focused on the supposed lack of a male breadwinner and identified this as the main issue and marker of socioeconomic inequality. Animated by white male anxiety about the Black maternal, the report sought to contain such menace by assimilating it into the white heteropatriarchal model against which Black mothers were (and are) evaluated and found lacking. Positing a culturally specific heteronormative and patriarchal family as the norm, the report assumed a narrow and provincial understanding of what constitutes mothering. Against this Western family ideal, in which the biological mother is assigned full responsibility for the children, the report evaluated maternal performance based on the "ability to procure the benefits of a nuclear family household" (Collins 181) and the (re)production of a liberal humanist understanding of subjectivity. It thus failed to recognize the communal networks of child-rearing support that Black women developed in order to mother in spite of racial terror. These networks often extended beyond the biological family to include "fictive kin," and, while woman-centered, they were "not predicated upon male powerlessness" (Collins 178). Once again, in a world dominated by racial violence, Black maternal praxis is erased and cannot be registered unless it is tethered to the pathological or the deviant: to imagine it otherwise would shake the onto-epistemic foundations of such an antiblack world.

For all its bashing of the supposedly matriarchal structure of African American families, the Moynihan Report never once mentions Black mothers, failing to acknowledge the labor of love they continuously perform or the strong networks of community-based childcare they manage to cherish despite harsh socioeconomic conditions: the Black mother remains a shadowy presence that haunts the Report throughout. This results in an erasure of Black mothering that sinisterly echoes and extends the one we have seen at work during slavery as it remains based on a paradoxical dynamic of present absence. Deemed unfit to mother, the Black mother is "rendered abject in both her absence and her presence" (73) as her maternal praxis is erased and disabled. Still disfigured, if only more indirectly, the Black maternal can become visible only as a locus for the undoing of subjectivities, remaining invisible as life-giving praxis: this sustains the creation of what Lorde has theorized as the "constant, if unspoken, distortion of vision" of racial terror (Sister 42).

In the dominant order, the maternal can only be understood through an economic lens and thus becomes an economically co-opted form that can potentially produce profit, this time in terms of "human capital," i.e., individuals that can be fully assimilated into the American economic market and thus become subjects recognized by the dominant society. The ruling ethos of capital accumulation requires a specific mode of understanding mothering that ensures it remains geared towards the (re)production of specific types of subjectivities and their correlative "non-subjectivities." It thus casts all alternative understandings of the maternal, which could threaten the stability of its symbolic order and its concomitant values and categories of the "human" and "nonhuman," as deviant or pathological. Always framed as in need of intervention, the Black maternal becomes the quintessential embodiment of a constructed "lack" that becomes tied to the reproduction of what are deemed "deviant" forms of the human. Not at all unprecedented in its conclusions, the Moynihan Report, as Spillers has observed, feeds back into the long history of the erasure and manipulation of maternal praxis, which can come into view only in economic terms as producing a space of capital accumulation rather than nurture with the result that, in this dominant order governed by racial (and maternal) violence, Black mothering, as Nash has documented, becomes tethered to crisis.

In her ground-breaking study *Killing the Black Body,* Roberts has traced the roots of these twentieth-century forms of maternal violence and co-optation to the enduring legacies of slavery, as the rhetoric surrounding debates over welfare and fetal protection attest. In welfare legislation, Black mothers have been often disciplined for alleged "failures" to perform "appropriate" mothering. Rendering the Black maternal invisible because it is unable to yield what can be considered as "valuable economic output" has allowed the attendant disregard for Black children's well-being. Ostensibly lacking "proper" maternal skills, poor women of color have been often forcibly deprived of their offspring. This is how Malcolm X described the maternal disruption his family suffered at the hands of the state, comparing foster care to the system of slavery: "Soon the state people were making plans to take over all of my mother's children [. . .] there was a crowd of new white people entering the picture—always asking questions [. . .] A Judge McClennan in Lansing had authority over me and all of my brothers and sisters. We were 'state children,' court wards; he had the full say-so over us. A white man in charge of a black man's children! Nothing but legal, modern slavery—however kindly intentioned." (21) Yates-Richard's observations about *Invisible Man*'s hospital scene can be applied here as this episode is a further instantiation of the maternal displacement that relegates "the process of rebirth to authoritative white male figures" (494). Ellison's womb-machine and Douglass's closet perform a similar displacement that erases the narrator's being through the severance of his maternal links, foreclosing not only Black maternal subjectivity but Black subjectivity altogether. Remembering when he visited his mother, Malcolm states that "she didn't recognize me at all [. . .] She didn't know who I was" (22). That is why he would never talk about her with anyone (22). The maternal is erased and displaced at the hands of a white man in an attempt to unmake Black subjects. As LaShonda Carter and Tiffany Willoughby-Herald have observed, "Black children's lives are available to be taken at any time under what Black people refer to as a regime of terror" (99). While disguised under different forms, racial violence still seeks to erase and co-opt Black mothering for ontological annihilation, engaging in various forms of racial and maternal violence that echo and extend those perpetuated by enslavers and their symbolic order.

In order to perform this erasure and co-optation, Black mothers have long been cast as irresponsibly procreating and lacking maternal skills, stripping them of their maternal identity. For example, a *New York Times* article entitled "Child Play Is Taught to Mothers in Ghetto" (1972) suggests that Black mothers need instruction in order to "properly" perform an "acceptable" form of mothering. Portrayed as either "welfare queens" or "crack whores," Black women are rarely referred to as mothers in public discourse. Even when they are, the term is immediately accompanied by adjectives that try to invalidate such an experience: "mother in trouble," "teenager," and "crack mom" immediately consign Black mothers to a marginal space and contest their inclusion into the white category of "good mother." As was the case in the Moynihan Report, Black mothers continue to be depicted as "caustic elements in the nuclear family" that are "antithetical to a conventional American way of life" (Césaire 518) as well as to a dominant mode of understanding the human.

It is in the context of this ongoing devaluation of Black mothering and the concomitant preoccupation with the policing of Black women's maternal skills that the media fixation with the figure of the crack mother during the Reagan administration must be read. Newspapers were keen to emphasize supposed maternal neglect, reporting stories about women who allegedly exchanged their children to buy crack.[2] Musing about how to protect the offspring, *The Washington Post* published an article entitled "Crack Babies: The Worst Threat Is Mom Herself." The *New York Times* suggested that "The Instincts of Parenthood Become Part of Crack's Toll": citing medical experts, this article claimed that "the maternal instinct gets blocked out because the only thing that matters is the addiction" (8). The *Los Angeles Times* quoted an expert who noted that "[t]he absence of a father is bad, but now the mother is missing" (35). The crack epidemic became an occasion for the press and the state to erase the Black maternal and then stage it as a site of "hereditary deviance," tapping into a longstanding tradition that, viewing Black mothering as a threat to the dominant order, has sought to erase and displace the maternal. The rhetoric around so-called "crack mothers" casts Black mothers as "purveyors of death and destruction" (Césaire 518) in an attempt to tether Black motherhood to a status of symbolic death, echoing a dynamic that originated in slavery.

As Black feminist scholars have shown, attaching the element of criminality to the trope of the "bad" Black mother, the racist stereotype of the "crack mother" is employed to justify not only the "disproportionate interventions into Black families by child services" but also "the over-criminalization and mistreatment of pregnant Black mothers" (Roberts 48). State prosecutors, legislators, and judges have taken a punishing stance against women who use drugs while pregnant by jailing them, forcibly depriving them of custody of their children, and prosecuting them after their children are born. As Roberts has noted, poor Black women are more likely to be reported to government authorities because of the racist attitudes of healthcare professionals and because they are under greater government supervision through welfare agencies and public hospitals. She understands these prosecutions as originating in the oppressive politics that devalued Black motherhood during slavery.

As the current trend of ever rising and disproportionate rates of incarceration for African Americans demonstrates, Black women continue to be deprived of their children through child welfare agencies and the prison industrial complex. As the maternal is erased and then displaced by white officials, the prison functions as a proxy womb that rebirths convicts to what Colin Dayan has termed "civic death," condemning them to inhabit a liminal status that echoes that of enslaved people: "the conversion logic" of slavery and its codes, which turned humans into things or socially dead nonpersons, remains at the basis of the mass incarceration program which condemns human beings to civil death. The erasure and co-optation of the Black maternal become the route through which such ontological annihilations are performed: echoing the dynamics of slavery, this conversion logic pivots around a displacement of the maternal that devalues Black mothering and delegitimizes it as a valuable site of subject formation. In an antiblack world, the Black maternal remains tethered to death and loss. If during slavery maternal praxis was erased and then harnessed to the production of social death, racial violence continues to transfigure Black mothering as a space of death—creating an environment in which Black women's "fear that their child could, at any moment [. . .] be subject to some form of racial terror," whether literal death or the civil death of the carceral state, impinges on their choice to have children, "which is another attack on their reproductive rights" (Césaire 521). Césaire, Melonas, and Jones have termed this form of racial violence aimed at the control of Black women's reproduction "Black maternal necropolitics," (522) a form of racially motivated maternal erasure, which extends the forms of "maternal violence" that Jones-Rogers has traced. In an antiblack world, maternal praxis remains marked by contradictions, ambivalence, and forms of racial terror that echo those we discussed in relation to slavery, making necessary the reclamation and reimagination of maternal practice as an alternative praxis of being that, while staged in the face of death and loss, manages to exceed them.

Constructed as unassimilable to white, middle-class, and heteropatriarchal standards geared towards the reproduction of human capital, i.e., workers who can comply and fit into the American labor market, Black women's maternal praxis cannot be registered as other than pathological and in need of control. Whether as "welfare mothers," "Black matriarchs," or "crack mothers," poor Black mothers often continue to be regarded as purveyors of various forms of death and deviance, and their maternal praxis is erased and transfigured as a site for the reproduction of "degeneracy," "unfitness," "civil death," or other forms of death-in-life. Invalidated as a site for nurturing what is regarded as symbolic life in the dominant neoliberal order, Black maternal praxis is co-opted for the creation of what are considered "wasted lives," "crack babies," or "civilly dead nonsubjects" whom the neoliberal society needs to relegate to the death-worlds of the prison or foster care, where their social links are further erased. Here these various forms of lives undone can then be disposed of or rebirthed at the hands of white officials, which happens in *Invisible Man*'s hospital scene.

Motherhood continues to be made into a forum where origin stories of the human based upon a brutal American grammar that upholds racial terror are affirmed. However, as the texts analyzed here suggest, these narratives that reify the human as Man can be challenged and, in the process, subjectivities reimagined. Attempting to untether Black motherhood from death and positing maternal praxis as a life-making practice staged against "Black maternal necropolitics," the literary works upon which this book focuses suggest that it is through a rewriting of maternal praxis that a rethinking of Man's origin stories and a remaking of the human can take place.

But what kind of subjectivities do these neoliberal narratives or origin stories seek to mold? If Black women's maternal praxis cannot come into view as a valid site of human-making so that it is regarded as deviant and pathological, what kind of human is maternal praxis supposed to be (re)producing? In other words, how is the human, and its corollary "archipelago of Human Otherness" (Wynter 321), constructed under neoliberalism?

To understand how neoliberalism (re)makes the human, we must extend our definition of the term, grasping its complexity as an ideology that embraces every sphere of life. Unable to legitimize noncontractual relationships, the neoliberal mode of reason recasts all relations in terms of the contractual exchanges of the market. Even though neoliberalism takes historically and geographically specific forms, constantly changing and adapting to different places and eras, viewing it more broadly as an all-encompassing, normative mode of reason, rather than just as a set of historically situated state policies, allows a deeper understanding of its ideological complexity. As Aihwa Ong has noticed, "[n]eoliberalism is merely the most recent development of such techniques that govern human life, that is, a governmentality that relies on market knowledge for a politics of subjection and subject-making that continually places in question the political existence of modern human beings" (13). As a normative order of reason dominated by unbridled individualism and free market capitalism, neoliberalism "transmogrifies every human domain and endeavor, along with humans themselves, according to a specific image of the economic" (Foucault 224–225; Brown 10). As Wendy Brown has underlined, for neoliberal reasoning, "[a]ll conduct is economic conduct, all spheres of existence are framed and measured by economic terms and metrics, even when the spheres are not directly monetized. In neoliberal reason and in domains governed by it, we are only and everywhere *homo oeconomicus*" (10). Refashioning noneconomic spheres, neoliberal reason redefines even social and ethical life according to economic norms, remaking the human into *homo economicus*.

Foucault in his "Lectures at the College de France" defined *homo economicus* as the "entrepreneur of himself, being for himself his own capital, being for himself his own producer, being for himself the source of [his] earnings" (226). Building on Foucault's work, Wynter argues that our genre-specific and auto-instituting mode of being human is rooted in a conception of Man as a bioeconomic subject whose salvation is postulated in economic terms (261): "[t]he new and present mode of salvation is, therefore, that of the unceasing mastery of natural scarcity by means of ever-increasing economic growth" (262). She goes on to observe how this genre of the human, Man2, is a bioeconomic subject "defined as a jobholding Breadwinner, and even more optimally, as a successful 'masterer of Natural Scarcity' (Investor, or capital accumulator)" (321). This "new descriptive statement of the human" calls for the concomitant creation of a class of "underdeveloped" or "economically damnés," and "in the Euro-Americas, it is the freed Negro, together with the Indians [. . .] who will now be interned in the new institution of Poverty/Joblessness" (321). These are the subjects unmade and rejected but whom *homo economicus's* mode of reason "cannot do without," and inhabiting "the edge of modernity, they return to haunt it as its constitutive, inner repudiation" (McClintock 72).

As we shall see, determined to escape from the archipelago of Human Otherness by molding themselves into the image of *homo economicus*, Jerome Johnson in *Praisesong for the Widow*, Macon Dead in *Song of Solomon*, and Luther Nedeed in *Linden Hills* all act in accordance with *homo economicus's* neoliberal praxis of being, which revolves around economic calculations and depends upon economic paradigms like capital and value. Their mode of practice co-opts the maternal, echoing slavery's processes of "thingification" and engendering the withdrawal of mothering that in *Zami* and *The Salt Eaters* becomes apparent in, respectively, maternal abjection and motherless landscapes.

But, in response to the maternal erasures occasioned by the neoliberal mode of reason and its narrative of the human, these texts conjure up a maternal grammar as they negotiate a maternal mediating space that recalls Jacobs's otherworldly loophole and that allows a reimagination of maternal practice in terms different than those imposed by *homo economicus*'s symbolic order. Turning to explorations of maternal praxes informed by an ancestral past, these narratives evoke her construction of an otherworldly loophole that enables her to mother otherwise, that is, according to a different mode of reason than that upon which the plantation was based, disrupting the economic co-optation of the maternal and its undoing of subjectivities.

Only from the point of view of Man's dominant order can one proclaim that the maternal is irretrievably lost. While this dominant order's archive has violently erased the maternal to enforce the ontological annihilation of Black life, Black women have often managed to preserve maternal ties and pass them down, even if official systems refused to acknowledge it. As Black feminist historians such as Tiya Miles have begun to demonstrate, Black women have (re)imagined, through their maternal praxes, a maternal archive of Black life or, to use Kevin Quashie's term, "Black aliveness." Attuned to its own maternal grammar and thus inaccessible through the lens of the brutal American grammar that Spillers has traced, it is this maternal archive that the texts analyzed here narratively recreate. But what does this maternal grammar look like and how does it rewrite the human?

A Maternal Grammar

In African American culture, the potential for both control and defiance that lies in the maternal has long been evident. As we have seen, historians of slavery have underlined that such a link was already apparent in the case of enslaved mothers, who cultivated an alternative maternal practice that challenged the basis of plantation life, a process narrativized in some slave autobiographies such as Jacobs's. In the 1970s and 1980s, a period that coincides with a "Black women's literary renaissance" as well as with the rise of neoliberal reason, African American literature often tends to focus on the maternal as a resilient force that can sustain life in the face of the deadly consequences of racial terror, evoking the potential of Jacobs's otherworldly loophole. Walker's understanding of freedom as an act of "fearlessly pull[ing] out of ourselves [. . .] the living creativity some of our great-grandmothers were not allowed to know," (242) in its reframing of freedom as a retrieval of the maternal, aligns itself with Jacobs's. In Walker's writing, as well as in many texts written by her contemporaries, Black motherhood becomes "synonymous with self-making, world-making, creativity, spirituality, and utopianism waged in the face of antiblackness" (Gumbs 10). Published in this period, the narratives upon which this book focuses revisit the link between maternal praxis and the creation of otherworldly loopholes that had been fundamental for the survival of the African American community since slavery, challenging neoliberalism as a normative order of reason and its perpetuation of racial violence.

By divergent means, each text analyzed here exposes the continuities between a post-civil rights United States and the antebellum South. However, if slavery, as Hartman writes, "established a measure of man and a ranking of life that has yet to be undone" (25), these texts reiterate the regenerative potential of ancestral maternal practices. Rupturing the maternal co-optation and related maternal abjection that like a *fil rouge* run throughout American history from slavery to the Moynihan Report and Reagan's rhetoric, these narratives reclaim the maternal as a means to remake the subjectivities undone by racial violence: against a brutal American grammar, they put forward a maternal grammar of the human. In their focus on the maternal, these texts situate themselves into a wider tradition of African American writing that aims at reclaiming maternal bonds and has its roots in the fraught historical context of slavery.

In *Song of Solomon*, Ruth's belated breastfeeding echoes the violent exploitation of enslaved mothers as wet-nurses while Aunt Pilate's and Circe's othermothering praxis is informed by the communal values enslaved women cultivated despite slavery's horrors. In *Linden Hills*, Willa's maternal ethics of care prompt her to look after the son her husband's economic logic killed, challenging his neoliberal mode of reason. *Praisesong for the Widow* contrasts Avey and Jay's descent into the symbolic underworld of *homo economicus* with Aunt Cuney's semiotic terrain where Pan-African connections can rupture the deadly effects of neoliberal reason, reimaging its signifying praxis as a maternal one. Attempting not only to construct a new narrative for herself but also to rewrite the subjectivation process, *Zami* reclaims the maternal connections that neoliberal forms of dehumanization, redolent of those perpetuated during slavery, severed. Against an urban environment devoid of the recreational facilities Black mothers and children need, *The Salt Eaters* conjures up a maternal playground to imagine Black being anew through a reclamation of playing as a maternal praxis.

1

Naming and Belated Breastfeeding

Maternal practices in Toni Morrison's *Song of Solomon* remain afflicted by the traumatic legacy of racial terror. Unveiling the painful contradictions that arise from mothering in a world of violent antiblackness where the maternal is co-opted by capital, this novel probes crucial questions. What does it mean to mother against the racial violence of an antiblack world founded upon a brutal erasure of Black subjectivity? Can the trauma caused by this brutality ever be fully overcome?

In this chapter, I argue that, striving to overcome these contradictions, the maternal practices in *Song of Solomon* strive to imagine an alternative space where mothering can take place outside white patriarchal authority. But they also attest to the impossibility of fully repairing the devastating effects of anti-blackness, rearticulating, through their ambiguous outcomes, the problematics of mothering in an antiblack world, rather than resolving them. While this novel suggests the necessity and achievability of a maternal otherworld, it also highlights its limitations against a context of racial terror. Conjuring up an otherworld defined by a nonlinear understanding of time and African-based cosmologies, Aunt Pilate's and Circe's maternal practices seem successful in aiding Milkman's development, but right after having glimpsed the possibility of enacting a relational mode of being, he dies. In spite of its hopeful movement towards a creative otherworld, mothering remains marked by tragic outcomes, echoing a similar dynamic in *Paradise* (1998).

Song of Solomon's concern with the relationship between motherhood and the violent history of antiblack terror becomes apparent in a scene of belated breastfeeding early in the novel, where Ruth keeps nursing her son even though he is four years old, taking pleasure in sensing his self-control: "She felt him. His restraint, his courtesy, his indifference, all of which pushed her into fantasy. She had the distinct impression that his lips were pulling from her a thread of light. It was as though she were a cauldron issuing spinning gold. Like the miller's daughter—the one who sat at night in a straw-filled room, thrilled with the secret power Rumpelstiltskin had given her: to see golden thread stream from her very own shuttle." (13–14)

The first sensuous sentences of this rapturous, troubling scene juxtapose "[h]is restraint" and "his indifference" with her "fantasy," emphasizing Ruth's physical sensations, which drive her imagination. The paragraph also draws a comparison between Ruth's nursing activity and the miller's daughter's magical spinning, underlining her feeling of empowerment and seemingly casting her breastfeeding as a nurturing practice with a transformative potential.

However, the comparison to "a cauldron issuing spinning gold" becomes problematic if we recall the mother-machine dynamic through which slavery disabled Black motherhood. The comparison the text is drawing has troublesome connotations since, while conveying a sense of empowerment for Ruth, at the same time it undermines such a reading by recalling the brutal exploitation of Black mothers during slavery. As we shall see, even the allusion to the German fairy tale of Rumpelstiltskin, while seemingly affirmative of Ruth's creative powers, problematizes such an interpretation since the imp threatens to take away the miller's daughter's child. Given the brutal history of racial terror and its co-optation of the maternal, the allusion underlines the disrupted and ever-fragile mother-child bond that Ruth is desperately trying to restore.

A celebratory analysis of Ruth's breastfeeding is also complicated by the sexual undertones of the scene.[1] Ruth's belated breastfeeding and her son's unwillingness reveal her neglect of him and open her to charges of incestuous behavior. Nursing her son on her own terms, she tries to reclaim him but she also objectifies him. The fact that the discovery of Ruth's breastfeeding leads to her son's renaming as Milkman is similarly ambiguous: while such renaming might seem to assert maternal agency and familial bonds, it also reveals Ruth's possessive and controlling drive as naming is a way to assert dominance.[2]

As we will see, the novel employs this dialectic dynamic to describe Ruth's approach to mothering. Milkman's conception and birth remain afflicted by similar paradoxes, and, while she proves able to nurture a watermark as if it were alive, she cannot relate to her son as a person. Her practice thus impedes a fully successful reclamation of human subjectivity and allows her "fitness" for the maternal role to be questioned. Casting her mothering in highly ambiguous terms as both empowering and disempowering, the text shows how Ruth's maternal practice remains afflicted by painful contradictions that echo those the system of slavery violently imposed upon enslaved women's decisions. Ruth finds herself struggling to mother and claim human status for herself and her son against a system of antiblack terror that transforms Black subjects into units of labor through a disruption of the maternal. Under these traumatic circumstances, Ruth's belated breastfeeding can only have discordant outcomes, calling attention to the meaning of motherhood when it occurs under forces that not only inhibit a mother's agency and power but also frustrate any attempt at claiming human subjectivity.

Through the depiction of Ruth's maternal practices, *Song of Solomon* reveals African American motherhood to be still affected by the violent legacy of racial terror. This novel centers upon the fraught history of the devaluation and exploitation of Black motherhood, and its maternal practices need to be understood in light of this commodification of Black mothers' bodies that started with slavery but by no means ended there. By considering this violent background in which breastfeeding becomes a practice of property development rather than nurture and women as midwives and conjurers are rendered obsolete by white healthcare professionals, this chapter analyzes the maternal practices in the novel. Through the description of such praxes, Morrison's text exposes the inadequacy of a model of subjectivity grounded on an individualistic and possessive idea of the individual, and its concomitant hierarchical order of being centered upon exclusions, highlighting the need to move beyond its representational grammar.

In the first section of this chapter, I will return to Ruth's maternal practices. Her nurturance of a watermark, her birthing of Milkman, her belated breastfeeding, and the subsequent renaming all endow Ruth with generative powers. Ruth's nurturing of the watermark is a key precedent for her breastfeeding since it highlights her creative abilities, stifled by her sterile marriage. I will suggest that, through this act of nurturance, she does prove able to remake her understanding of being, allowing her to imagine a transcendence of racial terror. But this attainment remains fleeting and temporary, never immune from the incursion of racial terror. What Hartman calls the "afterlife of slavery" continues to have negative effects, leading directly to Ruth's belated breastfeeding. This section shows how Ruth's maternal practices resonate with a brutal history of racial terror grounded in slavery's maternal violence, attesting to the impossibility of fully overcoming its abusive legacy.

In the second section, to consolidate my reading of *Song of Solomon,* I draw upon archival evidence that illustrates the practices of communal mothering and midwifery during and after slavery since the novel's portrayal of Pilate and Circe needs to be understood in light of this historical context. I interpret Pilate and Circe as otherworldly mothers whose characterization draws heavily on the historically powerful praxes of midwives—or "othermothers" as Rosalie Riegle Troester first described the "women who assist bloodmothers by sharing mothering responsibilities" (qtd. in Collins 192)—in plantation culture. Under the condition of slavery, it was paramount to develop networks to care for children communally, since mothers were often violently separated from their offspring. The novel similarly makes a case for the necessity of communal mothering for the upbringing of Milkman as Ruth needs to be assisted by Pilate and Circe.

In the third section, I will look closely at the influence of their maternal practices on Milkman's development. As a result of Ruth's disrupted maternal practice, Pilate and Circe need to complement her role. Pilate's cooking of an egg and her storytelling initiate Milkman's process of re-subjectivization, while Circe's revelations direct him toward his final quest, which leads him back to Pilate's teachings. Focusing on these two pivotal scenes in the novel, I will demonstrate how they allow Morrison's text to create a maternal otherworld defined by a nonlinear understanding of time and characterized by African-based cosmologies, where mothering can take place, allowing Milkman to imagine his subjectivity in different terms than those provided by racial terror. As an antidote to the isolated and incestuous breastfeeding of Ruth, the novel puts forward, through Pilate's and Circe's mothering, a collective maternal practice that echoes and extends that of enslaved women.

In the last section, I will move to a close reading of the end of the novel, which reveals motherhood to be still affected by the brutal legacy of racial terror. Milkman embraces the maternal practice of Pilate, singing to his dying aunt as she sang to him. As opposed to Ruth's non-developmental nurturing, Pilate's and Circe's mothering aids Milkman's development as an individual who can embrace a relational conception of subjectivity. But after having glimpsed this possibility, Milkman dies, surrendering to the destructive violence symbolized by his friend Guitar in a last flight towards death. Morrison's novel suggests that a creative otherworld can be achieved, as evidenced in Pilate and Circe's communal upbringing of Milkman. However, it also relates such an accomplishment to the giving up of life. The ending of the novel thus highlights racial terror's ongoing disruption of the maternal while admitting the possibility of a reclamation of mothering, however fleeting and temporary.

Maternal Reclamation?

Toni Morrison's work as a novelist reflects her intense engagement as in-house editor of *The Black Book* (1974), "'a scrapbook' of African American history" (Wall 105) that brings together disparate historical materials of the everyday. Her novels similarly engage in a recuperation of the intimate lives of common people, suppressed in historical accounts. *Beloved* is based on the story of a runaway slave, while the photo of a dead girl in James Van der Zee's *The Harlem Book of the Dead* (1978) sparked the writing of *Jazz* (1992). Her work recovers the collective history of a people through a creative reimagination of their "unwritten interior" lives ("Site" 238). As Morrison herself has acknowledged, her writing of *Beloved* was motivated by the "national amnesia" that surrounded slavery. Morrison states: "There is no suitable memorial or plaque [. . .] There's no small bench by the road [. . .]. And because such a place doesn't exist (that I know of), the book had to" ("Bench" 44). Written in a period when African American historical records amounted to "archives of silence" (Le Goff 182), *Song of Solomon*, like *Beloved*, constitutes Morrison's attempt to create a democratic site of memory, the bench by the road that had yet to be erected to memorialize the sufferings of many thousands gone. As Theodor Mason has noted, Morrison "is a writer particularly interested in depicting, and thereby preserving and perpetuating, the cultural practices of Black communities. [. . .] The novelist, then, is not a figure isolated from history and culture but rather is someone who conserves cultural forms and practices by depicting them in the public art of fiction" (172). In *Song of Solomon*, Morrison imaginatively rewrites maternal praxes that can be traced back to slavery.

While this novel, with its contemporaneous setting, might seem anomalous, it remains informed by Morrison's creative engagement with historical memory as the maternal practices in the novel need to be understood in light of the brutal history of Black women's exploitation. Morrison's text shows how they remain affected by this legacy of racial terror: even a middle-class patriarchal household located in a twentieth-century northern city, such as that of Ruth, cannot escape the maternal co-optation engendered by racial violence. Her text thus subverts and rewrites the national narrative of America as the land of the free, where human potential can be achieved through hard work and self-improvement. This "official" narrative of America as an inclusive and egalitarian country is a powerful story that gained even more prominence during the Reagan administration, and that can be seen at work in American public spaces, such as Washington's civic monuments.

The numerous classical allusions that underpin the novel—such as Circe's name, the Homeric quest, the flying motif, and the catabasis myth—recall the classical style of American civic architecture (Barnard 108; Roynon 1520). But they are merged with and subverted by references to African folklore: the flying motif, for instance, recalls both the Icarus and the Ibo Landing myths (Fletcher 405; Ramírez 108–9). Morrison's imaginative recovery of the past reinforces this disruption, imbuing the novel with the ghostly absences that haunt America's historical memory. The result is a complex narrative that fuses history and myth, past and present, and recalls America's classical monumentalism in order to subvert it, challenging its celebration of empire by highlighting its violent foundations.

Morrison's attempt to deal with the historical trauma of slavery is evident in the depiction of Ruth. Her portrayal of Ruth's maternal practices foregrounds their ambiguous nature, echoing the painful contradictions that enslaved mothers had to face in their struggles to overcome slavery's dehumanization. Her belated breastfeeding aims at regaining control over the body that was denied to enslaved women, whose breasts and milk were regarded as commodities. Much like enslaved women's mothering decisions, Ruth's ambiguous maternal practices try to transcend racial terror; yet they also end up invalidating these attempts, casting Ruth in neither heroic nor victimized terms. Through its ambiguous portrayal of Ruth's maternal practices, the novel reflects upon the disruption of the maternal perpetuated by racial violence.

In Morrison's oeuvre, the recurring themes of milk and breastfeeding are often charged with key and emblematic meanings. In her first novel, *The Bluest Eye* (1970), Pecola's growth is marked by the drinking of cow's milk from a Shirley Temple mug, indicating her internalization of her mother's self-loathing and white beauty standards. By contrast, in *Song of Solomon*, Milkman's development is represented by the drinking of his mother's milk, which has contradictory outcomes. Yet, critical discussions of breastfeeding in Morrison's work have generally centered on her novel *Beloved* (1987).

Even when analyzing maternal characters in *Song of Solomon*, much existing African American literary criticism has tended to revolve around Pilate and her status as an outsider while dismissing Ruth as a mere passive and pitiful victim of patriarchy.[3] Valerie Smith describes Ruth as "weak and pathetic" and interprets Ruth's behavior towards Milkman as selfish and objectifying, observing that "she uses Milkman as a way to fulfill her yearnings" (279). Yet the implications and motivations behind Ruth's mothering are more complex. Smith here dismisses the potential present in Ruth's maternal practices and the meaning her maternal practices acquire if understood in light of the horrific legacy of slavery. Wilfred D. Samuels and Clenora Hudson-Weems, while acknowledging that Ruth has an "undaunting strength" whose source is located in her complex sense of motherhood, nonetheless maintain that she has no personal identity and that "at no point does she rebel" (54–58). They do not further elaborate on the theme of mothering and do not analyze Ruth's maternal practices.

Alongside Hannah Zinker, Hirsch has been among the few who have paid due attention to the key scene of Ruth's breastfeeding in *Song of Solomon*, but theirs remain isolated and unusual critical statements. Hirsch recognizes Ruth's nursing as "secret and transgressive," unveiling its potential but also underlining the "incestuous confusion of distance" that characterizes it ("Knowing" 79). Yet, her analysis does not examine the key issue the depiction of Ruth's breastfeeding tackles, i.e., the meaning of motherhood in an antiblack world. Building upon her insights, my analysis is going to center on Ruth's maternal practices and their ambiguities, placing them against the context of the destructive legacy of racial terror.

As O'Reilly has observed, in Morrison's writing the patriarchal nuclear family "is structured both by male dominance" and the values of "money, ownership, individualism" (25). Ruth's household in *Song of Solomon* is no exception. The Dead family is portrayed as an example of a patriarchal nuclear family, a cultural construction of the Western world, which has been rendered normative and universal in spite of its sociohistorical specificity. Even though African American history radically challenges the very bases upon which this myth of the patriarchal nuclear family is based, in mainstream American culture, it constitutes the measure of success. Since the early twentieth century, especially for the northern bourgeoise, the two-parent family has symbolized class respectability (Stewart 6). Through assimilation, Black families, especially among the middle class, often seek "to emulate the hegemonic script of family relations in which the husband is dominant and the woman subservient and submissive" (O'Reilly 73).

Ruth's marriage is loveless and sterile as her husband's "hatred of his wife glittered and sparked in every word he spoke to her" and his glance emanates a "frozen heat" (*Song of Solomon* 10). He is so disgusted by his wife that he does not even want to sleep with her anymore: "in almost twenty years during which he had not laid eyes on her naked feet, he missed only the underwear" (16). The household is characterized by a lack of tenderness and communication as Ruth's husband, Macon II (from here on referred to as Macon), can speak to his son only "if his words held some command or criticism" (28). He beats his wife and is described as "a difficult man to approach—a hard man, with a manner so cool it discouraged casual or spontaneous conversation" (15).

Much like Luther in Gloria Naylor's *Linden Hills,* Macon is "a colored man of property" (23). He is a greedy man who treats everybody as an object, and his main teaching is "let the things you own own other things. Then you'll own yourself and other people too" (5). His focus on ownership and his objectification of human beings echo the distortions of enslaver-enslaved relations, recalling the reasoning that was at the basis of chattel slavery's transformation of people into property to be owned, sold, and exchanged. He unwittingly perpetuates the materialistic worldview that sustained the process of the "thingification" of black life represented by the systematic denial of personhood upon which chattel slavery was predicated. His rugged individualism and his investment in a patriarchal culture based on marketplace values makes him analogous to *homo economicus.* Through the description of Ruth's household, the novel creates a textual microcosm that echoes and extends the dynamics at play in slavery's processes of dehumanization.

But Ruth is not a powerless victim as she is sometimes able to subtly evade Macon's control. While she serves him non-nourishing meals, cooking chicken that is "red at the bone" and preparing food that he finds disgusting and "impossible to eat" (11–12), she nurtures an ugly watermark. Ruth's glance continuously searches for it, as it gives her a sense of security and stability: "She never set the table or passed through the dining room without looking at it. Like a lighthouse keeper drawn to his window to gaze once again at the sea [. . .] Ruth looked for the watermark several times during the day. She knew it was there, but she needed to confirm its presence" (11). Looking at the watermark makes her feel alive. Ruth is magically drawn to it, feeling a strange and powerful connection: "Even in the cave of sleep, without dreaming of it or thinking of it at all, she felt its presence" (11). An invisible umbilical cord, a mark of connection as well as separation, links Ruth to the watermark. Showing Ruth's attunement to an inanimate watermark, this scene highlights the complex interconnections upon which life depends, undermining the Western emphasis on the autonomy of the individual.

The text suggests that, in a world where the maternal has been co-opted by racial terror, such signs of interconnection must go underground. Ruth seems to be trying to get rid of the watermark, talking about her efforts to eliminate it, even though with her generative glance she secretly gives it nourishment and enables its growth: "she talked endlessly to her daughters and guests about how to get rid of it—what might hide this single flaw on the splendid wood [. . .] But her glance was nutritious; the spot became, if anything, more pronounced as the years passed" (12). Like a child, the watermark manages to gradually grow thanks to Ruth's nurturance. Caring for it as if it were her offspring, Ruth can magically transform the lifeless watermark into a living being pulsating with life: "it behaved as though it were itself a plant and flourished into a huge suede-gray flower that throbbed like fever" (*Song of Solomon* 13). As she creatively nurtures a watermark, she is endowed with life-giving powers. Through her meticulous caregiving and her sustaining touch and gaze, Ruth has given the watermark a life of its own, acquiring the power to infuse life into an inanimate flaw.

Magically endowing the lifeless watermark with life and beauty, Ruth has also infused life into herself: "She regarded it as a mooring, a checkpoint, some stable visual object that assured her that the world was still there; that this was life and not a dream. That she was alive somewhere, inside, which she acknowledged to be true only because a thing she knew intimately was out there, outside herself" (11). While Ruth creates the watermark, she is also in turn refashioned by it, becoming both creator and creation. If we conceive of the erotic as "the infusing of the everyday with a feeling of belonging to and expansively enacting a sense of alignment between self and world" (Tompkins 186), then Ruth's caring for the watermark becomes an erotic moment of self-creation. It aligns with Lorde's understanding of the erotic as a powerful force connected with creativity ("Uses" 45). Arising from a praxis that underscores a relational rather than instrumental conception of the other, the erotic is "a measure of the joy which I know myself to be capable of feeling," and it is "firmly rooted in the power of our unexpressed or unrecognized feeling" (44). As a means to cope with her sexless marriage, Ruth infuses her sterile life with an erotic force. In so doing, she demonstrates her willingness to engage in a relational and potentially self-decentering practice, in which both self and other are infused with new life and neither is objectified or instrumentalized: one gives life to the other in a reciprocal exchange that establishes a symbiotic relation among equals. The nurturing of the watermark provides Ruth with access to her creative powers, which otherwise remain unexpressed, buried under her loveless marriage. This scene thus contrasts with that of Ruth's breastfeeding: her nurturing of the watermark allows the novel to reclaim the nurturing and life-giving potential of the erotic that is absent in her nursing.

By highlighting how Ruth's practice nourishes and transforms a lifeless watermark into a beautiful living being, this scene challenges hierarchical conceptions of being. While "[d]isgust evaluates negatively what it touches, [and] proclaims the meanness and inferiority of its object" (Miller 9), working at maintaining hierarchies, Ruth's cultivation of ugliness troubles rigid dichotomies and affirms the fluidity of life. Through Ruth's magical nurturing of a watermark, Morrison's text conjures up an alternative space, an otherworld, where Ruth can transcend racial terror and reclaim the erotic as a creative force. Like Walker's mother, who can find a means to express her stifled creativity by transforming "whatever rocky soil she landed on" into a garden "magnificent with life" where "[w]hatever she planted grew as if by magic" (*In Search* 241), Ruth enjoys her life-giving powers by nurturing a watermark. Caring for it enables her to carve out an otherworld, where there is no hierarchical taxonomy of being and where she can joyfully embrace her creative potential.

Like the nurturing of a watermark, Milkman's conception is described as a magical practice since it is the result of the potions with which Ruth tricks her husband into sleeping with her. Manipulating Macon, Ruth administers to him the potions prepared by his sister Pilate and manages to give birth to her son in spite of her husband's efforts to the contrary. Aided by Pilate's magic, Ruth reclaims her control over her own body and reproductive capacities: "she had won over the castor oil, and the pot of steam that had puckered and burned her skin" (133). Given that castor oil was used as an abortifacient by enslaved women, Ruth's birthing of Milkman symbolizes her attempt to transcend racial terror. Magic empowers her and allows her to embrace motherhood on her own terms, honoring her creative powers.

But the novel also foregrounds the precariousness and unattainability of the magical otherworld created through Ruth's nurturing of the watermark and birthing of Milkman as it highlights her possessive and instrumental drive, which undermines the erotic source of power she found through her nurturing.

Ruth objectifies Milkman and uses his conception and birth as a means to re-kindle her husband's desire for her, hoping "to close the break between herself and Macon" (133). Even though that does not work out, Ruth still refers to her son as "her single triumph" (132–33), considering his birthing a violent rebellion gloriously completed in spite of her husband's attempts to make her abort. Theodor Adorno and Max Horkheimer have pointed out how Odysseus and Crusoe, both prototypes of *homo economicus*, regard other human beings "only in estranged forms, as enemies or allies, but always as instruments, things" (49). Here Ruth's behavior remains akin to theirs as she uses her son for her own ends. This underscores how *homo economicus*'s instrumental view of the other disrupts and co-opts Ruth's maternal praxis and its potentially lifegiving and erotically transformative force that we glimpsed in her nurturing of the watermark.

Before he is even born, Milkman is drawn into a power struggle between husband and wife, becoming "a plain on which, like the cowboys and Indians in the movies, she and her husband fought" (132). When Ruth discovers that Hagar wants to kill her son, she sees Hagar's action as an attempt to "deprive her of the one aggressive act brought to royal completion" (133). Her son constitutes a way to remind herself of an important victory in her struggle with Macon and evokes her long-suppressed desires, making her feel loved: "Long deprived of sex, long dependent on self-manipulation, she saw her son's imminent death as the annihilation of the last occasion she had been made love to" (134). Not only her son's birth, but also her son's death, are perceived by Ruth as being about herself and her affirmation of her life and power. Her behavior prompts Pilate to remind her that "[h]e ain't a house, he's a man" (138). While Ruth proves able to view an inanimate watermark as a living being, she, like Sethe in *Beloved*, remains unable to perceive her son as an individual, commenting that he has never been "a person to her, a separate real person. He had always been a passion" (131). Unveiling Ruth's possessive drive, the text foregrounds the limits of Ruth's maternal practice and its potential to conjure up an otherworld that can offer a different model of subjectivity.

Marked by the same contradictions that characterize Milkman's magical conception and birth, Ruth's belated breastfeeding intimates the necessity of such an otherworld while revealing its unattainability. The scene where Ruth nurses her son, quoted at the beginning, highlights her generative powers of nurturance but also shows how they become warped by the legacy of racial terror. If in *Beloved,* as Michele Mock has argued, nursing is a symbol of both ownership and loving communion (120), in *Song of Solomon*, it retains similarly contradictory connotations.

Ruth's breastfeeding constitutes one of her secret pleasures: she does it without her husband's knowledge. Much like the life-giving nurturing of the watermark, Ruth's belated breastfeeding is her attempt at finding her own way of mothering, and it allows her to embrace her generative powers. Ruth nurses her son in a secluded and intimate space, cut off from the rest of the house, where she can escape patriarchal authority. The room where she performs her nursing is characterized by the color green, suggesting fertility and rebirth: "A damp greenness lived there, made by the evergreen that pressed against the window and filtered the light" (13). Against the sterility of her marriage, Ruth takes pleasure in her maternal practice, and much like her nurturing of the watermark, this activity gives life to both her son and herself: her breastfeeding is described as "fully half of what made her daily life bearable" (14).

Nursing her son becomes a magical moment that spurs Ruth's imagination. Through the allusion to the German fairy tale of Rumpelstiltskin, the text foregrounds the magical power that characterizes Ruth's breastfeeding, which enables her to momentarily transcend her reality. The power of spinning gold gives the miller's daughter the means to escape from the tower where she is kept by the king in the same way that breastfeeding her son allows Ruth to leave behind her present circumstances. Placing Ruth's breastfeeding "in a heroic tradition of fairy tales" (Hirsch, "Knowing" 79), the text connects her breastfeeding to her initial nurturing of the watermark, highlighting the magical powers of transcendence that characterize Ruth's maternal practice.

Morrison's novel characterizes Ruth's breastfeeding as a magical practice that has the potential to free her from white patriarchal control, responding to the exploitation of the Black maternal upon which the system of slavery rested. The text creates a character that, by deciding when, where, how, and for how long to nurse her son, seeks to challenge the historical disruption and co-optation of mothering, casting her breastfeeding as an act of reclamation of a maternal heritage that has been violently denied to Black women. As we have seen, slavery erased and co-opted maternal practice for economic ends. Historically, as Jeffrey C. Stewart has observed—commenting on Alain Locke's bond with his mother—in the early twentieth century, maternal love was idealized and closeness between sons and mothers tended to be common in the Black community, "almost as compensation for the disruption of maternal relationships under slavery" (6).[4] Discussing liminal temporality in Morrison's neo-slave narrative, Kristen Lillvis argues that, overcompensating for slavery's maternal disruptions, "Sethe seeks through her mothering to strengthen her children's bodies in order to protect them—and their family link—from being appropriated by the white owner or, on a larger level, white culture" (*Posthuman* 17). Sethe's mothering decisions in the present remain influenced by the past.[5] A similar dynamic is at work in Ruth's breastfeeding. Attempting to reclaim the control over the breast, the milk, and the mothering experience that slavery took away from Black women, Ruth's breastfeeding seeks to tie her son to her, over-nourishing him in a desperate attempt to compensate for the historical disruption and devaluation of Black mothering this is the "too thick mother-love" we also find in *Beloved*. If read as a response to racist comments about the alleged "unworthiness" of Black mothers, Ruth's maternal efforts aim to challenge these. She is unconsciously seeking to prove her fitness for the maternal role and claim human status for herself and her son, first by giving birth and then by over-nurturing him.

Through Ruth's maternal practice, the text foregrounds the ongoing contradictions that characterize Black mothering in an antiblack world, placing her maternal practice in the context of a long history of racial violence. Gaining distance from the brutal context of slavery by placing Ruth in a 1970s northern context, the novel, through the description of her ambiguous maternal practice, shows the ongoing impact of racial terror. Much like enslaved women's mothering decisions, and echoing Sethe's ambivalent mothering, Ruth's maternal praxis remains marked by discordant outcomes that undermine her attempts at overcoming racial terror's co-optation of the maternal.[6] While hinting at the maternal as a practice with the potential to free Ruth's creativity, the novel at the same time links it to slavery and its legacy of racial violence.

Racial terror taints Ruth's generative powers: even the reference to the German fairy tale of Rumpelstiltskin acquires a sinister and less affirming meaning. The price the miller's daughter must pay for her magical powers is giving up her child. The miller's daughter is tricked by an imp, who is actually the one with the magical powers, into surrendering her child. The fairy tale thus not only symbolizes a mother-machine dynamic but also the disruption and denial of the maternal. Morrison employs a reference to a European fairy tale to hint at the historical context of slavery and its co-optation of motherhood, which subtends her portrayal of Ruth's maternal practice. Hence, when the brutal historical context of slavery and its aftermath are considered, the placing of Ruth in this tradition of fairy tales is not as "heroic" as Hirsch contends. While potentially liberatory, it highlights her vulnerability to racial terror.

As a result, the text casts Ruth's mothering as neither empowering nor transformative for both mother and son. As is the case with Milkman's conception and birth, the novel reveals the limits of Ruth's breastfeeding as her possessive and controlling drive, which undermines her humanizing efforts, becomes apparent. Considering her son as a means to an end, Ruth objectifies him: "she regarded him as a beautiful toy, a respite, a distraction, a physical pleasure as she nursed him" (13). She keeps breastfeeding him for her own pleasure, disregarding his reluctance: "he was old enough to be bored by the flat taste of mother's milk, so he came reluctantly, as to a chore" (13). Ruth continues to nurse her son to keep him dependent upon her, so that she can give her life meaning.

The novel shows how Ruth's attempts to transcend racial terror are hindered not only by her possessive drive but also by the suspicions that her belated breastfeeding engenders. In trying to be a good mother so as to challenge the historical degradation of Black motherhood, Ruth opens herself to charges of incest. Milkman muses that "[h]is mother had been portrayed as an obscene child playing dirty games with whatever male was near—be it her father or her son" (79). As Hirsch has argued, Ruth's breastfeeding violates "[s]ome appropriate but undefinable balance of closeness and distance," perpetuating the same "incestuous confusion of distance" that existed between Ruth and her father ("Knowing" 79). The novel never settles the question of whether these suspicions are true, but it does raise these doubts, which are often voiced by the patriarchal figure of Ruth's husband.

For Macon, Ruth has failed as a mother and as a daughter. His comments cast Ruth's relationship with her father as possibly bordering not only on incest but also on necrophilia: "In the bed. That's where she was when I opened the door. Laying next to him. Naked as a yard dog, kissing him. Him dead and white and puffy and skinny, and she had his fingers in her mouth" (73). Macon's account reveals his profound contempt for Ruth and her behavior, as he debases her to the level of brute animality, dehumanizing her. Macon's reaction reveals his investment in a bourgeois model of the individual: it expresses what Candice M. Jenkins calls "the salvific wish" typical, though not exclusive of the Black middle classes, and which she defines as "the desire to rescue the black community from racist accusations of sexual and domestic pathology through the embrace of bourgeois propriety" (45). As a self-made man of property, Macon, much like Luther, is anxious to maintain his fragile social position by conforming to white notions of respectability. What Macon views as Ruth's "deviant" behavior not only contradicts her humanizing attempts but also threatens to nullify his efforts to enter the realm of full citizenship—hence, his contempt as he tries to police her behavior.

The renaming that results from Ruth's belated breastfeeding displays similarly contradictory outcomes. Such renaming allows Ruth to disrupt patriarchal practices of naming, challenging the patriarchal power of name giving. In a patriarchal society, it is the male who bestows his surname on the offspring, and the family is constructed as "the vertical transfer of a bloodline, of a patronymic, of titles and entitlements, of real estate and the prerogatives of 'cold cash,' from *fathers* to sons" (Spillers, *"Mama's"* 74, emphasis added). Ruth's renaming ruptures this transfer from father to son, freeing the son from the father's ownership by connecting him to the mother "with a stream of milk, an alternative to the ink the fathers, white and black, use to write their children's names" (Hirsch, "Knowing" 85). Macon, which is also the father's name, would have constructed Milkman as a mirror image of his father, robbing him of his individuality, replicating a dynamic that we will find at work in *Linden Hills*. But Ruth's renaming casts her son under the mother's influence, creating a discontinuity in the father's line and substituting paternal blood with mother's milk.

Given the fact that Macon was a name given by a white man by mistake, the renaming constitutes a rebellion against not only patriarchy but also the legacy of slavery. Overturning the erasure and appropriation of the patronymic by the enslaver, it is an important refusal of white power, recalling a practice common in the second half of the twentieth century, when many African Americans changed surnames they traced back to the slaveholders of their first American ancestors and adopted new names or nicknames that designated their liberated status.[7] Ruth not only carries on her maternal legacy but also continues this tradition, substituting a name given by a white man with a maternal nickname that celebrates her and her son's humanity. The nickname functions as an assertion of human relatedness, emphasizing Milkman's connection to his mother and their interdependence as human subjects. Through Ruth's belated breastfeeding and the subsequent name change, Milkman's identity is shaped by not only the mother but also her human milk.

While the nickname can be understood as evidence of the community's scorn for Ruth's mothering, a closer analysis reveals that it constitutes their recognition of her and her son's belonging to the Black community. It is Freddie, "an important community figure in the book" (Fabre 109), who coins the nick-name. Trudier Harris pointed out that "in their studies of nicknames in black communities, scholars have focused on the tremendous value they have, the special recognition they bestow upon an individual for a feat accomplished, a trait emphasized, or a characteristic noticed" (72). The nickname honors Ruth's practice, functioning as a mark of acceptance and welcoming mother and son into the Black community. Freddie also links Ruth's practice to Southern tra-ditions of wet-nursing, remarking that "I don't even know the last time I seen that. I mean, ain't nothing wrong with it [. . .] Used to be a lot of womenfolk nurse they kids a long time down South. Lot of 'em. But you don't see it much no more" (14). Since in the novel, the South is cast as an ancestral home where "communal and mythical values prevail over individualism and materialism" (Smith 14), Freddie's comments emphasize the positive associations of Ruth's breastfeeding, casting her as connected to ancestral values in a manner similar to Pilate. While Freddie's intrusion can be interpreted as voyeuristic mockery (Hirsch, "Knowing" 79), it actually reconstructs the communal bonds that slav-ery violently erased, investing Ruth's breastfeeding with a positive value.

However, much like the birthing of Milkman, Ruth's renaming of her son, while a powerful act of recovery, also highlights her possessive drive as "the act of naming another reflects a desire to regulate and therefore to control" (Rigney 61). The enslaver exercised his authority through his power of nam-ing; the colonizer Robinson Crusoe's first action is to rename Friday, imposing upon him a name he does not choose, underscoring his wish to dominate him. Since names connote ownership, Ruth is reclaiming her son as hers, inverting rather than subverting patriarchal notions of familial inheritance and revealing the possessive ambition that underlies her relation with her son. The power to name is the power of the white patriarch and Ruth seeks to gain this phallic authority that—as attested by the circumstances of Macon's misnaming—not even the Black father had. Milkman's renaming substitutes the enslaver's name with that of the mother and recuperates the heritage erased by slavery. But even this final recuperation is not enough for Ruth to recover the mother-son bond that antiblack violence disrupted. Ruth herself comes to recognize that "he [Milkman] really didn't tell her anything, and hadn't for years," and then she muses: "who was this son of hers? This tall man who had flesh on the outside and feelings on the inside that she knew nothing of" (132–33).

The novel depicts Ruth's struggle against the brutal legacy of slavery as a constant dialectical process that seems to have no immediate resolution. Ruth's belated breastfeeding has the potential to transcend racial violence as it results in the reclamation of her creative powers, and in a renaming of her son that seeks to recover the maternal bond severed by racial violence. But Ruth's maternal practice at the same time reveals the possessive ambition that characterizes her relation with her son, which is far from subversive as she regards him as property. She fights with Macon to gain control over his life, without realizing that they are both competing for the phallic authority neither of them can claim because of racial terror. Following a materially possessive drive, which invalidates her humanizing efforts, Ruth's maternal practice cannot escape the devastating effects of racial violence. If, as Deborah Horvitz has suggested, "any attempt to possess another human being is reminiscent of the slave-master relationship" (161), then Ruth's relation with her son, much like the tormented mother-daughter bond in *Beloved*, "resurrects the slavemaster's monopoly over both word and body, enforcing the internalized enslavement that has become a legacy of institutionalized slavery" (Lawrence 196).

By highlighting the contradictory outcomes that characterize mothering in a world defined by antiblack violence, the text reveals the limitations of Ruth's maternal practice, attesting to the necessity of imagining a maternal otherworld. Through Ruth's initial nurturing of the watermark, the text seems able to conjure up an alternative space. Yet, the dialectical characterization of Ruth's belated breastfeeding also reveals the ongoing destructiveness of racial terror. Ruth's maternal praxis remains characterized by the prevailing capitalist property relations and their attendant values, failing to provide liberatory possibilities.

As a result, the novel points toward the othermother-midwife figures of Aunt Pilate and Circe, whose maternal practices attempt to find a resolution to the conundrum Ruth faces, challenging the property relations that remain at its basis. Suggesting the need for a communal mothering of Milkman, the text draws upon the important historical role of midwives both during and after slavery, when they not only delivered babies but also shared mothering responsibilities, contributing to the formation of woman-centered networks that challenged dominant values.

The Art of Catching Babies

Discussing the mother-daughter relationship in Marshall's *Brown Girl, Brownstones*, Rosalie Riegle Troester coined the term "othermothers" to identify those figures who "live different lives and exemplify values widely different from the biological mother," providing not only support but also a different perspective (13). She also notes how sometimes they can provide sexual initiation (13), as Circe does for Milkman. Drawing on Troester, Collins underlines the central role of othermothers in the African American community: while "[g]randmothers, sisters, aunts, or cousins act as othermothers by taking on child-care responsibilities for one another's children," often these networks of community-based childcare expand beyond biologically related individuals to include "fictive kin" (Collins 178–79). While these kin units tend to be mostly woman-centered, men can also be involved but to a lesser extent for reasons linked to male labor force patterns and sexist attitudes (Collins 182; Joseph 276). Providing crucial support for women "who lack the preparation and desire for motherhood" (Collins 179), this communal form of mothering can be traced to Central and West African traditions, which were adapted to a new setting in the slaveholding southern United States (Edwards 88).

In its characterization of Pilate and Circe, Morrison's novel draws upon the centrality of these othermothering praxes in African American culture, positioning them as necessary counterpoints to Ruth's. As we shall see, drawing upon African-derived forms of knowledge, Pilate and Circe embody different values: their praxes are described as rejecting the capitalist ethos that underpins Ruth's practice and thus make it possible for Milkman to envision different onto-epistemologies of the human not based on property relations.

Performing their roles as othermothers, Pilate's and Circe's practices recall those of midwives, paramount figures during and after slavery, when they attended births and helped in the upbringing of the newborn. Spiritual healers often called "grannies" or "conjurers," midwives were usually older Black women who passed on their ancestral knowledge about curative herbs to younger females, defying dominant Western medical practices (Bonaparte 157). Since they were "women who assist[ed] bloodmothers by sharing mothering responsibilities" (qtd. in Collins 192), in a manner not dissimilar to enslaved wet nurses, they can be thought of as performing an othermothering practice.[8]

Cheaper than a doctor, a midwife carried out duties a doctor would not have: she usually served not just as a birth attendant and nurse, caring for the mother and newborn, but she also prepared meals, looked after other children in the house, did the laundry, and performed other household chores; after their childbirths, she also stayed with the women to assist them. Midwives were expert users of herbal medicines for a wide range of body ailments, and they assisted the sick. In some communities, they "tended to the final washing and dressing of the dead," and ministering to extremely vulnerable bodies, they were involved "in the most potent stages of the life cycle" (Litoff 240). With no formal schools or training, midwives learned from practice and reached a high level of expertise in what they called "the art of catching babies" and "mother-wit" or knowing through intuition. This praxis constituted a shared system of charismatic knowledge and defied the rational practice of white healthcare professionals.

Midwifery rituals were linked to spiritual beliefs about the body and soul, aiming at rooting a baby's spirit to its body as well as to its mother (Wilkie 278). "Fussing," a traditional practice white doctors found problematic, is an example of such an attempt. "Fussing" referred to the second stage of labor, when the contractions were strong enough to be painful but not to trigger delivery. During this time midwives used to bring friends and family members into the room to care for the mother. Her body was massaged with perfumes and oils, her hair combed and scented in order not just to ease her pain but also to attract the baby into this world and keep away evil spirits, because "a baby whose spirit bound to its mother was more likely to stay rooted in the body" (Wilkie 278). Even after birth, practices derived from Central and West African traditions, such as the use of protective charms, continued to be employed to protect the child and keep its spirit tied up to its body and its mother (Wilkie 279). Connected to a spiritual set of relationships among the midwife, the pregnant woman, God, the family, and the community at large, midwifery was not just a secular craft (Litoff 248). Rooted in non-Western onto-epistemologies, it comprised a whole set of communal spiritual praxes, learned and passed on, that foregrounded a sense of relatedness, forging maternal bonds that included fictive kin and extended well beyond the Western nuclear family. Related to many aspects of life, these praxes foregrounded alternate ways not only of mothering but also of being in the world, putting forward a spiritual sense of relationality.

After Emancipation, midwifery continued to be widely practiced. In the North, this practice was common among poor and immigrant women, while in the South, the great majority of midwives were African American women and the craft of midwifery was identified as a "black trade" (Litoff 239). Midwives were often portrayed as "dirty," "ignorant," "evils," and "inveterate quacks" (Litoff 239). In the North, there were some concerns about the growing numbers of midwives and the belief that they administered abortions; in the South, the superstition and folklore of the midwives were underlined as they were allegedly "so gross in many cases as to rival voodoism" (quoted in Litoff 239). Towards the beginning of the twentieth century, the medicalization and regulation of childbirth began to take place, and the authority of the male-controlled medical profession eroded that of midwives, rendering their practice obsolete. Their historical role and their competence in reproductive medicine were "relegated to near-total obscurity" through the use of racist healthcare initiatives (Tunc 404).

Between 1910 and 1930, white physicians began to campaign against midwives, linking them to uncleanliness, disease, and the high mortality rates of mothers and infants. In the South, "the large number of Negro maternal deaths" were attributed not to "economic conditions but to the fact that Negroes were attended by Negro midwives" (qtd. in Litoff 250). While physicians purported to be fighting for women's and infants' health, their midwifery-control crusade was entrenched with wider issues of race, gender, and class as they aimed at taking the birthing process "out of women's hands" and cleansing it of "its racial stigmata," erasing not only the competition of the midwives but also the "linkage of childbirth to empirically untrained, usually unlettered black women" (Bonaparte 156). The rhetoric was racialized as the emphasis was placed on the "symbolically purified bodies of white physicians and nurses," and the "cultural hygienization of reproductive health care had its material component in scientific medicine's emphasis on the sanitary and safe conditions offered by physician-attended hospital births" (Bonaparte 160). While midwives' hands were "instruments of healing" (Wardi 204), the campaign against them, centering on the alleged dirtiness of their hands, not only conflated Blackness with filth (Lee 36) but also transmogrified these instruments of healing into alleged tools of death.

White healthcare professionals linked the "midwifery problem" with other social ills, mingling racial and scientific reasons in an attempt to medicalize pregnancy and childbirth, paving the way for the cultural understanding of birth as a medical event. The campaign exploited the negative historical associations between midwifery and African American culture with the intention of raising the birthing process to a scientific realm while simultaneously putting white patriarchy in control of it and erasing the authority and knowledge of the Black midwife.

Otherworldly Mother-Midwives

Because of racial terror, Ruth's role must be complemented by that of Pilate and Circe, the otherworldly mother-midwife figures who aid her in the upbringing of Milkman. Aunt Pilate is portrayed as the typical figure of the outsider, and the neighbors regard her as "the one who was ugly, dirty, poor, and drunk" (37). Hers is a matrifocal family reminiscent of that of Eva Peace in *Sula*: she defies societal norms, choosing not to marry and living an unconventional life in an all-female household with her daughter Reba and granddaughter Hagar, who both call her "Mama." She regards Hagar and her nephew Milkman as brother and sister, and when her daughter reminds her that they are cousins she responds: "Same thing [. . .] what is the difference, Reba?" (44), disregarding patriarchal and nuclear conceptions of family and kinship. As Kimberly W. Benston has noted, "the imperatives of genealogical hierarchy, with its burden of cultural taboo, are casually breached" (99) as even Milkman refers to both Reba and Hagar as Pilate's daughters. Embracing the tradition of community-based childcare, as evident through her othermothering of Milkman, Pilate challenges the capitalist property relations that her brother Macon upholds in his household and that are manifested through Ruth's mothering.

Giving up "table manners or hygiene" and showing "no interest in or knowledge of decent housekeeping" as "no meal was ever planned or balanced or served," Pilate lives in a cabin with no comforts and where every object is used for some other purpose than that for which it is built (20–29). It is there that she makes the wine she sells for a living so that "the odor of pine and fermenting fruit" pervades everything (39). The house is full of candles, and it has no electricity or gas as "they warmed themselves and cooked with wood and coal [. . .] and lived pretty much as though progress was a word that meant walking from a little farther on down the road" (27).

Pilate's disregard for Western values is revealed not only by the organization of her household but also by her beliefs about life and death. Able to see and communicate with the dead, Pilate is not afraid to die: "since death held no terrors for her (she spoke often to the dead), she knew there was nothing to fear." Her mentor is her dead father "who appeared before her and told her things" (150), and she keeps his remains in a green sack hanging from the ceiling in her home. Adopting "African cosmological views of the reciprocity that exists between [the] world of the living and the living dead" (Samuels and Hudson-Weems 77), Pilate creates an otherworld characterized by non-Western understandings of time and no opposition between past and present, life and death.

Recalling the othermother figures of Aunt Cuney and Lebert Joseph in Marshall's *Praisesong*, Pilate's difference is also manifested physically. She is a strong and powerful woman whose appearance eludes gender norms as she dresses with both men's and women's garments, attesting to the fluidity of gender and embodying ambiguity: her short hair is "cut regularly like a man's," and she wears "unlaced men's shoes" with a "long-skirted black dress" and an earring (36–38). Like the trickster Lebert Joseph, she possesses magical healing powers of regeneration and manifests a protean quality. When she rescues Milkman from jail, she becomes smaller and her voice is different, but when they drive her home, "there was a change. Pilate was tall again [. . .] And her own voice was back" (207).

But Pilate's most striking feature is that she has no navel, a "frightening and exotic" (148) characteristic that confers her an otherworldly quality: "It was the absence of a navel that convinced people that she had not come into this world through normal channels; had never lain, floated, or grown in some warm and liquid place connected by a tissue-thin tube to a reliable source of human nourishment" (27–28). It is her navel-lessness that is believed to be responsible for her magical powers: she "was believed to have the power to step out of her skin, set a bush afire from fifty yards, and turn a man into a ripe rutabaga—all on account of the fact that she had no navel" (94). Her navel-ness does not only make her, like Sula, a pariah: "It isolated her [. . .] Men frowned, women whispered and shoved their children behind them" (148). It also removes the most evident sign of connection to the mother, who died when birthing her so that Pilate had to birth herself: "After their [Pilate and Macon's] mother died, she had come struggling out of the womb without help" (27). As was the case with Ruth's nurturing of the watermark, in a context in which the maternal has been co-opted by racial terror, signs of connection to the mother must go underground.

Pilate's spiritual and anti-materialistic values, her caring attitude—as a "natural healer" with "a deep concern for and about human relationships" (*Song of Solomon* 149)—and her matrifocal household stand in stark opposition to Macon's materialistic values and his patriarchal and nuclear family. Her brother feels uneasy in her presence, and, preoccupied with respectability, he regards her as "filthy" and as a "regular source of embarrassment," critiquing her appearance: "Why can't you dress like a woman? [. . .] What's that sailor's cap doing on your head? Don't you have stockings? What are you trying to make me look like in this town?" (*Song of Solomon* 20). Estranged from Pilate, he does not want his son to enter her house. Even though Macon admits that "[a]t one time she had been the dearest thing in the world to him," he describes her as "odd, murky, and worst of all, unkempt" and wishes she would "show some respect for herself. Could get a real job instead of running a wine house" (*Song of Solomon* 20). As with Ruth, Macon's comments manifest the "salvific wish," since he is afraid that "the white men in the bank" might discover that "this raggedy bootlegger was his sister" and that he is related to a "collection of lunatics who made wine and sang in the streets" (*Song of Solomon* 20). He fears Pilate's unconventional appearance will compromise his precarious middle-class respectability in the eyes of white people. The stark opposition of Macon's and Pilate's households, and the respective worldviews upon which they are based, highlights not only the exclusions upon which Macon's patriarchal order is based. It also emphasizes, as attested by Ruth's practice, the inadequacy of such a model and the impossibility of reclaiming the maternal and reimagining Black subjectivities within its confines. It is Aunt Pilate's alternate praxis that acts as catalyst for Macon's growth, stifled by Ruth.

Despite Macon's attitude, from the beginning, Aunt Pilate is a fundamental presence in Milkman's life. Having access to ancestral practices derived from Africa, she aids his birth with her potions, songs, and hoodoo tricks, protecting Milkman before he is even born: it is her practice, not Ruth's, that "brought him into the world when only a miracle could have" (210). Like a root doctor, Pilate supplies Ruth with "some greenish-gray grassy-looking stuff to put in his [Macon's] food" (125) in order to make her husband sleep with her. When Macon attempts to make Ruth abort, Pilate resorts to the use of hoodoo dolls, placing in Macon's office a "male doll with a small painted chicken bone stuck between its legs and a round red circle painted on its belly" (132). When Ruth is giving birth to Milkman, Pilate sings the ancestral song that, as Milkman will discover, recounts the legendary story of their ancestor Solomon who escaped from slavery by flying, recalling the myth of the Ibo Landing.[9] Even after Milkman is born, Pilate keeps paying visits to Ruth, helping her take care of the baby by singing to him. She can be viewed as acting as a midwife and othermother figure, protecting both the child and the mother by using practices derived from West African cultures. Described as "the woman who had as much to do with his future as she had [with] his past" (36), Pilate is able not only to guard ancestral knowledge but also to conjure up an otherworld where mothering can take place. It is here that she can nurture Milkman and aid his maturation by passing on her wisdom.

Despite his father's intimations not to visit Aunt Pilate, Milkman enjoys going to her house as it makes him feel happy and loved: "His visits to the wine house seemed [. . .] an extension of the love he had come to expect from his mother" (*Song of Solomon* 79). A key scene and a catalyst for Milkman's journey of self-discovery is his first meeting with Pilate, when she cooks a soft-boiled egg for him and his friend Guitar. First unable to speak, then hesitant, Milkman feels uneasy at the presence of "[t]he queer aunt whom his sixth-grade schoolmates teased him about" (*Song of Solomon* 37). Pilate's men's shoes catch his attention, and she looks to him "as though she were holding her crotch" (*Song of Solomon* 38). This only heightens his sense of uncertainty as he is unable to make sense of her ambiguous appearance. In spite of his reluctance to fully abandon himself to her influence, Milkman perceives an irresistible force attracting him to her: "nothing—not the wisdom of his father nor the caution of the world—could keep him from her" (36).

Pilate's cooking and storytelling nurture both their bodies and minds, and the two boys feel as if they were under a soporific spell: "The pebbly voice, the sun, and the narcotic wine smell weakened them, and they sat in a pleasant semi-stupor, listening to her go on and on" (*Song* 40). She gives cooking instructions and then starts talking about Macon and their childhood, leaving Milkman "spellbound" and wishing she would not stop (35). With her magical powers, Pilate challenges Macon's control over his son, as she did when Milkman was a newborn. Against the co-optation of breastfeeding as a practice of property development, Pilate reclaims her nourishing powers, which makes her household a relational space of nurture rather than capital accumulation so that Milkman can grow and claim a new subjectivity, one that is ready to embrace the maternal.

Milkman's first encounter with Pilate marks his initiation into her otherworld, which will only be completed at the end of the novel, when he (re)embraces and performs her maternal praxis. Pilate's sustaining acts of cooking and storytelling propel him forward in his journey, supplying him with precious knowledge about his past. This experience is an important step in Milkman's maturation: "today he had seen a woman who was just as tall [as his father] and who made him feel tall too" (*Song of Solomon* 50). It is this realization that prompts Milkman's first courageous confrontation with his father, when Milkman continues the discovery of his past that Pilate's storytelling initiated.

But Pilate is not the only othermother figure able to conjure up an otherworld with her maternal praxis. Aunt Pilate and Macon themselves, after their parents' death, are cared for by another powerful figure, the midwife Circe, who works for white people on a farm. She helps deliver Macon and Pilate, and then she takes care of them, surreptitiously feeding and hiding them inside the house of the white man who killed their father. She is a "[h]ealer, deliverer," who "risked her job, her life, maybe, to hide them both after their father was killed, emptied their slop jars, brought them food at night and pans of water to wash" (246). In doing so, Circe courageously challenges the white man's control, and asserts her life-giving powers over his deathly authority. In a prison-like house, Circe manages to conjure up a secluded and alternative space, reminiscent of Jacobs's otherworldly loophole, where she can nurture the life racial terror negates. Like Pilate's, her practice is an instance of the otherworldly mothering that Milkman will learn to perform at the end of his quest.

Milkman meets Circe in a surreal encounter, where she is described as a spectral witch-like figure. Named after the eponymous character in the *Odyssey*, this othermother-midwife figure is, as Adorno and Horkheimer argued with respect to Homer's epic, an agent of the mythic world opposed to the rational one of Odysseus or *homo economicus*.[10] Adorno and Horkheimer interpret the magical tale of Circe as corresponding to "the actual stage of magic," which "causes the self's dissolution" (47).

Morrison's Circe is a very old woman with filthy gray hair who lives in poverty, in a dilapidated, dark house, which is what remains of the white man's mansion, surrounded by the dogs she feeds. Charmed, Milkman is compelled to follow her "like a small boy being dragged reluctantly to bed" (240). Rather than being transformed into a pig like Odysseus's men, Milkman reverts to a child-like state as a result of his abandonment to Circe's magic. Meeting her reminds him of scary but also arousing dreams he used to have as a child. He is repulsed but at the same time sexually attracted to her as she emanates a powerful erotic force: he remembers that when he used to have dreams about witches when he was a child, "he would wake with a scream and an erection" (239), and Circe's embrace does cause him a sexual arousal. Unlike the *homo economicus* figure of Odysseus, back to a childlike status, Milkman is bewitched by Circe and cannot defeat the power of her othermothering magic. He does not withstand Circe; instead, he succumbs to her power of self-dissolution: when "he saw the woman at the top of stairs there was no way for him to resist climbing up toward her outstretched arms" (239).

Milkman seems unable to decide whether Circe is dead or alive, referring to her as both. He remarks that "[t]his woman is alive," but then he also links her to death: "Circe is dead [. . .] although the woman was talking to him, she might in any case still be dead—as a matter of fact, she *had* to be dead," and he describes her face as "so old it could not be alive" (240, original italics). Circe

is not only both dead and alive but also both young and old. Her "strong, mel-
lifluent voice of a twenty-year-old girl" sharply contrasts with her "toothless
mouth" and wrinkled face, making Milkman feel even more uncomfortable:
"[i]t was awful listening to that voice coming from that face" (240–41). He
cannot decide whether she is dead or alive and neither can he establish her
age: "seventy-two, thirty-two, any age at all, meant nothing whatsoever to her.
Milkman wondered how old she really was" (241). Her presence itself concret-
izes the reciprocity between the world of the living and the dead. As Derrick
Mashau and Themba Ngcobo have observed, many traditional African religions
regard the spiritual world of the ancestors and the physical one of the living
as interconnected and constantly interacting with each other: when one dies,
"one is expected to maintain close bonds with the living" (37). Circe's praxis is
rooted in a similar sense of relatedness between the living and the dead.

Embodying ambiguities, Morrison's Circe is characterized by indeterminacy. Poised between life and death, young and old at the same time, Circe has
no sense of time, existing in an alternative space, the otherworld she conjured
up with her witchlike powers, where death and life can coexist. Like Pilate,
Circe defies Western linear understandings of time. She lives in the present and
in the past at the same time, bewildering Milkman as he cannot make sense of
these embodied contradictions. A sense of ambiguity and shifting nature is a
signature also of Homer's Circe, as Adorno and Horkheimer have shown: "in
the story she appears by turns as corrupter and helper" and, being the daughter of Helios and the granddaughter of Oceanus, even her lineage is ambiguous. In the *Odyssey*, Circe and her connection to an ancient mythical world
are construed as threats that must ultimately be dominated and left behind
by Odysseus/*homo economicus* so that he can continue his "ruthless pursuit of
[his] atomistic interests" (Adorno and Horkheimer 43). However, in Morrison's
novel, Milkman must learn Circe's art of maternal interconnection and fully
abandon himself to her magical powers in order to be birthed anew through
the maternal.

Echoing Circe's prophecies about the Sirens in Homer's epic, Morrison's
Circe gives Milkman precious details about his ancestral past, revealing his
grandmother's name: Sing. Thanks to Circe, Milkman rediscovers "the name of
the mother, supposedly lost both to the past's violence and to the equally violent
efforts to forget the past" and is delivered from the father's ghost (Benston 105).
With her knowledge about the maternal past, Circe guides Milkman, leading
him toward the path that will enable him to rediscover his ancestral roots and

embrace the maternal. While in the *Odyssey*, Circe's prophecies "only serve the purposes of male self-preservation" (Adorno and Horkheimer 45), in *Song of Solomon*, Circe's maternal wisdom guides Milkman towards his final transformation: his journey, which Circe's othermothering spurs, is not aimed at "self-preservation" like Odysseus's, but at an undoing of the self in order to remake it. While he sets out to find gold, in the end, it is his maternal connection and heritage that he reclaims together with a new way of being in the world.

Unlike her Homeric namesake, Circe is not a "powerless sorceress" (Adorno and Horkheimer 47) and always remains in control, never letting Milkman define the terms of their relation and behaving as "a contractual lord" like Odysseus (Adorno and Horkheimer 46). Milkman initially shows Circe a patronizing attitude and assumes that she needs his help: like Odysseus when he meets his mother in the Underworld, Milkman "maintains a purposive patriarchal hardness" (48). But, unlike the blind, powerless, and speechless Anticlea, Circe speaks back, making it clear she is perfectly able to look after herself: "You think I don't know how to walk when I want to walk?" (246). She scolds him for his inability to listen: "You don't listen to people. Your ear is in your head, but it's not connected to your brain" (246–47).

Milkman thinks Circe's decision to stay in the white man's house after the enslaver's death and her taking care of their dogs attested to her loyalty towards them, but her choices derived from her long-suppressed rage: she is not a helpless victim. After the white people who owned the house died, she remained there to feed the dogs that would help her tear it apart, recalling Jim Bon's fate in William Faulkner's *Absalom, Absalom!* (1936):

> They loved it [the house]. Stole for it, lied for it, killed for it. But I'm the one left. Me and the dogs. And I will never clean it again. Never. Nothing. Not a speck of dust, not a grain of dirt, will I move. Everything in this world they lived for will crumble and rot. [. . .] And I want to see it all go, make sure it does go, and that nobody fixes it up. I brought the dogs in to make sure [. . .] You ought to see what they did to her bedroom. (247)

Circe nourishes the dust and breeds the dogs that will dismantle the enslaver's house from its foundations. Echoing Circe's power to transform men into pigs, Morrison's Circe has become a midwife for dogs: "Birthed just about everybody in the country, I did. Never lost one either [. . .] Now I birth dogs" (243). While she used to attend to life, she now tends to death as those dogs are the

harbingers of destruction. Circe's life-giving powers as a midwife are now harnessed to the destruction of white power, symbolized by the mansion. It is as
a result of racial terror that her caring and life-giving powers are devoted to
destructive purposes: "She [the white mistress] saw the work I did all her days
and *died*, you hear me, *died* rather than live like me. Now, what do you suppose
she thought I was! If the way I lived and the work I did was so hateful to her
she killed herself to keep from having to do it" (247). As her account of the mo-
tives behind her acts demonstrates, Circe's destructive drive is the result of the
enslavers' exploitation of her, which consigned her to a death-in-life. But her
violent magic is, like that of Homer's Circe, ambiguous: her destructive drive is
at the same time a creative one as, through her praxis, she seeks to destabilize
the very foundations upon which racial violence is built so as to conjure up an
otherworld based upon different premises.

Pilate's and Circe's creative othermothering practices, connected with the
spiritual, offer them sources of knowledge alternative to those dominant in U.S.
society. Through the portrayal of such practices, informed by an ancestral maternal wisdom that threatens the dichotomies of man/woman, young/old, dead/
alive, and enslaver/enslaved, the novel questions Western dualistic thinking. By
conjuring up a maternal otherworld where such distinctions do not hold and
where past and present, death and life coexist, the text shows how Pilate and
Circe challenge the structures of domination and seek to escape white patriarchal authority, freeing the maternal from the co-optation of racial violence.
Nurturing Milkman, they help his maturation as an individual who can embrace the intricate web of interconnections the world is built upon.

Milkman's Flight

At the end of the novel, Milkman is able to perceive his mother in a new light,
no longer seeing her as a selfless and asexual being, but as a separate person.
He acknowledges her sexuality and perceives her not in opposition to, but in
relation to, himself: "The best years of her life, from age twenty to forty, had
been celibate, and aside from the consummation that began his own life, the
rest of her life had been the same. He hadn't thought much of it when she'd
told him, but now it seemed to him that such sexual deprivation would affect
her, hurt her in precisely the same way it would affect and hurt him" (300). He
recognizes her suffering and the tenacity breastfeeding has granted her: "His
mother had been able to live through that by a long nursing of her son [. . .]

What might she be like had her husband loved her?" (300). He does not view her as a threat, as the castrating Black matriarch derived from white patriarchal notions of masculinity.

By contrast, earlier in the novel, Milkman observed that "[n]ever had he thought of his mother as a person, a separate individual, with a life apart from allowing or interfering with his own" (75). Showing the same patriarchal hardness he displayed with Circe, he described his mother as "a silly, selfish, queer, faintly obscene woman" (123), and is suspicious about her inappropriate conduct as a mother and daughter: "if she did that [breastfeeding] to me when there was no reason for it [. . .] then maybe she did other things with her father?" (78). His perceptions of his mother were mainly characterized by his sense of her neediness and by his own anxiety regarding his masculinity. This is evident in his impulse to punish his father for beating Ruth but even more so in a troubling dreamlike vision of her that he recounts to his friend Guitar. In it, Milkman is watching Ruth planting red tulips that suddenly grow uncontrollably and submerge her: "Milkman thought she would jump in fear—at least surprise. But she didn't. She leaned back from them, even hit out at them, but playfully, mischievously. [. . .] And she merely smiled and fought them off as though they were harmless butterflies. He knew they were dangerous, that they would soon suck up all the air around her and leave her limp on the ground. But she didn't seem to guess this at all." (105)

In his dream, he sees his mother as a victim needing help, even though, as Guitar notices, he does not offer her any. He is unable to think of his mother as capable of fighting back and reads her serenity as childish naiveté, infantilizing her. In this scene, his mother is characterized as powerless and speechless since Milkman imposes upon her his own perspective. He cannot hear her voice nor recognize that Ruth is not scared as she is embracing her creative powers. As is the case with the watermark, she is engaging in the creation of an otherworld where she can generate life.

As the dream reveals, Milkman kept projecting his own anxieties upon his mother, afraid of conceiving of himself in terms different from those dictated by normative white masculinity. Michele Wallace, in her controversial book *Black Macho and the Myth of the Superwoman* (1979), has underlined the misogyny that underscored the Black Power movement, connecting their assertion of African American masculine power to the devaluation of Black women perceived as complicit in the oppression of Black men. To some extent, she might be right in denouncing the movement's sexism; however, as Robyn Wiegman has underlined, their claims for Black masculine power need to be understood as "a broader representational strategy" that, however limited, historically tried to challenge the "exclusionary logic of white masculine power" (110). We must remember that, especially in the United States, the status of Black masculinity remains precarious as Black men have historically been emasculated in order to conceal the threat of masculine sameness. It is only at the end of his journey that Milkman overcomes his masculine anxieties by seeing his mother as a fully rounded, complex, passionate, and sexual woman, and by learning how to perform maternal acts.

Milkman's reconciliation with his mother is based on his recognition of his own failures and his inability to connect with her. Embracing the love and nurture of Ruth and Pilate, he acknowledges them both as his mothers and displays an awareness of his shortcomings: "From the beginning, his mother and Pilate had fought for his life, and he had never so much as made either of them a cup of tea" (331). It is this newly found wisdom that brings him closer to the maternal love of Ruth and Pilate, restoring his own nurturing abilities and allaying his anxieties. Milkman can now nurture others while taking care of himself. As his relationship with Sweet demonstrates, he ceases to regard people as instruments or things: by the close of the novel, he has been transformed into a new version of *homo*, ready to re-embrace the maternal.

This reconciliation with the maternal allows him to feel deeply connected to multiple places, where he can find the same homely atmosphere of Pilate's house. Reminiscing about it, he senses that, although no material articles of comfort were there, nonetheless "peace was there, energy, singing, and now his own remembrances" (301). During his trip, he muses that "there was something he felt now—here in Shalimar, and earlier in Danville—that reminded him of how he used to feel in Pilate's house" (293), suggesting that his conception of home has expanded. Like Pilate, Milkman is no longer bound to a stable sense of place anymore: "Pilate had taken a rock from every state she had lived in—because she *had* lived there. And having lived there, it was hers—and his, and his father's, his grandfather's, his grandmother's. Not Doctor Street, Solomon's Leap, Ryna's Gulch, Shalimar, Virginia" (*Song of Solomon* 329–30, original italics). His concept of home disperses across various spaces as he becomes able to acknowledge his ancestral maternal connections to multiple places, abandoning his claim to any single location. He comes to understand homeland not on the basis of "settlement and fixed property," like Odysseus (Adorno and Horkheimer 57), but of deep maternal bonds. Pilate's maternal practice reveals its impact upon Milkman: even away from her house, he can now experience an expanding sense of relatedness.

Through his narrative journey, which reverses the usual trajectory of antebellum slave narratives, Milkman has built connections not only to various places but also to people, extending kinship relations in a jumble of intimacies: "He closed his eyes and thought of the black men in Shalimar, Roanoke, Petersburg, Newport News, Danville [. . .] Their names. Names they got from yearnings, gestures, flaws, events, mistakes, weaknesses. Names that bore witness" (330). Imagining himself as part of a wider community, he reclaims "the sorts of social spaces, and caring, playful relationships, that would serve as the condition of possibility for such naming, such proximity rendered in language" (Bennett, *Being* 81). He feels powerful links connecting him to those people "as though there was some cord or pulse or information they shared" (293). He now sees himself in relation, rather than opposition, to others, and he can perceive his interconnectedness with the wider world, not just with his mother, reforging communal links. Against the social death enforced by racial terror, his embracement of the maternal allows him to reclaim social life.

This new awareness of relatedness enables Milkman to rewrite his family history: he learns that his journey is not powered by a greedy quest to find material riches, as he assumed, but by a spiritual need to gather the fragments of his ancestral heritage. He discovers that the song Pilate has been singing recounts "a story about his own people" and this realization makes him feel "as eager and happy as he had ever been in his life" (302), signaling his joyful embracement of his ancestral past. Milkman's quest ends as he is able to decipher the song that narrates his family history and recognize Pilate's important role: through her singing she preserves and passes on ancestral wisdom and family history like a West African *griot*. Pilate and Circe's communal mothering is effective as Milkman reaches an individual identity but also acknowledges his reliance upon others and his connections with multiple places, both in the past and present.

Through his quest, Milkman uncovers the whole narrative of his family and embraces the maternal values of Pilate. In the last scene of the novel, Milkman takes up the nurturing role of Pilate as he celebrates her creative practices. Unlike Odysseus or Crusoe, he is finally able to break away from his radical alienation, embracing the maternal. After his friend Guitar shoots her, Milkman mothers his dying aunt, acknowledging their mutual dependency and showing his newly found ability to nurture: "He dropped to his knees and cradled her lolling head in the crook of his arm [. . .] He pressed the fingers against the skin as if to force the life back in her, back into the place it was escaping from" (335–36). Nurturing himself and his aunt, he performs the ancestral song Pilate sang when Ruth was giving birth to him. Preserved by maternal figures, this song represents his maternal inheritance and functions, much as it does in *Iola Leroy,* "to mark its bearers with knowledge of and from the mother, and to connect scattered kin" (Yates-Richard 486). Through the performance of a creative maternal act akin to that of Pilate, Milkman embraces her otherworldly maternal powers. Like the young boy Gan, the male protagonist of Octavia Butler's short story "Bloodchild," Milkman gets access to "the tradition of non phallic maternal authority that developed out of black women's experiences during slavery" (Lillvis 8).

Having uncovered his ancestral heritage and embraced the maternal, Milkman can fly, reenacting the Ibo Landing myth also central to *Praisesong.* Like Pilate, he is not afraid of dying because he has learned to recognize the reciprocity between life and death. The dream he previously had of flying and "sailing high over the earth," which imbued him with a "sense of lightness and power" (*Song of Solomon* 298), becomes a reality. Knowing that "[i]f you surrendered to the air, you could *ride* it" (337, original italics), Milkman willingly succumbs to the violent destruction symbolized by Guitar, who killed Pilate with a rifle: "'You want my life?' [. . .] 'You need it? Here.' Without wiping away the tears, taking a deep breath, or even bending his knees—he leaped. As fleet and bright as a lodestar he wheeled toward Guitar" (337). Pilate and Circe's othermothering praxes thus seem to have allowed Milkman to reimagine his subjectivity; however, his flight has problematic and less liberatory aspects that underscore the ambiguous nature of mothering in the novel.

Since "black men are the summary of weight" and "the epitome of embodiment" (Weaver 43; Weheliye 26), through his transcendental flight, Milkman seeks to flee the constraints of the body to challenge the historical imposition of extreme corporeality on the Black male subject and leave behind the negations forced upon bodies as signifiers of identity. As Wiegman has observed, Enlightenment thought constructed the social category of the citizen as a rhetorically disembodied entity, with the result that "the white male was (and continues to be) 'freed' from the corporeality that might otherwise impede his insertion into the larger body of national identity" (94). By contrast, for the African American male, "the imposition of an extreme corporeality [. . .] defined his distance from the privileged ranks of citizenry" (94). Wiegman interprets the lynching of Black male bodies after Emancipation as a white male attempt "to reclaim and reassert the centrality of black male corporeality, deterring the now theoretically possible move toward citizenry and disembodied abstraction" (94). Read under this light, Milkman's flight constitutes a rejection of the body in an attempt to escape this imposed corporeality and claim the right to the rhetorically disembodied abstraction of the white male, leaving behind the specific racial markers of disempowered identity.

Milkman's effort to claim the transcendental subjectivity of liberal humanism attests to his inability to claim a different form of subjectivity, resulting in his death. The text thus highlights the limitations of his potentially liberating mythical flight as the body politic does not allow for the recognition of Black people's subjectivities. His flight remains marked by failure and death as the heaviness imposed upon Black masculinity "prevents something like flight or a legible form of social mobility" (Bennett, *Being* 45). As Hartman has noted, "the freedom of liberal personhood accorded to Black Americans by the 14th Amendment proved a vastly diminished prize" (28). African Americans "have been denied the right to create a recognizable public self" (Davis 6), and the novel suggests that overcoming this denial demands the full relinquishment of liberal humanism's conception of the subject: while Milkman's performance of the maternal offered him the means to do so, he ultimately remains unable to claim a new subjectivity. The ending of the novel highlights the unattainability of Black male subjectivity if we insist on retaining a Western bourgeois definition of the human, yearning for a different mode of being rather than a fuller recognition within liberal humanism's terms. In Morrison's novel, the very moment in which Black people seek to lay claim to a liberal humanist ideal, its limitations become clear.

Many critics read Milkman's flight as a spiritual reawakening, equating his flight with transcendence. Deborah Guth, for instance, argues that "[i]n this one moment he finally repossesses his mythic heritage" and "gives it new meaning" (5). According to Manuela López Ramírez, "his flight signals a spiritual epiphany in the hero's quest for self-definition in the black community" (105). However, flight, an important theme in the novel and the African American literary and cultural tradition, does not have a completely positive association in Morrison's text. Foregrounding the novel's obsession with failed flight, already evident in the opening scene, Joshua Bennett argues that even birds "come to signal a certain boundness to earth, a certain abundance that limits all possibility of escape or futurity" (49). As Morrison herself has noted, Solomon's and

Milkman's flights are both "ambiguous, disturbing" (xiii). To attain transcendence, his ancestor Solomon had to leave behind his children, flying away from his responsibilities and severing his familial connections: "he [Solomon] disappeared and left everybody. Wife, everybody, including some twenty-one children" (326). Barred from deriving his sense of worth from "traditional modes of accruing wealth," the Black male must find "alternative means of producing self-esteem and dignity" such as flight and mobility (Bennett, *Being* 116). While this is "a positive, majestic thing," as Morrison has observed in an interview about her writing of *Song*, "there is a price to pay" (46). According to Hirsch, Solomon's flight is "an act of paternal irresponsibility and abandonment" so "heroic soaring is also antiheroic evasion" (76–77). Reenacting his ancestor's flight, Milkman seeks to connect to an ancestral tradition of transcendence, but his death brings to the fore the limitations and problematic nature of such an endeavor, which encodes a rejection of the body and its relationality, as the ancestral warning of Milkman's grandfather underlines: "[y]ou just can't fly on off and leave a body" (*Song of Solomon* 332). As is the case with Ruth's breastfeeding, the text complicates and problematizes a celebratory analysis of Milkman's flight as it employs a similar dialectic modality in its depiction.

Song of Solomon portrays maternal practices that, while potentially liberating, do not fully deliver their promise of transformation: even Pilate's and Circe's practices at the end cannot escape the dialectic dynamic that we have seen at work in Ruth's mothering. Their practices bring death instead of life since Milkman dies right after having envisaged the possibility of remaking his subjectivity and performing a relational and caring mode of being. The novel suggests that a creative otherworld, albeit attainable, remains out of reach: over such a fleeting accomplishment death still looms large for both mother and son. Pilate dies and the ghostly Circe remains surrounded by an aura of death. Ruth, buried in her sterile marriage, keeps living a death-in-life as her relationship with her husband does not change: "relations between Ruth and Macon were the same and would always be" (335). The novel suggests that, in the context of violent antiblackness, imagining an otherworld where maternal practice can become a praxis of being is possible, but such an achievement remains linked to death as racial violence keeps warping the maternal.

Through the portrayal of Ruth's maternal practice, the text has shown the ongoing disruption of the maternal perpetuated by racial terror and the limitations of a liberal humanist model of the human. Consequently, it has created a corollary network of maternal support, symbolized by Pilate and Circe, opening up the possibility for Milkman to claim a relational subjectivity. Through Pilate's and Circe's maternal practices, the text has managed to create a space of possibility where mothering can enable a creative remaking of the human. However, the novel's ending problematizes such an accomplishment as Milkman's flight results in death: in an antiblack world, the result of maternal praxis can only ever remain fleeting and temporary since the liberatory possibilities of the maternal remain constrained.

But, through the writing of the novel itself, Morrison has been able to reclaim a literary space of possibility, an otherworld, where she has rewritten and reanimated an archive of maternal praxis. In her text, she has drawn upon and reenacted the ancestral art of "mother-wit" conjuring up the practice of midwives, carrying their voice and wisdom, and making it a model for her own literary practice of interconnection. As we have seen, weaving together history and myth, past and present, she has rewritten the "official" narrative of American exceptionalism and individualism to create her own, which centers upon ancestral othermothering and midwifery praxis as the main catalysts for the male's journey to remake his subjectivity. In so doing, she has transformed herself into a midwife figure. In a conversation with Naylor about her writing of *Jazz*, Morrison has described her narrative practice as a "process of reclamation" that can give new life to the dead. Her writing becomes the medium through which the dead can come back to life: "Bit by bit I had been rescuing her from the grave of time and inattention. Her fingernails may be in the first book; face and legs, perhaps, the second time. Little by little bringing her back into living life. So that now she comes running when called—walks freely around the house, sits down in a chair; looks at me, listens [. . .] She is here now, alive. I have seen, named and claimed her—and oh what company she keeps." (567)

Similarly, through her writing of *Song of Solomon*, she has brought into being midwife-othermother figures, and with them their ancestral practices. In writing the novel, Morrison has engaged in a form of maternal performance rooted in Black women's othermothering traditions: her writing itself has become a maternal praxis inspired by their "mother-wit."

2

· ⁄

Human-Making Mourning

In her book *In the Wake: On Blackness and Being,* Christina Sharpe defined "wake work" as "hard emotional, physical, and intellectual work that demands vigilant attendance to the needs of the dying, to ease their way, and also to the needs of the living" (11). As historians have documented, this is the work Black people have been trying to perform in spite of, and because of, racial terror. Historian Vincent Brown has reported that in 1786, on board the slave ship *Hudibras,* enslaved people fought hard to be allowed to mourn the death of another enslaved woman. He describes how the other women, refusing to be herded below decks, started a "'loud, deep, and impressive' rite of mourning" (1231). This wake work was necessary to assert the value of not only the deceased's life but also theirs in the face of racial violence: it was an attempt "to make social meaning from the threat of anomie," an example of how enslaved people "have often made a social world out of death itself" (Brown 1232–33).

Engaging in the performance of such acts, enslaved people sought to reclaim a sense of communal life, as enslavers strove to enforce social death by not allowing them "to anchor the living present in any conscious community of memory" (Patterson 5). Since funerals occurred only occasionally on slave ships as the dead were usually thrown overboard unceremoniously, enslaved people "confronted a dual crisis: the trauma of death and the inability to respond properly to death" (56).[1] Jones-Rogers has documented how enslavers denied enslaved mothers the right to publicly mourn, attempting to "render invisible" their grief to make them more marketable (121–22). She describes such forms of racial terror as another type of "maternal violence" akin to the forced separations of enslaved mothers and children and their exploitation as wetnurses (122).

Even throughout the twentieth century, Black people have oftentimes been barred from the performance of mourning. After the 1921 Tulsa race massacre, the victims were buried without a funeral in mass graves. In the aftermath of the 1928 Lake Okeechobee hurricane, whose devastating effects on the poor Black communities of Florida are depicted in Hurston's *Their Eyes Were Watching God*, caskets were reserved for the corpses of white people—who received a proper burial service—but the corpses of Black people were burned or thrown into mass burial sites. As Karla FC Holloway has documented, white undertaking establishments generally did not provide services to the Black community, and, when they grudgingly did, they treated them in a disparaging and demeaning way: white morticians "would keep the bodies of whites upstairs [. . .] as they awaited burial, while dead blacks were hidden in the basement" (qtd. in Holloway 21). These "[m]emories of the disrespect for Black bodies ran deep [. . .] and [were] generationally passed on" (Holloway 21). More recently, it has transpired that the remains of two Black girls who died in the 1985 MOVE bombings in Philadelphia were used in an online anthropology class, sparking outrage and the call to bury their remains.

Considering such acts of racial terror, the performance of mourning rituals carries significance as a way to reimagine the humanness that racial violence attempts to undo. If, as Judith Butler reminds us, "[a]n ungrievable life is one that cannot be mourned because it has never lived, that is, it has never counted as a life at all" (*Precarious* 4), the insistence on mourning despite racial terror becomes a processual reclamation of lives undone—both those of the grieved ones and those of the grievers. If racial violence creates a symbolic order that, erasing the value of Black life, negates the very possibility of mourning for the loss of such a life, Black people, engaging in efforts to mourn such losses, have at the same time also brought forth an onto-epistemic order that can allow the untethering of Black being from "social death." Much as during slavery, the performance of communal mourning by Black people not only affirms the life of the deceased but creates the "social world" racial terror negates (Brown 1232–33) wherein both the life of the griever and the grieved find new meaning. Echoing Sharpe's definition of "wake work" as attending to the needs of the living and the dead, such mourning rituals create a caring community that can reclaim both from the social death created by racial terror.

In this chapter, I want to suggest that it is a similar kind of labor, which I will call human-making mourning, that Gloria Naylor's second novel, *Linden Hills*, performs in an attempt to rewrite the onto-epistemic terrain of the human. Her novel engages in a narrative practice of human-making mourning directed inwards, towards the Black community. This praxis humanizes both griever and grieved through a communal caring ritual that bonds the living with the dead, attempting to rewrite the social links that racial terror erased.

I argue that Willa's mourning practice is a human-making praxis based on a relational ontology that highlights a different genre of the human, challenging what Wynter has called the overrepresentation of the human as Man. Through the portrayal of Willa's praxis, which, reminiscent of slave rituals, is based upon a communal responsiveness to the needs of others, both living and death, and a reshaping of social relations, or what I will term her maternal ethics of care, the novel summons up the intimate experiences of Black people. Together with *Song of Solomon*, it attempts to build a democratic site of memory, where Black people can find alternative origin stories for themselves and refashion their subjectivities. Describing Willa's grieving process, the novel itself, I will argue, performs a literary equivalent of the graveyard art that characterized the funeral rituals of enslaved people and that had its roots in West African traditions (Holloway 210). Commemorating the lived experiences and spiritual lives of the deceased, Naylor's novel establishes a connection between the world of the living and the dead. In doing so, not only does it memorialize the slave past and humanize Black lives, but it constructs an alternative historical narrative that problematizes economically driven accounts such as those offered by Fogel and Engerman in *Time on the Cross* (1974). It also rewrites our genre-specific narrative of the human as a bioeconomic subject (Wynter 265): if the human is also "*homo narrans*" or a narrative being, so that the laws that engender our empirical reality are "storytellingly chartered" or implemented through a storytelling praxis (Wynter 268), then this novel is not only rewriting history but the human itself.[2] It provides a way to unthink the ontological constraints that structure our "monohumanism" or genre-specific sense of being human, which has been historically shaped by ideas and concepts of the Enlightenment and ratified in our narratives.

My understanding of what I term maternal ethics of care as a responsiveness to other people's needs and an ability to foster social bonds and cooperation is informed by feminist philosophical analyses of ethics and morality that emphasize a relational conception of persons. This stands in contrast to the (apparently) self-sufficient, rational, and self-interested individuals posited by dominant moral theories whose conception of personhood was developed mainly for liberal political and economic theory (Held 15). According to these feminist analyses, moral agents are "embedded," "encumbered," and embodied, revealing the illusory nature of the myth of the independent, "self-made" man (Held 47). However, these theories often tend to disregard non-Western traditions of thought that are based upon alternative onto-epistemologies and to treat the human as a given; by contrast, Naylor's novel draws upon such traditions, regarding the human as the object to be creatively reassessed and reimagined rather than the context of investigation.

Based upon a Black Atlantic nonlinear temporality and aimed at fostering connections, the novel's narrative practice of human-making mourning highlights maternal care as an alternative "way of being in the world" (Hamington 2) that is rendered necessary by a socially produced vulnerability. This maternal praxis underscores an understanding of the human as a relational being that has its roots in the African ethical concept of Ubuntu, which "is based on the idea that as human beings we depend on other human beings to attain ultimate wellbeing:" it is in our interconnectedness with each other that we acquire humanness (Murove 39). Upholding this relational ontology, the novel's maternal praxis posits relationality as a starting point to rethink what it means to be human, destabilizing Western ontological categories. It thus functions as the "demonic ground" that, as Wynter has theorized, will enable us to reimagine humanness so that the human will no longer be conceived in "biocentric-liberal monohumanist terms" (277) as *homo economicus*.

A key scene early in the novel illustrates the questions that animate my analysis. In a state halfway between asleep and awake, imprisoned in the basement-morgue, Willa tries to come to terms with the grief for her son's death:

> She blinked her mucus-caked eyes rapidly in the dim light and looked at the dead weight on her chest, her chilled body actually feeling warm against the coldness and rigidity of the flesh she held. She eased the child from her; its muscles had stiffened around the shape of her body so that the limbs were permanently spooned toward her. [. . .] She would leave it all very soon, but there should be somebody to pity this. And there would be no one. Their bodies would be carried away, dumped somewhere, and left unmourned because no one would know. But didn't she know? (90)

She recognizes that her and her son's lives will remain unmournable unless she tells her story and remembers the past, both personal and communal. Manifesting, through her maternal ethics of care, an enduring concern for her dead son, Willa is determined "to let them know that she cared," and she seeks suitable materials with which to bury her son (92). This search enables her to uncover funerary objects with which she conjures a caring community of foremothers. Her maternal ethics of care spur a mourning praxis that fosters relationality, mutual recognition, and interdependence, compelling a renegotiation of the human and paralleling the narrative work of human-making mourning the novel itself performs. Linked to enslaved people's "wake work" and their related summoning up of a "social world" out of death, her mourning ritual enables her to connect to the lived experiences of her maternal ancestors, humanizing both herself and her son. In so doing, she engages in an insistent act of "radical humanization" that, according to Miles, Black women have been performing throughout history as they preserved maternal links from one generation to the other (4).

The first section of this chapter will trace the textual microcosm the novel creates through the portrayal of the Northern middle-class neighborhood of Linden Hills and the power his "creator" holds over it. Luther has built a world according to the dictates of a profit-based white patriarchal bourgeois society: much like Macon in Morrison's novel, he is the epitome of Foucault's *homo economicus* (226) and Wynter's "monohumanist Man2," which corresponds to our present genre-specific praxis of being human (268). Luther's house-enterprise is driven by an economic logic according to which people can be bought and sold, and children are just another form of capital. Motherhood is reduced to a mere mechanical function so that women become vessels whose main purpose is to deliver a son fit to inherit the Nedeed's business. Like Willa, the previous Mrs. Nedeeds are condemned to a death-in-life that recalls the condition of slaves as the value of these women's lives continues to be gauged against purely economic interests. When Willa gives birth to a son who shows a maternal connection, Luther's economic mode of reason can only apprehend his life as deselected and disposable. According to his economic worldview, his "unfit" son has no value and becomes a fungible object, whose death he is unable to mourn: "[o]nly under conditions in which the loss would matter does the value of the life appear" (Butler, *Precarious* 14).

However, as the second section will make clear, the birthing of Willa's son has initiated a disruption of Luther's house-enterprise. Against Luther's devaluation of their son's life, Willa's determination to mourn him recasts his life as grievable and worthy of life. If "[a]n ungrievable life is one that cannot be mourned because it has never lived, that is, it has never counted as a life at all" (Butler, *Precarious* 38), then Willa's mourning practice humanizes her son. Accessing a space outside of linear time, where past and present, death and life coexist, Willa manages to create a funeral procession for her son and prepare his body for burial. Much like slave funerals, her care-driven practice functions as an assertion of communal caring bonds and as a way to humanize not only her son but also herself, shaking the foundations of Luther's control over their lives.

The third section turns to the shattering of Luther's economic world catalyzed by Willa's maternal ethics of care. Giving the previous Mrs. Nedeeds the life they were denied, she reflects on her own death-in-life existence, in a process that culminates in her rebirthing of herself assisted by these women's ghosts. Willa is able to destroy the capitalistic heritage of Luther in a last action reminiscent of slave insurrections and connected to the disruptive nature of Black funerals. Her care-driven practice results in a destructive fire in which both she and Luther die, but which also dismantles Luther's house-enterprise and provides hope for rebuilding Linden Hills on noneconomic premises. As attested by the bewildered reaction of Willie and Lester, the "pile of charred woods" to which Luther's mansion is reduced can become the "demonic ground" that Wynter theorized as a locus for a redefinition of our present conception of Man as a bioeconomic subject and its "monohumanism" or its reification of Man-as-human.

Luther's Economic Logic

Naylor's text characterizes Luther as the epitome of *homo economicus,* whose conception of the world revolves around economic paradigms such as capital and value. According to his economic logic, which he learned from his forefathers, "[l]ife is in the material. Success is being able to stick an "er" on it. And death is watching someone else have it" (9): every aspect of life, even life itself, is understood in purely materialistic terms so that "all dimensions of human life are cast in terms of a market rationality" (Brown 40). Even people can be bought and sold, as the first patriarch "sold his octoroon wife and six children for the money that he used to come North and obtain the hilly land" on which Linden Hills grew, and then he bought her back (4).

In many ways, Luther resembles *Song of Solomon*'s Macon: he too is a self-made man, a businessman, and "a man of property" (123) at the head of a patriarchal household-enterprise. He pursues economic success, adopting a materialistic worldview: he is described as "a wizard" who has turned "our iron chains into gold chains" (12). His ancestors, "a whole line of men who had shown Wayne County what it was possible to do with a little patience and a lot of work" (16), accumulated money and land where they built houses to rent. They managed to become wealthy and retain their riches despite racism and even through the Great Depression, when "America's nervous breakdown" confirmed that "nothing was closer to the spleen and guts of the country than success" (9). The world he inhabits is imbued with economic modes of valuation, which he absorbs in his attempt to assimilate into *homo economicus's* order, identifying with this figure. Following in the footsteps of his forefathers, Luther's actions are driven by a possessive drive: "the omnipresent, omnipotent, Almighty Divine is simply the *will* to possess" (17, original italics). The fact that he is a mortician underscores his upper-class status and materialistic outlook since during the twentieth century, "the black undertaker emerged as a businessman in a community of few independent black-owned businesses:" his high social status was earned "through his appearance and his acquisitions," especially the accumulation of cars and ownership of property (Holloway 23–24). But, if viewed in the context of the novel's employment of Dante's hell as a structural model and the series of deaths that punctuate the plot, Luther's occupation also functions to underscore how Black death is as central an occurrence to the social order of the plantation as to that of *homo economicus's* neoliberal America. What Vincent Brown has called the "mortuary politics" of the plantation still loom large in Luther's *homo economicus's* order, to which he aspires to belong.

Engaging in conspicuous consumption and approaching his entire life in the mode of an entrepreneur, Luther adopts an economic logic that performs specific types of ontological erasures, transforming women into fungible objects that can easily be replaced when no longer fulfilling their purpose: "His father was right: breaking in a wife is like breaking in a good pair of slippers" (67). Objectified, women are viewed as investments to be made to ensure the continuity of an enterprise; they "are maintained at a distant/inferior position to be psychically milked [. . .] to provide a life-giving substance for their masters" (Lorde, "Uses" 54). Her identity erased and reduced to a mere function, Willa is expected to "[j]ust come into his home and respect him [. . .] Work along with him to continue the tradition of several generations" (68). Luther does not even refer or think about her as a person because to him she is just a "long neck, small breasts, thick waist" (19) woman whose main purpose is to conceive a child who will share not only the father's physical appearance but also his materialistic values. Woman and mother become interchangeable terms.

Luther's entrepreneurial mode of reason devalues the maternal, reducing it to the action of reproduction alone and seeking to strip it of its ontological achievement. It thus becomes a mere mechanical activity primed first and foremost to deliver a potential economic output: "women are encouraged to [. . .] reproduce entrepreneurial forms of self-governance by producing babies emotionally primed to navigate an economic system that prioritizes flexible, mobile, and adaptable workers" imbricating women "in ever-more-dense networks of authority, expertise, and government" (Johnson 400). In the neoliberal order, the main aim of mothering becomes the reproduction not of human beings but of human capital, and its value rests on economic evaluations of the utility of such capital: the maternal becomes transfigured as a space of capital accumulation. Mechanically performing what is viewed as just another economic pursuit, mothers are reduced to mere reproductive vessels, becoming lifeless machines used to reproduce capital and then discarded. As Brown has observed, women are constituted as "the invisible infrastructure for all developing, mature, and worn-out human capital" (105). They are made to sustain "a world of putatively self-investing human capitals" who actually remain "dependent upon invisible practices and unnamed others" (104–6). This is what happens to the various Mrs. Nedeeds, condemned "to fade against the whitewashed boards of the Nedeed home after conceiving" a son who is an exact replica of the father (18). Their lives cannot be understood outside of an economic schema, and they cannot be apprehended as living; they acquire value only in so far as they can bear and raise a healthy male offspring that can be assimilated into a neoliberal marketplace.

Even children are assigned value only to the extent to which they show the potential to become useful according to strictly economic calculations. Luther's son, like Willa, is reduced to a mere object to be possessed and exploited, as Luther sometimes refers to him with the impersonal pronoun "it" (68). The value of such an objectified son is measured against purely economic parameters, its purpose being that of successfully taking over the father's business: "it [the materialistic dream of Luther's predecessors] could go on forever through his son" (18). To take his proper place in Luther's enterprise, his son needs to share his father's economic logic. He becomes a means to an end: the reproduction of economic capital through the investment in human capital.

In Luther's household-enterprise, sex becomes a mere profit-making activity, deprived of its erotic power and akin to work. Lorde defined the erotic as "our most profoundly creative source," which is perverted in Western society (54). This creative energy is missing from the Nedeeds' lives: "If spontaneity and passion didn't exist in the rooms they ate in, entertained in, and sat in, how could she expect it in the room she slept in?" (148). Willa and Luther keep sleeping in separate bedrooms because that is "*[t]he way it's always been done here*, he'd said" (148, original emphasis). But "then he would come at night. Enter and leave her body with the same quiet precision that she saw when he balanced his accounts, read his newspaper, or dissected his steak" (148). For Lorde, in a profit-based society, both work and sex, robbed of their erotic value, are reduced to a "travesty of necessities, a duty by which we earn bread" (55): this is what happens in Luther's household-enterprise. Like his forefathers, he records "dates and times of penetrations, conceptions, and births" (19) so that the sexual act is transfigured into a mechanical activity to be performed according to specific rules, devoid of passion, and only valuable if harnessed to a specific economic purpose: the reproduction of an economic heir fit to become a copy of the father.

After Willa has conceived, Luther brusquely stops his nightly visits and becomes obsessed with her wellbeing. Her days are filled with "his growing concern about her health and diet" as he keeps track "of her visits to the doctor and the punctuality with which she took her vitamins and exercise" (149). Luther's biopolitical control aims at ensuring that Willa gives birth to a son who is "fit" to inherit his business. Extending a neoliberal logic to all domains of life, even the "activities concerning the health of individuals" become investments in human capital since they are conceived as ways to improve it (Foucault 230). Regarding Willa as a reproductive machine and his son as capital, Luther's preoccupation with her wellbeing derives from economic calculations, which transform human life into an economic good to be gauged according to a materialistic schema.

Having failed to generate the capital expected by Luther, Willa has not fulfilled the function for which he brought her home, becoming "a constant irritant" to him (19). The son must be discarded, and she is regarded as "a whore" that must be punished and turned into a wife (19); only then will she be able to deliver a son who can become economically valuable. Unable to leave behind his materialistic stance, Luther cannot understand "what had gone wrong. He had never been cruel or abusive to her. He must have given her at least six lines of credit in his name, never questioning what she bought or why" (68). Luther finds no other way to make sense of his son's "unfitness" but to blame Willa for her alleged infidelity and ingratitude: "Somewhere inside her there must be a deep flaw or she wouldn't have been capable of such treachery. Everything she owned he had given her—even her name—and she had thanked him with this?" (19). Marrying Willa, he invested in a machine, which needs to be fixed to be useful for his house-enterprise.

Luther can only apprehend Willa and his son as "abilities-machines which will produce income" (Foucault 229), condemning them to live a death-in-life that reduces them to figures of the walking dead. They become "the literal embodiment of those dispossessed and socially dead others borne of late capitalism" (Bauman 59), echoing and extending the zombie-like condition that, according to Dayan, resulted from "the experience of slavery and the sea passage from Africa to the New World": "the reduction of human into thing for the ends of capital" (49). As Walter Mignolo has argued, "[e]conomic dispensability of human lives is a practice" that was applied "during the slave trade and exploitation of labor engendered by the European discovery [. . .] of the New World" (74). Luther's objectification of both his wife and son extends the "instrumental, 'mechanistic' view of slaves as little more than means to promote their [the enslavers'] wealth" (75). His entrepreneurial *homo economicus* mindset guiding the management of his house-enterprise in an unnamed northern city reveals the links between the supposed modernity of a free, post-Emancipation, post-Civil Rights North and the alleged backwardness of an equally mythical notion of "the Old South" as pre-capitalist. Historians such as Walter Johnson, Edward E. Baptist, and Adam Rothman have shown that slavery was central to American economic growth. Schermerhorn, among others, has dismantled the idea of a supposed "cavernous divide between a Free North and a Slave South," showing how slavery was a business built on "credit and investment, paper money, and promises" (1–4). Luther's treatment of his wife and son exposes the interconnections not only between North and South but past and present as well: the practice of neoliberalism's *homo economicus* echoes and extends that of enslavers.

Luther's economic mode of being can be traced back to the first Luther Nedeed, whose legacy has been handed over from father to son. Recounting the origins of Linden Hills, the beginning of the novel highlights the close connection between father and son that is replicated with each generation. Every time, the Nedeeds' rigorously male offspring is given over "to the stamp and will of the father" (18) so that the patriarch can teach the son the economic logic with which to run an house-enterprise. Each child is given the same name as the father and grows up to be physically indistinguishable from his father: "It seemed that when old Luther died in 1879, he hadn't died at all, especially when they [the neighbors] spoke to his son and especially when they glanced at those puffed eyelids and around those bottomless eyes" (4–5). The forefathers' practice results in "the erasure of intelligible, legitimate alternatives to economic rationality" (Brown 68) and removes any sense of maternal relationality or continuity as every son imbues the same values as those of the father, replicating a *homo economicus* worldview. The maternal, while central to the mechanical reproduction of this enterprise, is erased and replaced by the paternal, which fosters an illusory relationality based upon a paradoxical sense of individuality that makes everybody the same yet detaches them from the (m)other.

But Willa's son displays his disconnection from *homo economicus*'s mode of reason: he is not the carbon copy of his father. He has the potential to unveil the maternal connections that, repressed, must go underground in Luther's household. His appearance alone testifies to his maternal heritage: "You look like your grandmother. And the mother before that. And the mother before that" (93). Trying to figure out how "such havoc" was brought into his house, Luther reaches the conclusion that his son must be a "bastard" since "there was no way this child could be his son" (18–19). He has the potential to carry over the maternal legacy that the Nedeeds repressed, as Luther does not even remember his mother's name: "everyone—including his father—had called her nothing but Mrs. Nedeed" (18). Unlike the other Luthers, Willa's child goes "unnamed and avoided by his father" (18). It is Willa who chooses his name, Sinclair, further setting him apart from the previous line of Luthers, all as identical in name as in appearance (294). With his limbs "permanently spooned toward her," even in death, Willa's child retains a powerful connection with his maternal heritage: it is because of his maternal affinity that Luther transforms him into a disposable object.

Having absorbed an economic logic, Luther cannot recognize his son's life as worthy of life: to him he is but "a ghostly presence that mocked everything his fathers had built" (18). He perceives his son as the harbinger of "the destruction of five generations" because he cannot inherit his material riches: "How could Luther die and leave this with the future of Linden Hills?" (18). Economic calculations lead to his decision to dispense with the life of his son, which loses value because of his alleged economic unfitness. In his household-enterprise, Luther's power is evident in his right to decide who can live and who can die, i.e., whose life is valuable and whose life is dispensable. Since Luther bestows value according to a materialistic scheme, he regards his son as a fungible object, one for whom he can no longer find a suitable use and can thus dispose of as he pleases. Luther's son becomes a "deselected other" reduced to what Giorgio Agamben has called "bare life," or life devoid of value, which can be annihilated without punishment (139). While he grants Willa the power to name his "deselected" son, in his house-enterprise, Luther still exercises the right to dictate who may live and who may die as he defines his son's life as unworthy. In the fictional microcosm the text creates through Linden Hills, the authority he holds over his household-enterprise translates into a form of biopower, i.e., a control over the life and death of Willa and his offspring.

The novel shows Luther's economic practice to have a dehumanizing power that renders "deselected" lives disposable since his economic logic cannot value them. Like enslavers who, when it was "too late to get a good market for them [the slaves]," selected "the most sickly of the black slaves, and ordered them to be thrown overboard into the sea, in order to recover their value from the insurers" (qtd. in Mignolo 74), Luther, finding Willa and his son no longer economically useful, throws them down in the basement. This provokes his death, which Luther is unable to mourn: for him, "the child's death" is "an expedient turn of events" as "he hadn't really thought about what to do with it [. . .] It certainly couldn't have stayed in his home" (68, emphasis added). Referring to his child with the impersonal pronoun "it" and regarding his death as a convenient occurrence that let him get rid of a useless object, Luther cannot grieve for his death. In Luther's economic framework, there is no possibility for his son's life to be apprehended as a life and, hence, to be mourned and grieved. As Butler observes, "[i]f certain lives do not qualify as lives or are, from the start, not conceivable as lives within certain epistemological frames, then these lives are never lived nor lost in the full sense" (*Precarious* 1). Like those slaves violently tossed into the sea, his son is left in the basement unmourned because his father's economic worldview cannot register the loss of a life he did not recognize as such.

But Willa begins a human-making mourning. If Luther's practice, driven by economic values, undoes the humanity of his son, Willa performs a human-making praxis, based upon her maternal ethics of care, that undoes Luther's objectification of their son, revealing that, as Wynter contends, "*humanness* is no longer a *noun. Being human is a praxis*" (263, original emphasis). If Luther's economic practice cannot offer the means to mourn the death of his son and apprehend his life as a life worthy of life and, thus, a grievable one, this is what Willa's care-driven practice accomplishes. In doing so, she humanizes not only her son but herself as well, in a process that mirrors the novel's narrative work of human-making mourning.

Willa initially wishes to adhere to the patriarchal and heterosexual rules of respectability laid out in "her piles of *Cosmopolitans* and *Ladies Home Journals*," which advise wives to shut up and be patient (148). This prompts her useless trips to New York and her walks "down miracle mile" (149). Unlike Ruth who is helped by Pilate, Willa searches for assistance in the perfumes and lipsticks of a neoliberal society that constructs each human being as "human capital tasked with improving and leveraging its competitive positioning and with enhancing its (monetary and nonmonetary) portfolio value across all of its endeavors and venues" (Brown 10). But, after her son's death, she realizes that Fifth Avenue and its shops cannot deliver their promises. Even though "Lancôme had told her to 'believe in magic'" (150), no change is on the way for Willa, at least not through the illusory and ephemeral magic offered by the neoliberal rationality through which her husband constructs the world.

Willa's Conjuring

As regards the character of Willa, critics have offered contrasting interpretations, remaining undecided about the nature of her resistance. Some scholars, including Teresa Goddu, interpret Willa's death as a sign of her "self-destruction and disappearance" without discussing its rebellious undertones (225–26). Margaret Homans comments that "the novel institutes no counter-tradition of strong womanhood to oppose the destructive legacy of patriarchy," and while she concedes that the dead Mrs. Nedeeds can potentially "expose the destructive truth," she then concludes that "they offer no hints for constructing a new one" (396). For her, the line of foremothers "can at best only suicidally negate them [the fathers]" (396). By contrast, Catherine C. Ward characterizes Willa's death as "triumphant" (80), even though she does not elaborate further. According to K.A. Sandiford, Willa discovers "in her subterranean exile the power of absence, a passive yet potent method of resistance" (134–35). Paula Gallant Eckard remarks that the novel "portrays female resistance that eventually brings down the House of Nedeed" (795). I argue that Willa's practice actively resists Luther's dehumanization, as evidenced by her human-making mourning which affirms the humanity negated to her and her son.

Against Luther's profit-driven logic, which reduced their son to a "worthless" corpse, Willa retains a care-driven practice, managing to transform her maternal grief into empowerment. While Luther is unable to value his son and mourn his death, Willa keeps caring for him also in death, behaving according to a maternal ethics of care that undermines Luther's economic logic. Being able to mourn her child constitutes Willa's defiant act against Luther's economic values, which will culminate in the final burning of his house-enterprise: "Through some sort of twisted willfulness, she had not only disrupted his home but almost managed to destroy lifetimes of work, to erase the labor of those proud, strong men" (68). Through her human-making mourning, Willa challenges Luther's dehumanization of her son and herself: she (re)builds a social life and recognizes the presence of an ancestral community of carers, echoing the funeral and burial rituals of enslaved people.

The scant literary evidence about slave rituals in the colonial South suggests the retention of West African patterns (Frey and Wood 394; Holloway 175). Enslaved people made do with the scarce resources available to them, carrying the corpse, "which if not in a coffin would be wrapped in cloth," and organizing, with or without the enslavers' permission, long processions characterized by singing and dancing that had its roots in West African traditions and often disgusted white observers (Frey and Wood 396). Black women usually took care of the corpse by shrouding it in white cloth and looking after it: no undertakers served the slave dead and "[p]reparation of the dead body, which consisted of thorough washing and shrouding, [. . .] fell to slaves—mainly women," who kept constant watch over the corpse (Roedinger 169). Archaeological excavations in the Chesapeake and Lower South regions have revealed that "talismans, beads, and similar objects that probably had a profound religious significance" were buried with the body together with food, drink, and sometimes also artistic objects (Frey and Wood 396). A father buried with his son "a piece of white muslin, with several figures painted on it in blue and red, by which, he said, his relations and countrymen would know the infant to be his son, and would receive it accordingly on its arrival amongst them" (qtd. in Frey and Wood 396). The funeral and burial rituals were extremely important for the slave community as the care enslaved people showed for their dead challenged the enslavers' order of meaning: "The significance of proper funerals for the slaves lay, not in the peripheral if real danger of conspiracy, but in the extent to which they allowed the participants to feel a human community unto themselves. To that extent, the slaves decisively negated the mythical foundation of the slaveholders' world" (Genovese 195; Frey and Wood 384). Engaging in a "reassertion of the central continuity between past, present, and future generations," (Frey and Wood 394) through such rituals, enslaved people reforged the social life racial terror negated. They recognized that ways of dying were also ways of living so that "respect for the dead signifies respect for the living—respect for the continuity of the human community and recognition of each man's [sic] place within it" (Genovese 202): Willa's mourning practice echoes and reimagines these rituals.

After her son's death, Willa has a dream in which she sees "pale women wrapped in lace bridal veils" dancing "around the cot" and throwing "flowers on the stale blanket" where her son lies (90). Representing the previous Mrs. Nedeeds, they chant "[m]ourn *our* son. Mourn *our* son" (90–91, emphasis added) and spur her to arrange a proper burial. Much like enslaved people, Willa makes do with the limited resources she has at her disposal to arrange a funeral procession, complete with the singing and dancing that characterized slave funeral rituals and that had its strongest corollary in the twentieth-century jazz funerals of New Orleans (Holloway 175). Crafting Willa's mourning praxis as similarly performative, communal, and participatory, the novel recovers the caring community of which she and her son are a part. Upholding a worldview based upon relatedness, the Mrs. Nedeeds' intimation echoes a popular adage in Ubuntu "which says that 'Your child is my child'" and underscores a relational view of the human (Murove 40). Employing the plural form of the possessive, these women regard Willa's son as their own and cast her mourning praxis as communal othermothering. Extending the caretaking role of so-called "church mothers" or "nurses" who assisted the bereaved (Holloway 162), Willa's foremothers are placed within a powerful tradition of othermothering, which the novel aims to reimagine through the performance of a mourning praxis that forges a deep sense of relationality based upon an ancestral maternal continuum. Willa's mourning practice conjures her son's maternal ancestors, enabling her to feel part of a wider mothering community while establishing her son's storied place in their maternal history. The maternal narratives Willa is about to uncover are thus also part of his life-narrative, recreating the sense of communal storytelling that has often characterized Black funerals (Holloway 165). Restoring the social life that Luther's economic praxis erased, Willa's mourning practice allows her and her son's lives to be apprehended as human and grievable through the rewriting of maternal ties.

After the dream, Willa decides that "she could bury him [her son]" and "Luther didn't have to know" (92). She is committed to care for him in a way that recalls enslaved people's determination to properly mourn their dead: while the enslavers' symbolic order made it impossible to recognize enslaved people's grief, their mourning praxes, affirming their social life, conjured up an otherworld where such grief could not only be registered but also form the basis for a reimagination of being. Finding the blanket on which he lies smelly, "coarse and cheap" (92), she begins to search for a more suitable material with which to wrap the body of her dead son: "She went to the corner and opened a trunk of old clothes, remembering silk dresses and brocades in her search for extra blankets weeks ago. Her hand touched a gauzy film and she pulled out the end of a long bridal veil trimmed in yellowing lace. [. . .] She could wrap him in this—yards and yards of finely tatted lace and pearls" (92–93). Willa's mourning practice echoes the rituals performed during slave burials as the wedding veil with which she wraps her son serves a community-building function similar to that of the white muslin an enslaved father buried with his son. Since the veil belongs to one of the other Mrs. Nedeeds, it attests to her son's communal kinship, serving as a token of maternal recognition.

She had previously conceived of mourning as impossible: "She couldn't mourn her son," but after she has wrapped the body, Willa recognizes that the "mourning had begun" (92–94). Through her processual reclamation of her son's life as grievable, Willa begins to mourn: her recreation of her and her son's connection to a maternal community, or their social life, aids the process. But mourning means remembering a history, to use Alice Walker's phrase, "cruel enough to stop the blood" (171): "[T]o mourn she would have to remember. That alone would kill her" (91). As we will see, what she will need to remember and then rewrite is the grief of her maternal ancestors. Steepled in an African American funeral tradition that, while trying to build a sense of community, also attested to the "racialized violence done to black bodies," (Holloway 25) her mourning practice triggers an unconscious remembering not only of the slave past but also of the painful daily experiences of her maternal ancestors who lived a death-in-life not dissimilar to that of enslaved people. However, in engaging in such memorializing, Willa's mourning praxis also seeks to rewrite a different text for Black life, one that does not uphold racial terror's ontological annihilation.

Challenging the claim that "[t]he sites of loss and mourning are timeless zones, where the dead do not seem dead, where the past intrudes into the present" (Miller 471), her mourning praxis creates a space that, rather than being timeless, defies linear, teleological conceptions of time and calls for a way to conceptualize time in a more accumulative fashion. Recalling slave funerary rituals rooted in West African traditions, Willa's mourning practice troubles Western conceptions of temporality and the division between life and death:

mourning her son, Willa transforms the basement-morgue into an otherworld outside linear time, where death and life, past and present coexist and accumulate, blurring the lines that divide each category. This opens up the possibility to apprehend history "not as a series of causal events that proceed logically, one from the other, but rather as a *constellation* in which past and present are enmeshed and the future necessarily ensnared" (Weinbaum 114, original italics). Rejecting "the socially normative (linear) time" and the corollary maternal separations it enforces (Rody 59), Willa's praxis enables the imagination of other, nonlinear temporalities that disrupt the linear time of history, which, according to Kristeva, makes maternal abjection evident. It is in such an onto-epistemological order, which eschews *homo economicus's* mode of reason, that the ghostly existences of her maternal ancestors can be released from the limitations and separations imposed by normative time and imbued with new life while Willa is rebirthed anew.

Echoing West African funeral traditions "in which the family and the deceased were honored with visitations that indicated respect and esteem" (Holloway 25), Willa's praxis is aided by the presence of the previous Mrs. Nedeeds. She conjures up her community of foremothers through the unearthing of objects that act as funerary talismans and guide her journey: an old and personally annotated Bible, cookbooks, and an album of photographs, all belonging to the Nedeed women. Each of these objects is connected to the mourning rituals of the African American community: the Bible symbolizes the historic role of the Church and Black preachers in the creation of a "space of balm and solace," even a "sanctuary" or "haven" (Holloway 150);[3] the cookbooks with their detailed descriptions of abundant food recall the funeral banquets common especially in the South; and the photographs allude to the tradition of taking pictures of the dead, especially children, in life-like poses to "construct a memorial of the dead [. . .] that contradicted the fact of the event" (Holloway 28). However, as we shall see, during the lives of their owners, the function of these funerary objects was co-opted since they served to contradict the fact of their lives, attesting to their death-in-life status. It is this ontological erasure, which violently assigned her foremothers' lives to the condition of spectrality, that Willa seeks not only to uncover but also to rewrite through her mourning praxis.

Unwrapping the wedding veil, Willa finds an annotated Bible belonging to Luwana Packerville, the "child's great-grandmother or one of the many mothers that Luther never talked about" (93). She is the one with whom the cyclical pattern of subordination of the maternal to an economic logic began. Much like

Bluebeard's wife, Willa exhumes a series of forgotten corpses who lived a death-in-life, which, as she gradually begins to realize, mirrors not only the condition of enslaved people but also her own. Since the Bible is regarded as the greatest conjure book in the world (Hurston 293), with Luwana's Bible, Willa continues the maternal conjuring that had begun with the birthing of her son, endowing her foremothers' ghosts with a voice and a body that can undo Luther's dehumanizing practice and its maternal erasures.

Reading the old Bible, Willa has "the key to Luwana Packerville's buried memories" and is able to reconstruct the "fragments of this woman's mind" (117–18). From her scribblings in the margins, she learns how the first Luther buys Luwana as a slave and keeps "the papers that were signed over to his agent" as confirmation of her status (117). Owned by her husband, Luwana muses: "can it be that I have only exchanged one master for another?" wondering whether her scribblings are "the diary of a slave" (117). She becomes his property together with her offspring so that one of her main functions continues to be that of (re)producing economic assets that can be owned: "Luther told me today that I have no rights to my son. He owns the child as he owns me" (117). The laws that apply under slavery continue to be valid since Luwana's child follows the condition of the mother according to the legal doctrine of *partus sequitur ventrem*. Like enslaved mothers, Luwana becomes "both mother and mother dispossessed" as enslavement displaces maternity (Spillers 80). Even Luther's fears resemble those typical of slaveholders. Having heard about a woman who poisoned her enslaver and fearing Luwana would do the same, Luther employs a new housekeeper, paternalistically claiming to do that for her sake. But she knows "it is not for me, because last week the papers told of a woman in Tennessee who was hanged for poisoning her enslaver's soup, and Luther seemed much agitated over the account [. . .] he and the child would eat from her [the new housekeeper's] hands" (119).

Mother and son become more and more estranged as "the child is constantly with his father" and "grows more like his father with each breath," increasing the alienation and loneliness of Luwana: "I thus live with two Luthers in truth, and so I live alone" (121). Such uncanny resemblance makes her question her own sanity: "Believe me, I am not losing my mind but it is not just that he is Luther's son, he *is* Luther" (123, original italics). Realizing she has never owned her son, who is his father's "in flesh and now in spirit," Luwana is unable to distinguish between the two: "the two are now inseparable. And what is worse, they are becoming inseparable in my mind" (121).

By tending the flowers in her garden, Luwana manages to create a place of her own where she can cultivate the creative life that Luther's economic logic has crushed. The garden represents her access to another temporality, made up of the slow, cyclical rhythm of plants: taking care of a garden requires a patient attunement to this circular time. Her gardening threatens Luther's control and he attempts to destroy it, but Luwana resists: "I only managed to save my garden from the hands of some vile outsider by flinging myself on the ground in the yard and refusing to be moved. Yes, I screamed like a banshee at the feet of Luther and the new gardener, threatening to water the soil with my blood if I could no longer tend the flowers in it" (121). In her gardening Luwana sees the possibility of cultivating the creative power to which her death-in-life does not give her access. In her essay "In Search of Our Mothers' Gardens," Walker documented her mother's ability to hold on to the possibilities that cherish life, "feeding the creative spirit" against the spiritual waste to which racial violence has reduced Black women's lives (404–8). Her mother's creation of a garden "magnificent with life and creativity" constituted "work her soul must have" and amounted to a reordering of "the universe in the image of her personal conception of Beauty" (408). Luwana's gardening performs a similar nurturing function for the creative life stifled by Luther's economic practice. Acknowledging the connection between her life and that of the flowers, and refusing to submit to Luther's control of life and death, she looks after her flowers with a strong determination to care that recalls Willa's and foreshadows her final rebirth.

However, Luther takes the pleasure of gardening away from Luwana, so that she starts losing her sense of corporeality. She fears she is becoming a stranger not only to her family but also to herself: "they are trying to push me out of this house by making me a stranger to my husband and a stranger to my son. And the true horror is that I am becoming, sister, a stranger to myself" (123). The housekeeper taking on many of her responsibilities and her son now under the father's tutelage, Luwana perceives herself as being useless, feeling as if "I could leave this world tomorrow and no one in this house would miss me" (120–21). Her life becomes disposable in Luther's household-enterprise, which is governed by an economic scheme of valuation. In her study of slavery, *Scenes of Subjection*, Hartman has identified fungibility as crucial to slavery's process of "thingification," describing it as the "abstractness and immateriality of Blackness characterized by the replaceability and interchangeability of Black people within the logic of the commodifying practices of enslavement" (21).

Through Luwana's recollections, the novel links this dynamic of slavery to *homo economicus's* commodifying logic, which renders her fungible and disposable.

As the letters addressed to herself reveal, her fungibility reduces her to a phantom who lives a death-in-life: "I cannot talk to this man [. . .] I know it is only contempt which prompts him [Luther] to question me of my days when he knows they are those of a corpse [. . .] I have already left this house and believe me, there are no tears" (123). Condemned by *homo economicus's* mode of reason to living a death-in-life, her loss cannot be mourned because the value of her human life is not recognized outside of purely materialistic concerns. Her existence echoes the form of death-in-life that Mbembe identified as characteristic of enslavement, inhabiting the liminal condition of the slave who "appears as the perfect figure of a shadow" dwelling in "a phantomlike world of horrors" (21). Never questioned or asked about anything, Luwana does not speak except for greetings, passing "one full year without talking to my husband and my son" (123–24). To give the lie to Luther's claim that these are all "the delirious fantasies of a foolish woman," she carves a line on her chest with a pin every time she is called upon to speak (123–24). But her attempts at asserting her corporeality and her authority over her own body are in vain against the Nedeeds' objectification of her, which enforces both a bodily and linguistic disempowerment: Luwana recounts how her son could easily mistake a shawl for herself and address it. Turned into a purely economic resource to exploit, in the Nedeeds' household, in which a materialistic logic rules, she has value only as a vessel for human capital: "I fear that I have been the innocent vessel for some sort of unspeakable evil" (123). Once that function is performed, her life becomes worthless, impossible to be recognized as a valuable life, reducing her to a mute phantom of herself: "the woman seemed to have disappeared" (124).

But, through her letter writing, Luwana asserts control over the words with which to recount and remember her experiences, prompting the beginning of a similar process for Willa. Reading Luwana's reflections, Willa recalls episodes of her own life as the narrative shifts backward and forward between her reminiscences and Luwana's, creating close parallels. Luwana's recollections of her marriage and bridal ring prompt Willa to remember her own wedding gown and band. Her description of the gown underlines its phantom-like nature, which made her look empty and without substance: "He wanted her all in white [. . .] with loose brocade panels that hid her breasts and the outline of her waist and hips; the cloudy veil so dense and folded she could barely see out and surely no one could see in. All in white—even her hands were covered with thick kidskin gloves as she carried the ivory roses and baby's breath. She shuddered at the ghostly image—a strange beginning" (Linden Hills 118). The repetition of "all in white" and the imagery—cloudy veil, ivory roses, baby's breath—underline Willa's vulnerability and invisibility. Her veil is "dense" and her gloves "thick," which make her body disappear: reduced to a ghost, no one can see her. Matching the color of her skin, the wedding band too seems nonexistent as Willa notes repeating Luwana's words: "It is as if I wear no ring" (118). Willa even wonders whether her marriage took place at all: "Was she so busy being needed that it never dawned on her she wasn't being married?" (118). Not only her body and existence but also her lived experience is called into doubt and assumes a ghostly aura.

Luwana's letters prompt Willa to reflect on her alienation, solitude, and social death as it becomes clear that she herself is being transformed into a surreal phantom condemned to live a death-in-life, like her predecessor. When Luther shows up at various social gatherings, no one notices her absence: "she had been dead to them for years" (Linden Hills 121). Marginalized from social life, Willa's condition under Luther's homo economicus's rule extends the social death that characterized slavery: slaves had "no socially recognized existence" and were reduced to "social nonpersons" (Patterson 183). Since she is condemned to living the death-in-life of a phantom, Willa's existence cannot be apprehended as life, and thus, she could not be mourned if she died.

Uncovering "dusty, yellowing cookbooks" belonging to Evelyn Creton Nedeed, Willa first identifies the kitchen as a locus for the performance of the creativity Luwana was negated: "she [Evelyn] didn't know that a woman had gone insane because she was barred from the very kitchen that Evelyn Creton later filled with her damned cookbooks [. . .] Evelyn Creton had obviously found joy in that kitchen as she filled her shelves with these recipes" and fed herself (140). However, as Willa continues to carefully read those cookbooks, which record "with a fanatical precision" even "the dates on which she [Evelyn] purchased and used the ingredients for each recipe" (139), it becomes clear that whatever joy the kitchen could have provided her is corrupted into madness: "none of it made any sense [. . .] The woman cooked as if she were possessed. What drove her to make that kitchen her whole world? Between the buying, baking, and recording she had to be in that kitchen all day—and probably all night. There were only three of them in this house, so they couldn't have eaten all of that food" (140–41). Willa's conclusion is that Evelyn "must have been a bewildered woman. Driven by the need to spend so much time in the kitchen" (188).

Willa finds no suitable language with which to express Evelyn's needs "as she watched the relentless accuracy with which this woman measured her anguish" as if she were a machine (190): "She [Evelyn] had to cringe at each meal, wondering if he could taste traces of those things in his food [. . .] She probably lay awake in that empty canopied bed, preparing a thousand explanations; but she would have been hard-pressed for the language to explain their need. She had watched the twentieth century bring a multitude of new words to Linden Hills without one to validate these types of desires in a Mrs. Evelyn Creton Nedeed." (188) An economically driven society, symbolized by Luther's house-enterprise, cannot provide a language with which to make sense of Evelyn's noneconomic needs of care. Those necessities become "raw and personal needs that the woman herself had probably wanted to forget" (187), because the language of productiveness and rational explanations cannot take such needs into account. Like scientific knowledge, this language "enumerates, measures, classifies and kills," and employing it means that "mankind *depersonalized* itself, *deindividualized* itself" (Césaire 19, original italics). Recalling the practice of double-entry bookkeeping that enabled a cost-benefit analysis and the concomitant transformation of "*personality* into *property*" (Spillers, "Mama's" 67), Evelyn's impersonal recipes—detailed with precise measurements, dates, and accurate annotations of ingredients purchased and used—exemplify the words such a language can provide: "*Potato Casserole* June 5th—Purchased: 50 pounds of potatoes, 12 pounds of cheese, 10 pounds of onions, 16 pints of cream. June 5th—Used: 37 pounds of potatoes, 9½ pounds of cheese, 10 pounds of onions, 12 pints of cream" (140). Her annotations meticulously record food transactions as debits and credits without any personal comments: through them, Evelyn's subjectivity is erased.

Seeing the world through the framework that the language of economic rationality provides can only result in the reduction of everything, even of Evelyn's life and death, to mere mathematical and technical calculations devoid of any emotion: "It would only take minutes to calculate the average capacity of the human stomach, then the maximum potential of calories in what she could have consumed, and subtract from that the minimum effectiveness of each of these purgatives [. . .] And leaving room for a small margin of error, the computer could still pinpoint the exact year, if not month [of Evelyn's death]—yes, it could probably do that." (190) Not only her life but also her death become impossible to apprehend through a scientific, logic-driven language, which reduces it to a mere number that erases Evelyn's lived experience. This echoes the language that enabled the cold determinations of value of the slave trade and deemed some people "worthy of living only a life of want" (Kennedy 522). Through "the rationalized science of human deprivation," it became possible to "determine scientifically the cost of an impoverished life" (504). Not "savage rage or desire," but rational calculations, enabled the Middle Passage and slavery's "consumption of African bodies," reducing them to social death (Kennedy 505; Woodard 259).

Such a rational language can only find economic explanations for Evelyn's cooking, scientifically analyzing her practice according to a cost-benefit economic logic: "Maybe she was selling those things. But how could you sell gravy?" (141). When such rationalizations fail, her experience is dismissed as "fanatical" (140) and her cooking as "black magic," dangerous and regarded with suspicion. In neoliberal reason, "those who acted according to other principles [not economic] are not simply irrational, but refuse 'reality'" (Brown 67) and are thus labeled as "mentally unstable." Evelyn is one of those women whom Walker memorialized in her essay "In Search of Our Mothers' Gardens": dreaming "dreams no one knew—not even themselves" and seeing "visions no one could understand," they might have been artists but were turned into "lunatics" and "suicides" that "no one mourned," condemned to wander aimlessly (232). As her intimate experience becomes unimaginable, Evelyn's life is reduced to that of a wandering ghost living a death-in-life, and her progressive death goes unremarked, remaining unmourned. Erasing Evelyn's subjectivity, the language sustaining a linear, rational, and economic conception of the world makes it impossible for the delivery boy to notice Evelyn's distress and deadly thinness. On the day of Evelyn's death, "[w]hen he received his tip, he wouldn't have thought anything about the fact that it was extraordinarily generous. [. . .] he smiled at how nice she was to appreciate the fact that he had been smart enough to hurry and make Tupelo Drive the first call on his route—since he was also bringing her a quart of vanilla ice cream" (191). He could only make sense of Evelyn's large tip through the economic reasoning and cost-benefit analysis of which such language is an expression: a large tip is a reward for his efficiency in performing his job.

The last pages of Evelyn's book contain her records of purchase dates for household medications—"[t]he epsom salts, mustard powder, castor oil, and calomel" that Evelyn mixed with food and used as laxatives—measuring them with "relentless accuracy" (189). Recalling Ruth's maternal praxis, in the Nedeeds' house, cooking fails to provide adequate nourishment: the vast amount of recipes Evelyn records contrast with her ever-growing thinness, caused by the laxatives she takes in with her food. While she bakes "dozen cakes or casseroles" (189) and "[i]n one day she had made forty quarts of chicken gravy, and the next day, turned around and made another forty with onions instead of mushrooms" (141), such food becomes a vehicle for death rather than life. Despite this abundance, Evelyn's face "was becoming sunken, her arm skeletal" (190). By taking laxatives and mixing the amounts "until it was staggering," she "eat[s] herself to death," while nobody notices or even cares (190). Eating and cooking, a means of survival and a life-giving praxis, instead lead progressively to a death-in-life, the only life Evelyn could ever have dreamed of in the neighborhood of Linden Hills, the realm of *homo economicus*. The more she eats, the ghostlier she becomes, until she is reduced to "a pile of bones" (187). Hers is "the hunger of feeling, the hunger of life" that, according to Césaire, gnaws scientific knowledge from within (19): "the flesh on her thighs, hips and breasts fallen away, so that the stiff corsets, high-necked collars, and heavy skirts she was buried in were no longer enough to mask the empty cavities that had been living all along the covers of this book" (187–88). Like Luwana, Evelyn is progressively reduced to a living corpse, whose clothes become her grave. Evelyn's existence haunts her cookbooks, infusing them with the ghostly presence they strive to conceal and deny.

Through her hunger and growing thinness, she unconsciously reexperiences a crucial phase of enslavement: malnutrition. The horrific process that transformed Black people into slaves or "social nonpersons" involved meticulously calculating the amount of food provided and controlling the ritual of eating itself: rationing food and regulating how, what, and when enslaved people could eat "was part of the slaveholder's toolbox for enhancing social death" (506). Food deprivation "was a weapon used by the slaveholder to sever bonds between parents and children," stealing "not only nutrients but an important expression of love and care" (Kennedy 520). Like breastfeeding and other maternal practices, under slavery, the ritual of eating was co-opted for the ends of capital as "food function[ed] only as fuel to ensure the running of a cotton-producing machine" (515). Evelyn's written records highlight these "mundane calculations that depleted enslaved people's bodies and disrupted their social relations" (510). Recalling a similar dynamic in Ball's slave narrative, in which he catalogs food received and denied, Evelyn's body haunts her narrative.[4] Alienated, and undernourished both physically and emotionally, Evelyn's condition recalls that of enslaved people as eating, similarly transfigured into an economic practice, becomes the enabling force in her transformation into a living corpse.

The contrast between abundance of food and lack of proper nourishment echoes the stark opposition of food abundance and malnutrition that, as Andrew Warnes has observed, was a prominent feature of slavery: "[s]laves and sharecroppers experienced food shortage while producing food surfeit" (4). Douglass observed that, while he and other slaves lived "in the midst of plenty," they suffered "the terrible gnawings of hunger" (qtd. in Warnes 2). He also characterized slavery as a condition of "starvation, causing us to eat our own flesh" (48). The paradox of malnutrition amid abundance was even more evident for slave cooks working in the Big House kitchen; they produced staggering amounts of food but could not eat it as they were prepared for the enjoyment of white mouths. A visitor to a Louisiana plantation described breakfast in Lucullan terms: "There is on the table a profusion of dishes—grilled fowl, prawns, eggs and ham, fish from New Orleans, potted salmon from England, preserved meats from France, claret, iced water, coffee and tea, varieties of hominy, mush and African vegetable preparations" (qtd. in Genovese 541). As Genovese has pointed out, such foods were prepared by enslaved cooks, but it was the white mistress who took credit for such banquets (540). As a result, the mistress's presence shadowed the unacknowledged one of the Black cooks who prepared her food and influenced her cooking: "What Missus knew, she usually learned from her cook, not vice versa" (Genovese 540). This history of suffering haunts Evelyn's life, manifesting itself in her growing thinness and her reduction to a living corpse, which paradoxically results from her over-abundant cooking.

Like a conjurer, Willa manages to summon up the ghostly presence that Evelyn's tomb-like clothes and cookbooks hide: "[t]he real Evelyn Creton. She could see her now" (188). Mixed with the recipes, Evelyn recorded instructions on how to make hair masks and face creams, enabling Willa to "almost see her [Evelyn's] slender fingers massaging that pale face with glycerin, almond paste, and pigeon fat" (150). As is the case with Luwana, Willa's conjuring enables Evelyn's presence to come to light, acknowledging the traumatic legacy of the consumptive nature of slave economy. Through her creative reading, Willa reclaims the life hidden behind the impersonal words of her recipes, putting together the remains of her interiority and reconstructing her painful story. She relates to Evelyn's experiences as if they were happening in the present: "She could see her now, turning the corner from the grocer's where she ordered her bushels of fruit and sacks of flour" (188). Willa's mourning performs a human-ization of phantoms, "providing them with the agency of physical bodies to tell the story of a death-in-life" (Holland 4) and giving them the life they were negated. Willa fears Evelyn might come out of the shadows at any moment to confront her, demanding an explanation: "she glanced toward the shadows each time she turned as if expecting someone to jump out [. . .] The rational side of her mind knew it was impossible, but there was an impulse to guard herself against being caught [. . .] If Evelyn Creton stepped out of the shadows at that moment, she would have no excuse to give for not having the decency to close the book once she realized what it contained" (*Linden Hills* 187). What it contains is Evelyn's painful record of her death-in-life, which Willa reinfuses with life, setting in motion a process of mutual recognition wherein each can give validity to the other's life. The cookbook becomes a conjuring device akin to Luwana's old Bible, containing the key to Evelyn's intimate life of suffering and enabling her to reimagine both her and Evelyn's life.

From an album of photographs, "a pair of soft, compassionate eyes" (205) suddenly meets Willa's: it is another Mrs. Nedeed, Priscilla McGuire, whose life resists oblivion. Portrayed before her marriage to Luther in a posture in which "there seemed to be so much life," it is as if she had been waiting for Willa: "the slender arms seemed poised to spring her body off the cushioned seat as if her full lips were caught in the act of saying *I knew you would come, and I'm so pleased to meet you*" (205, original emphasis). Holding her attention, those eyes full of life bewitch Willa, who under their magic spell, turns the pages of the album "[a]lmost against her will" (*Linden Hills* 206).

Priscilla has a fiery and combative nature mirrored in the "dark fire" in her eyes and a firm willingness not to let others speak for her, wanting to live her life according to her own rules: "she had her own way of thinking or acting, her own definition of important or trivial" (208). She keeps her own name, and no one calls her Mrs. Nedeed. Championing for the rights of Black women, admiring the work of Ida B. Wells while despising Darwin and reading D.H. Lawrence and Ibsen (208), Priscilla is an emancipated woman, well versed in feminism and African American struggles for civil rights. However, although "[t]hose rigid rooms upstairs couldn't contain her," she cannot escape the fate of the previous Mrs. Nedeeds.

Looking at the album of photographs, Willa comes across those of Priscilla and Luther's wedding and is struck by the physical resemblances between him and her husband: "[h]is dark immobile, protruding eyes, and short barreled torso sent an immediate shock of recognition through her, defied only by reason and the man's clothes" (206). The following pictures confirm that Priscilla and Luther's son bears hardly any resemblance to the mother and is instead "a miniature of the man, in almost identical poses with their matching tweed suits and vests" (207). He looks so different from Priscilla that "only the veiled anxiety and awe in her eyes could proclaim her as the mother"; by contrast, "even the blindest fool could see that the man standing beside them was the father" (207). These pictures further attest to the maternal erasures performed by the praxis of *homo economicus*, symbolizing the assimilation of Priscilla's son into the market logics imbued by and transmitted through the father who has exploited her reproductive capabilities and then discarded her.

Looking at the pictures organized around the son's age, Willa notices that Priscilla's presence starts fading as son and husband cast a shadow over her that grows bigger and bigger over the years, forming a veil that gradually engulfs her. The photographs no longer record the growth of her child but her phantom-like status: "the only thing growing in these pictures was her absence" (209). In contrast to the first photographs, these pictures attest to Priscilla's death-in-life. Always in the same pose, she is reduced to a shadow of herself, a "beige blur" that loses any resemblance to humanity: "Her face was gone [. . .] and without her features, she was only a flattened outline pressed beneath cellophane" (249). Priscilla records her own disappearance, writing in the hole in the last picture the word "me," striving to (re)write her absence into presence. Like Luwana and Evelyn, Priscilla is robbed of her corporeality as her body is severed from its will. Resorting to rationality, Willa denies Priscilla's disappearance and blames herself for losing her mind: "there was no way this wasn't done on purpose. Cleaning fluid. Bleach. A drop of hot grease" (*Linden Hills* 249). She then labels Priscilla as another mad, twisted woman like her predecessors: "What other kind of woman would have kept something like this?" (249).

Priscilla's pictures constitute her attempt to grieve for the loss of both herself and her child, who grows ever more distant from her, becoming a miniature of *homo economicus*. However, Willa initially finds herself unable to find the means to articulate such grief, so similar to her own, because she still resorts to the kind of brutal American grammar that, as we have seen, cannot accommodate the recognition of Black people's grief and that originated and sustained slavery's racial and maternal violence. As Jones-Rogers notes, "White southerners developed a special terminology to describe enslaved people's emotions, terms and phrases intended to render their pain, grief, trauma, and emotional loss invisible" (121). For instance, enslavers constructed enslaved mothers' emotional responses to losing or being separated from their children as pathological, referring to their grief as "the sulks" or "a form of madness—'vices,' 'flaws,'" which made them less desirable in the slave market (121). As a result, in their advertisements, they tried to render enslaved mothers' grief invisible as they marketed "a particular kind of maternal sentience along with enslaved women's maternal labor" (Jones-Rogers 121). According to this brutal American grammar, which Willa ventriloquizes, Priscilla's pictures can only be the result of "madness." In such a symbolic order, her grief for losing her own subjectivity and her son to the maternal violence of a market logic that makes her son a carbon copy of the father while distancing him from her allegedly useless life cannot be registered.

But Priscilla's photographs undermine such attempts to invalidate maternal grief and loss, spurring Willa's recognition of her death-in-life: they function as "a realization of loss," a *memento mori*, reminding the viewer of death (Prosser 23). Unlike the funeral portraits of Black infants, such as those by James Van Der Zee, which were constructed in order to "contradict the tragedy of [. . .] death" (Holloway 28), Priscilla's pictures, while they do seek to create a memorial of the dead, contradict her sense of corporeality, and thus, the fact of her life uncovers her death-in-life status in the realm of *homo economicus*. Her photographs spur Willa's awareness of her own death-in-life existence as she perceives herself as "a dying body": "She knew she was dying [. . .] lung tissues that disintegrated a little with each breath; heart muscles that pumped and weakened" (266). Willa identifies herself with Priscilla: entombed alive in the basement-morgue and confronted with Priscilla's photographs, she acknowledges that "she was born dying" (266), trapped in a similar ghostly existence, living a death-in-life. Asserting the interdependency, rather than dual opposition of life and death, Priscilla's photographs not only function as *memento mori*, they disrupt linear temporality, prompting Willa to link the moment of birth to that of death in a circular concatenation of beginnings and endings that eschews linear interpretations of life as a sequence of stable, individual events such as birth, maturation, and death.

Fearing she will disappear like the other Mrs. Nedeeds, Willa doubts her own corporeality as she desperately searches for a means to validate her own existence. She touches her own face, then finds an aluminum pot full of water to use as a mirror: "[h]olding the pot as still as she could, she found that an image would form if she brought it down to her waist. As the water came to rest, a dim silhouette appeared in front of her. Rimmed by light, there was the outline of her hair, the shape of her chin [. . .] this was enough. No doubt remained— she was there" (267–68).

Having assured herself of her corporeality, Willa reviews her life while looking into the pot of water, which functions not only as a reassuring mirror but also as a conjuring device. A tank of water has a similar purpose in Walker's short story "The Revenge of Hannah Kemhuff" where a conjure woman, Tante Rosie, peers deep into it to get information about her clients. Here, though, it is her own self and her agency that Willa is summoning up; she starts with her name and age, revealing these details to the reader for the first time: "Her name was Willa Prescott Nedeed [. . .] Thirty-seven years ago she had been born and given the name Willa," a name her mother chose because it was "lyrical and delicate" (277). By contrast, "the name Prescott had come from her father"; then, she married Luther and had a son, becoming Willa Nedeed: a wife and mother (278–79). She details the evidence for that, i.e., her feeding and taking care of the child and Luther, and "with that evidence, she could be tried by any court in this galaxy or the next and be acquitted" as a good wife and a good mother (279). While "[f]or six years, she could claim that identity without any reservation," in the basement, which functions as a tomb for both mother and son, Willa leaves that identity behind, being "no longer anyone's mother or anyone's wife" (279). She concludes that "[i]t happened because she walked down into [. . .] a room that was cold and damp" like a tomb, and that "she had started walking down them [those basement steps] from the second she was born" (*Linden Hills* 280). She recognizes that her life is not dissimilar to that of her foremothers as she is leading a death-in-life.

However, what sets her existence apart is her caring attitude towards her son, which leads her to the destruction of her golden prison. By making her son's life a grievable one, and thus affirming it as a life worthy of life, Willa also manages to humanize herself through a process of rebirth. Not only does grieving, as Butler contends, humanize the deceased; it also humanizes the griever. If care is "a set of relational practices that foster *mutual* recognition" and interdependence (Gordon et al. xiii), then Willa's mourning praxis driven by her maternal ethics of care rebuilds her communal ties, reconstructing her social life. Recognizing herself and her life in these women, she can rebirth herself and remake her subjectivity, untethering it from a state of social death. If "the construal of *homo economicus* as human capital leaves behind not only *homo politicus*, but humanism itself" (Brown 42) so that "[t]he West has never been further from being able to live a true humanism—a humanism made to the measure of the world" (Césaire 73), through Willa's care-driven practice, the novel seeks to rewrite the human, rethinking its ontological categories.

Willa's Final Rebirth

In a scene of reverse birthing that recalls both the matricidal scene in Morrison's *Beloved* and the birthing scene in Faulkner's *Wild Palms*, Willa starts laughing while she coughs up and spits blood and phlegm: "She bent farther over her knees and coughed up phlegm and blood but she couldn't stop, so she laughed and spit. Laughed and spit, her raw throat pulsating. It would be enough to kill her. She threw her head back and screamed with laughter, small tears running down her temples. Her stiff sides ached terribly" (91). "The blood and mucus," as Eckard has noted, "resemble 'bloody show,' an unmistakable sign heralding the onset of labor during childbirth," foreshadowing "the rebirth of self that she is to undergo" (803). During her destructive drive, Willa is described as a woman in labor: "she wanted to scream from the sensation building within her. Her breathing was labored and her forehead clammy as she forced her tired arms to keep going" (204). Ripping the photographs, she assumes "a kneeling position that is not uncommon in woman-controlled childbirth" (Eckard 805). Willa's rebirth is aided and made possible by the ghosts of the previous Mrs. Nedeeds, who act as midwives, recalling the role of Pilate and Circe in *Song of Solomon*. As she is rebirthed with the aid of her foremothers, she transforms the basement from a deadly womb-as-prison to a womb as a source of regeneration and new life.

Rebirthed anew in a process that echoes the one Avey undergoes in *Praisesong*, she is not the Willa of the beginning as the denouement of the novel will reveal. Her newfound determination spurs her to escape from her entrapment and confront Luther. Willa's trudging on like a "wingless queen amidst a horde of army ants [. . .] watching the deadly tarantula, the sleeping crocodile, the rifle-bearing hunter eaten away in front of her eyes" forebodes the utter destruction she will leave behind. Willa now asserts her will against Luther's: "whenever she was good and ready she could walk back up" (297–80) without waiting for his permission. While her husband had previously claimed he had given her everything, including her name, she now challenges his assertions, declaring that she chose the name "Willa Nedeed" because she wanted it and that it is her right to get it back (297). She displays a determination to fight

Luther's power over her life and that of her son, holding on to her ethics of care: she continues to care for her dead son, securing him close to her body, reclaiming the maternal.

Finding the door unlocked, Willa enters the kitchen, still holding the child. Facing her, Luther has no means to apprehend the new life mirrored in her eyes, so he perceives them as evidence of her insanity: "He has never encountered the eyes of a lone army ant, marching in defiance of falling rocks and rushing water along the great Amazon, the wingless queen who cannot fly from danger, blindly dragging her bloated egg sac as long as at least one leg is left uncrushed; so the dilated pupils in front of him registered insanity" (300). Willa no longer shows passivity and condescension, and a fight ensues between husband and wife: "[h]er fist lashed out and caught him across the Adam's apple, making him bend and choke" (*Linden Hills* 300). When Luther reaches for the child, touching the wrapped body, Willa's "arms loosened for one to shoot around his neck, the other his waist, and the three were welded together. Luther tried to wrench free, but they breathed as one, moved as one, and one body lurched against the fireplace" (300). Her determination to keep the child, even in death, free from Luther's grasp precipitates the final destruction of Luther's economic legacy. The veil, in which her dead son is wrapped, catches fire, destroying Luther's house-enterprise, which is reduced to "a pile of charred wood" (303).

Flying from imprisonment through death, "the wingless queen who cannot fly from danger" (300) magically acquires the wings that can liberate her. Much like Bertha Mason, who in *Wide Sargasso Sea* finds in death by fire her only escape from a death-in-life, Willa's only way to elude Luther's control over her life is through death. Prompted by her determination to care for the son that Luther's economic logic had deemed unworthy of life, her death brings about the destruction of his house-enterprise. Dying on her own terms, Willa takes back the control over her life that Luther claimed.

Willa's death by fire echoes the arsonist and suicidal acts that enslaved people used as practices to challenge the enslaver's power over their lives. Her final action recalls those of enslaved people, who sometimes resorted to arson, "one of the most significant tools of resistance" (Rodríguez 26), and set the enslaver's house on fire to rebel against their enslavement. Her resulting death summons back the desperate gestures of many African captives during the Middle Passage, when they committed suicide hoping to go back to Africa. Faced with the horrific conditions of slavery, many slaves considered death as the only way to free themselves, articulating not only "a conception of the slave subject as an agent" but also "a principle of negativity that is opposed to the formal logic and rational calculation characteristic of modern western thinking" (Gilroy 68). By dying on their own terms and retaining their African beliefs, enslaved people were able to challenge "the total authority over their persons" (Frey and Wood 384) that enslavers claimed. For historian Michael Gomez, the suicide of African captives "was perhaps the ultimate form of resistance, as it contained within it the seed for regeneration and renewal," creating "a portal [. . .] to the land of the dead and spiritual Africa" (qtd. in Brown 137). Willa's suicide links her to this ancestral tradition of transformative suicide.

That Willa's final destructive fire and suicide are an indirect consequence of the mourning of her son is significant given that slave insurrections were often plotted at Black funerals, often regarded as subversive. Colonial legislators considered them dangerous, and there were laws that forbade night funerals. As historian David R. Roediger has reported, Gabriel's Rebellion near Richmond "arose in part out of a meeting held at a funeral ceremony," prompting a careful survey of slave funerals (164). A similar reaction was provoked by Nat Turner's Rebellion, in response to which "the Virginia legislature banned black preaching at unpoliced funerals" (Roediger 165). At the beginning of the novel, one of the first Luther Nedeeds proclaims that "[h]e'd cultivate no madmen like Nat Turner" in Linden Hills (11): Willa's final action undermines such claims, dismantling the Nedeeds' economic legacy, and linking her suicide to the revolutionary tradition of slave revolts plotted during Black funerals.

Placing Willa alongside this powerful history of slave funerals, rebellions, arsons, and suicides, the novel constructs her practice as part of what Stuart Murray termed *thanatopolitics* or "an oppositional politics that uses death as a means of resistance to the biopolitical as such" (204). Willa, like her foremother Evelyn, kills herself in a desperate act of rebellion, destroying the mansion and challenging *homo economicus's* biopolitical logic through her death. However, Naylor's novel reveals Willa's practice to be not only a means of rebellious destruction and resistance but also a harbinger of change: her death has the potential to bring forth new life. Like Circe's, her praxis is simultaneously destructive and creative, finally transforming death into life. According to Angela Davis, racial terror forces Black people to "constantly carry deceased children while simultaneously negotiating imagined futures" (14): through her mourning ritual, Willa has gathered the energy to carry on her mothering praxis, rebirthing herself and her son, even in the face of death. In doing so, she not only destroys Luther's world but also sets the foundations for alternative possibilities. Joshua Bennett, analyzing Williams's work, notes how it performs "a poetics of demolition" that brings forward a *"revelation, or opening"* wherein Black life can flourish so that apocalypticism also becomes Afrofuturism ("Where," original italics). The same could be said of Naylor's novel: through its depiction of Willa's maternal praxis of human-making mourning, *Linden Hills* sets out to rupture *homo economicus's* realm so as to imagine an otherworld.

Having lost faith in their senses, Willie and Lester, the two young men who witness the fire, are "[s]uspended in a world where reality caved in" and cannot find the parameters with which to evaluate the scene: "Where were the guidelines with which to judge what they had left behind that door? [. . .] There would have been no question of smashing in that door if their world were still governed by the rules of cowboys and Indians, knights and dragons—black and white. But their twenty years immobilized them in a place where they were much more than boys, but *a long way from being men*." (299, emphasis added) This scene signals a caesura, an opening up of a space for something other than what they had previously known, and that might allow a nonhierarchical and nonteleological mode of being human. Luther's profit-driven world has collapsed, and these men are lost in the space, governed by different values, that Willa's mourning praxis has managed to envision: in this otherworld, they are not men, not in the meaning given to it by *homo economicus*. Having disrupted the rules by which Luther's house-enterprise is built, her maternal ethics of care prevail over his patriarchal economic practice and offer the means to imagine an alternative understanding of being human. Investing Willa's act with a transformative potential, the text presents it as a form of "revolutionary suicide" as "it conveys an awareness of reality in combination with the possibility of hope—reality because the revolutionary must always be prepared to face death, and hope because it symbolizes a resolute determination to bring about change" (Newton 6). Fire being a symbol of regeneration and purification, the "pile of charred wood" (303) becomes both a sign of destruction and reconstruction, conveying the hopeful possibility to rebuild Linden Hills on different premises. Through its apocalyptic Afrofuturism, the novel casts Willa's mourning praxis as a form of "revolutionary mothering" answering "death with utopian futurity" (85).

If Luther's practice, driven by economic values, undoes the humanity of his son, the novel shows how Willa is able to envision and perform a human-making practice that disrupts this objectification. Luther's economic practice cannot offer the means to apprehend his son's life as a life worthy of life and, thus, a grievable one: it is Willa's care-driven human-making mourning that accomplishes this, humanizing both her son and herself. Accessing an otherworld outside linear time—where past and present, death and life coexist—Willa conjures the previous Mrs. Nedeeds and establishes a mutual identification on the basis of care. With their help, she develops her mourning praxis, managing to create a funeral procession for her son and prepare his body for a proper burial. Her human-making mourning is based on a recognition of the interconnections between her son's life, hers, and that of the previous Mrs. Nedeeds, giving validity to their lives and rebirthing herself in the process. Her maternal care-driven praxis defies our current genre-specific narrative and its concomitant mode of being human—based upon a neoliberal, seemingly independent and autonomous individual—bringing forward an alternative, more relational and caring model. Thus, the final "pile of charred wood," to which her maternal praxis has reduced Luther's mansion, becomes the "demonic ground" that, according to Wynter, will enable us to reimagine what it means to be human, so that humanness will no longer be synonymous with being Man.

Wynter's demonic project can start, *Linden Hills* suggests, with a maternal rewriting of our genre-specific historical narratives. Writing about Willa's mourning process, this novel creates a humanizing historical narrative that opposes not only Luther's but also contemporary accounts such as those of revisionist cliometricians, among them Fogel and Engerman. Rising to prominence during the mid-1970s, these historians proposed an economic and "emotionally detached" analysis of slavery (Fogel 28), which relied heavily on the interpretation of economic data garnered mostly from slaveholders' documents, disregarding slave autobiographies. Reiterating violence by reducing lived experiences to the purely economic, their historical analysis made it impossible to think about enslaved people as "subjects that lived and dreamed other ways of being human" (Weheliye 123). As Césaire commented in another context, such accounts could at best offer "an impoverished knowledge" for an "impoverished humanity" (18). Like Ishmael Reed's *Flight to Canada* (1976), *Linden Hills* challenges this kind of historical analysis, creatively rewriting the lives of the enslaved through the mingling of different temporalities and spatialities, and the blurring of the separation between life and death. Portraying the management of Luther's house-enterprise as redolent of slavery, the novel exposes the modernity of the antebellum South and its economic efficiency in a way that might seem to align it with Fogel and Engerman's findings. However, while Fogel and Engerman had a hard time trying to grapple with the economic viability of a system as violent and brutal as slavery, the novel reveals neoliberalism to be similarly based on an economic co-optation of the maternal, underlining slavery's affinity to a capitalistic logic as well as the violence upon which neoliberalism continues to rely. Creatively re-narrating history, the novel offers a way to rethink the categories of not only space and time but also the human, making it possible to grieve for the losses that such dehumanizing systems frame as unmournable.

In writing an alternative human-making narrative, *Linden Hills* aligns itself with Black mourning rituals that seek "to make death more than a mere statistic" (Thompson 259), reclaiming "deselected lives" (Wynter 331). This novel constitutes a literary equivalent of the wood sculptures and broken crockery with which enslaved people decorated their graves: it is commemorative art that celebrates personal lives and engages in a creative remaking of the human directed towards the Black artist's community, providing the means through which to reimagine the lives of the living and the dead. This "art for the dead" (Thompson 260) had a narrative mourning function since the broken objects were linked to the daily activities of the dead: it attempted to "distill the life of the deceased in an artistic statement atop the grave," continuing "the West African tradition of viewing the funeral as the climax of life" (Roedinger 168). These intimate artistic decorations, whose meanings often eluded Westerners, were related to a West African understanding of death rituals as linking the living with the dead. They rendered possible for the Black community to nurture "a spiritual belief in the spiritual life of their loved ones" against a context of racial terror which constantly sought to devalue such beliefs and violently erase Black being both physically and ontologically. Discussing African American mourning stories, Holloway has noted that, if only occasionally, even at the end of the twentieth century, in some southern Black burial grounds, one could still find "plots decorated with the remnants of broken dishes, glassware, bedframes, and shells," which echoed the customs of enslaved people (210). Naylor's novel takes part in this powerful tradition of African American mourning rituals whose roots go back to West Africa and whose sustainable and memorable text remains centered on the daily lived experiences of Black people.

In its description of Willa's praxis as connected to the burial rituals of enslaved people, *Linden Hills* rewrites the past in a novelistic translation of enslaved people's funerary art, providing a creative way to remember and mourn the slave past and ancestors while attempting to reforge communal links. Alongside Morrison's *Beloved* and *Song of Solomon,* this novel narratively participates in The Bench by the Road Project, constructing intimate sites where Black people can reimagine history and feel part of a wider community. Transforming Black lives into grievable ones, it rewrites an alternate origin story so as to remake the ontological category of the human.

Through the portrayal of Willa's mourning practice, driven by her maternal ethics of care and reminiscent of slave rituals, the novel captures traumatic experiences in a way that an economic and rational analysis could not. Such a narrative eschews Western conceptions of time as it is based upon a nonlinear, accumulative temporality that complicates the categories of a stable past and present, death and life, and that is an element *Linden Hills* shares with a range of texts from the Black diaspora: from Derek Walcott's *Omeros* (1990) and Kgositsile's poetry to Toni Morrison's *Beloved* (1987). Linking the past with the present—the urban North and the antebellum South, the living with the dead—*Linden Hills* offers a creative way to re-narrate history, not reducing deselected lives to numbers, and allowing unrecognized losses to be not only registered but also mourned: apprehended as lives, they become grievable.

In the process, both the grieved ones and the grievers are remade through the establishment of a mutual recognition that can forge the broader communal links or social life that racial violence erased. Challenging the division between life and death and the individualistic, self-interested conception of the subject posited by much of Western philosophy, the novel's maternal praxis upholds an understanding of the human as a being in relations, which echoes the relational ontology at the basis of the African concept of Ubuntu: "it is in our dependence and interdependence with each other that we attain the fullest of our humanness" since we "exist within a perpetual state of symbiosis with others" (Murove 38).

The novel itself performs an improvised mourning ritual that enables a relational understanding of the human and produces alternate forms of subjectivities, not only engaging in an ontological resistance to an antiblack world, but in the process, rewriting the figure of the human. Naylor's novel thus performs a human-making mourning that parallels Willa's, and that makes it possible to rewrite an alternative narrative rooted in a maternal praxis that destabilizes given ontological categories, problematizing and relativizing our genre-specific conception of the human as Man. If we are *"homo narrans,"* i.e., "a biological-storytelling species" so that the laws that engender our empirical reality are "storytellingly chartered" (Wynter 268), the novel rewrites not only history but also the ontological category of the human itself, establishing a specifically *maternal* demonic ground from which to reimagine its meaning.

3

Performing a Pan-African Semiotic

As we have seen in Toni Morrison's *Song of Solomon,* maternal practice is able to withstand racial terror, albeit in severely distorted forms. In Gloria Naylor's *Linden Hills,* Willa's maternal ethics of care challenge Luther's *homo economicus's* worldview, destroying his patriarchal household through her suicide. In this chapter, I want to suggest that Paule Marshall's *Praisesong for the Widow* ends on a more idyllic note than either of those novels, but the maternal remains central to that utopian-like attainment. The novel presents us with a series of pre-Oedipal othermothers who can be thought of as Signifyin(g) Monkey or Eshu figures. Their praxis enables Marshall's protagonist, Avey, to reconnect with a repressed Pan-African semiotic, which will lead to a reimagination of the signification process.

As my discussion will show, Marshall's novel exceeds and problematizes Julia Kristeva's theorization of the semiotic as a maternal, heterogeneous, and pre-discursive libidinal economy as well as her related conception of the abject. In her *Revolution in Poetic Language* (1984), Kristeva postulates the existence of an embodied and preverbal dimension of language, which she terms the semiotic and links to the bodily contact with the mother before the paternal-symbolic order enforces the separation between subject and (m)other. For her, refusing this "founding separation of the sociosymbolic contract" can lead to psychosis (52). But can this subversive refusal generate instead an alternate and coherent system of meaning not predicated upon maternal separation, becoming "an effective or realizable cultural practice" (Butler, "Body" 114)? Kristeva's framework, as Butler and others have argued, precludes such a possibility, in part because her theory continues to assume a genre-specific understanding of the human and its attendant cultural configurations of language and the maternal. As I argue, the possibility of an alternate practice of signification is what Marshall's novel explores, putting Gates's discussion of the African American praxis of signifyin(g) in dialogue with Kristeva's analysis of the maternal-semiotic while exceeding both.

As I develop a theoretical framework partly derived from psychoanalysis, I am mindful of the limitations of this discipline, especially with regards to the African American context. In this context, as Spillers has suggested, the traditional symbolics of gendered identity cannot be applied: psychoanalytic models of subjectivation remain inaccessible. However, rather than shunning psychoanalysis altogether, I will instead attempt to break "the disciplinary cordon sanitaire between psychoanalysis and history" (72), as Anne McClintock did with respect to the postcolonial, by asking how Marshall's novel can help us rethink Kristeva's psychoanalytical framework. Putting it in dialogue with Gates's theory of signifyin(g) through my reading of her text, I want to probe the possibility of rewriting and reframing psychoanalytic concepts related to the signification process in more sociohistorically informed ways.

As J. G. Brister has suggested, Kristeva's theory of the semiotic comes close to Gates's theorization of the complex African American rhetorical praxis of signifyin(g). In signifyin(g), which centers upon a figurative language use, "meaning goes beyond" dictionary entries (qtd. in Gates 89): like the semiotic, this practice "displace[s] the Logos, which represents the univocal signifier, the law of identity" for the "heterogeneity" that for Kristeva characterizes the maternal terrain (67). Construing abjection as an irruption of the maternal into the patriarchal logic of the symbolic, Kristeva defines the abject as "something rejected from which one cannot part:" it is that which the symbolic cannot comprehend as it defies its power (1–31). Being "[e]verything that must be excluded for meaning to remain coherent and linear," the abject comes to bear in the process of signifyin(g), which "wreaks havoc upon the Signified" (Gates 58), allowing the abject to resurface and perform its disruptive function.

But signifyin(g) constitutes much more than a fleeting and momentary disruption of the dominant order: "rather than merely one specific verbal game [. . .] it is a pervasive mode of language use," which constitutes an exceptionally complex "second language" that Black parents teach children (Gates 87). It refers to a consciously acquired and complex system of communication based upon indirection and implication that derives from an elaborate rhetorical manipulation of the dominant language in a way that eschews prevailing modes of signification: while from the perspective of the dominant order it might seem meaningless, it is full of meaning. This praxis highlights the very "possibility of other cultural expressions no longer constrained by the [paternal] law of noncontradiction" (118) that Butler finds lacking in Kristeva's theory. Unveiling the existence of "a simultaneous, but negated, parallel discursive (ontological, political) universe," signifyin(g) allows the maternal realm of heterogeneity to permanently disrupt and even coexist with the symbolic, rather than remain repressed or be allowed only momentary respite.

While in Kristeva's framework, entrance into the symbolic necessitates the repression of the semiotic, Gates's theory of signifyin(g) underscores how an embracement of the semiotic results in the creation of a coherent system of meaning that can be sustained without resulting in psychosis, chaos, meaninglessness, or the breakdown of cultural life, as Kristeva would have it. This alternate signification process can be framed as meaningless only by those not proficient in it because it cannot be comprehended or deciphered through a recourse to the signifying practice performed in the dominant order.

But what are the dynamics that engender the learning and performance of these praxes of signification? It is this question that Marshall's novel explores, positing the Signifyin(g) Monkey as a pre-Oedipal othermother figure and signifyin(g) as an eminently *maternal* praxis enabled via the reactivation of what I call a Pan-African semiotic. As Marshall's novel suggests, the performance of signifyin(g) can bring into being its own parallel discursive realm through an embracement of, rather than a separation from, this semiotic with the figure of Eshu and their African American equivalent, the Signifyin(g) Monkey, performing a mediating role between this realm and the dominant one.

While Kristeva suggests that the semiotic is a realm beyond culture and signification, Marshall's novel posits the semiotic as culturally constructed and its abjection as performatively (re)enacted through a culturally specific mode of signification. Her text unveils how *homo economicus's* praxis and system of meanings, encoded in its dominant narratives, require the creation of a symbolic order predicated upon the construction and subsequent repression of a maternal-semiotic that, rooted in the communal transmission of oral knowledge from a variety of Afro-diasporic contexts, is framed as antithetical to the ethos of *homo economicus*. Linked to a status of death-in-life, this semiotic needs to be re-embraced and (re)signified as a source of new meanings.

Through the narrative performance of semiotic rituals rooted in Afrodiasporic traditions, Marshall's novel engages in a maternal praxis of signifyin(g), not only disrupting the dominant order but also conjuring up an alternate realm of signification where the maternal is not repressed and Black subjectivities can be reimagined as other than ontological aporia. Enabling a different performance of the human and its signification process, Marshall's text opens up the possibility of (re)writing a maternal otherworld that (re)signifies *homo economicus's* symbolic underworld of death-in-life as a maternal realm where Black life can thrive.

The usefulness of Kristeva's work in a Black Atlantic context is certainly limited by the fact that it tends to remain Eurocentric and individualistically oriented, as Eric Morales-Franceschini has shown in his essay "Tropics of Abjection: Figures of Violence and the Afro-Caribbean Semiotic" (2019).[1] If Kristeva's theory is to remain useful for a discussion of Marshall's text, it needs to be revised vis-à-vis a Black Atlantic context: to denote such a revision, he uses the term "Afro-Caribbean semiotic" (510–13). Since Marshall's novel evokes semiotic connections that encompass a much broader terrain than the Afro-Caribbean, my own term "Pan-African semiotic," while drawing upon his, is also informed by Jerry Gafio Watts's definition of Pan-Africanism as "a social consciousness [. . .] that generates and sustains affective links to all black people," allowing them to (re)define themselves "as members of a larger 'we' group" (894).

While Morales-Franceschini does show how the works of some Caribbean writers exceed and problematize Kristeva's theory, he does not fully discuss the wider implications of a rethinking of her theory vis-à-vis a Black Atlantic context. Here, I want to show how Marshall's novel further complicates Kristeva's theory by putting it in conversation with Gates's discussion of signifyin(g). I aim to broaden Morales-Franceschini's analysis by highlighting the potential for a sustained, rather than fleeting and episodic, semiotic disruption of the symbolic that does not result in the breakdown of social life but rather in a rethinking of the signification process—a possibility that Morales-Franceschini does not fully develop in his essay.

Remaining so focused on the individual, Kristeva's theory refers mainly to the connection between a child and its biological mother-wit no consideration of communal bonds and othermothers. However, as we have seen, in Black diasporic communities, othermothers were as involved in childrearing practices as bloodmothers. Derived from West African practices of communal child rearing, othermothering was essential for the survival of Black communities during slavery and throughout the twentieth century. Marshall's novel performs a narrative reimagination of this tradition through the description of the othermothering praxis of the pre-Oedipal maternal figures of Aunt Cuney, Lebert Joseph, and Rosalie Parvay, whom I interpret as enacting the mediating role of Eshu or the Signifyin(g) Monkey. Connected to a Pan-African semiotic, these figures reactivate a portal to the maternal, initiating Avey into a realm of nonunivocal signifiers and enabling her, at the end of the novel, to engage in a maternal praxis of signifyin(g). Creatively rewriting the othermothering tradition through a number of pre-Oedipal figures that undermine fixed identities, Marshall's novel complicates Kristeva's account, showing that what I term a Pan-African semiotic is not only about the individual's connection with the biological mother but with a wider Pan-African community of othermothers that can withstand the racial and maternal violence of the symbolic, supporting the individual by offering a sustained anti-imperial semiotic praxis based upon ancestral traditions.

The maternal practices of Aunt Cuney and Lebert Joseph rely upon a rich historical heritage of Pan-African semiotic rituals handed down from generation to generation, while the novel itself engages in a similar praxis as it draws from a rich repertoire of sources from Caribbean, African, and African American cultures: the trope of the living dead harks back to the figure of the zombie so central to Haitian folklore and literature, while the character of Lebert, as some critics have pointed out, recalls the Yoruba trickster figure of Eshu, which Gates has connected to its American heir, the Signifying Monkey (57).[2] According to Wendy W. Walters, the novel is based upon a "collection of Gullah folktales from the Georgia Sea Islands," (19) from which Marshall takes the myth of the Ibo Landing.

Characterized by "ambivalence" and pre-Oedipal processes that—connected to music, singing, and oral storytelling—are predominantly oral, embodied, sensual, and aural, this maternal praxis is a communal one that relies on strong maternal links to be passed down from one generation to another in order to retain its power to transform subjectivities and become more than a fleeting moment of disruption. Enabled by the broader connections that unite the African diasporic community, it results in "a new and original dimension allowing each person to be there and elsewhere, rooted and open, lost in the mountains and free beneath the sea, in harmony and in errantry" (Glissant 34).

It is this strong element of Pan-African communalism, so central to Marshall's novel and its semiotic, that can account for its potential to present a sustained disruption of the patriarchal and imperial symbolic, providing the basis upon which to create a parallel realm of signification not predicated upon maternal abjection. While, as some critics have pointed out, in Kristeva's theory, the semiotic remains transitory and subordinate, always doomed to be surmounted by the symbolic, Marshall's text suggests a more momentous and resilient disruptive praxis as the semiotic refuses to be reabsorbed into the symbolic, generating its own alternate discursive order where the relation between the semiotic and the symbolic is reinvented.[3] Rooted in a Pan-African communalism, Marshall's semiotic generates an alternative relational praxis of signification. While that of the dominant symbolic order is predicated upon separations, the signifying praxis that this Pan-African semiotic brings about is based upon an embracement of the maternal.

Marshall's text manages to conjure up a parallel realm, most clearly symbolized by the island of Carriacou, with its own alternate order of meaning, which can be accessed only by the initiated, or those who are reconnected to and learn to perform the novel's Pan-African semiotic and its praxis of signification. While the novel's ending seems to imply that such an attainment retains an almost utopian character, a reading reinforced by the fact that Aunt Cuney's Tatem is a fictional town; it also hints at the possibility of recreating this otherworld in New York through the performance of the maternal praxis of signifyin(g) as passed on to Avey by Aunt Cuney.

Much like Aunt Cuney's retelling of the myth of the Ibo Landing, *Praisesong* seeks to reactivate a maternal portal to a repressed Pan-African semiotic, where communal connections can thrive in spite of the separations violently imposed by the dominant symbolic order and the racial and maternal violence these require and sustain. Reenacting a Pan-African semiotic based upon a heterogeneity that defies the hierarchical taxonomies of being responsible for racial terror, the novel engages in a maternal praxis of signifyin(g) to re-imagine *homo economicus's* symbolic underworld as an otherworld where Avey can be rebirthed anew. It thus provides a way to unthink the semantic closures that structure our genre-specific sense of being human (Wynter 337) based upon a symbolic order established by a rejection of the undecidability of the semiotic for the "univocally signifying signs" that form the domain of the symbolic (Kristeva 56) and that uphold racial terror: in this dominant order, human can only mean Man.

In the first section of this chapter, I will trace the Pan-African semiotic that the novel charts. According to Kristeva, the maternal semiotic can resurface and manifest in the symbolic order as various contradictions, meaninglessness, and disruptions. However, while related to Kristeva's conception of the semiotic as a realm of heterogeneity and ambivalence, the novel's semiotic draws from a Pan-African epistemology and connects Avey to her maternal ancestors and the Black diasporic community. Aunt Cuney's appearance initiates her process of reclamation of this long-repressed Pan-African semiotic and its praxis—where different places, past and present, life and death merge—offering Avey a way to unveil the violent separations of the symbolic, evident in her ghostly encounters on the cruise ship that suddenly becomes a stage for racial terror.

In the second section of this chapter, I will link the rich cultural life Avey and her husband used to enjoy to the notion of the Pan-African semiotic established in the previous one. Avey's dead husband, Jay Johnson, appears to her, making her reflect on their decline into "the snowy wastes" of the symbolic, where they are condemned to death-in-life, a descent paradoxically initiated by Avey's pregnancy. Absorbed in their race for middle-class status, they repress the rituals that connected them to a Black diasporic community and shielded them from a symbolic underworld founded upon a rejection of the semiotic. Having a similar function to the secret gatherings of slaves, these rituals infused their bodies with new life and enabled them to cherish the relational semiotic that Aunt Cuney passed on to them. But a horrified repulsion of maternity constitutes the pivotal moment when they enter a symbolic underworld inhabited by death-in-life figures: substituting their rituals with mechanical, lifeless ones, they undergo ghostly transformations that echo those enabled by the process of enslavement.

The third section of this chapter will explore Avey's new childlike awareness of her surroundings and her encounter with another of her pre-Oedipal othermothers, Lebert Joseph, who displays a strong connection to the Pan-African semiotic that Aunt Cuney urged her to performatively embrace and that similarly troubles fixed identities. Lebert manifests a protean quality, inhabiting a semiotic terrain where, as opposed to the symbolic underworld of *homo economicus*, heterogeneity reigns and distinctions no longer hold. He appears genderless and ageless but can be more accurately interpreted as inhabiting a realm that eschews fixed categorizations where the limitations imposed by the law of noncontradiction that characterizes *homo economicus's* order do not apply. Residing in a state of deep connections where relationality rather than oppositions thrive, he can be a whole array of personas and experience different places and timeframes at the same time, defying the rigid hierarchical taxonomies and constrictions of *homo economicus's* symbolic order.

The fourth and final section will trace Avey's final rebirth aided by the pre-Oedipal othermother Rosalie Parvay, Lebert Joseph's daughter, who, like him, performatively inhabits a Pan-African semiotic characterized by indeterminacy and interconnections. While she bathes, touches, and massages her body, she assumes the semblances of Avey's mother and a nurse, performing a midwife role and reanimating her lifeless flesh. Joining the dances taking place on the island, Avey experiences Pan-African connections irradiating throughout her body as she transforms herself through the embracement of the semiotic heterogeneity and relationality of her pre-Oedipal othermothers. Her rebirth culminates in her renaming and subsequent determination to keep performing a maternal signifyin(g) praxis, initiating people into Aunt Cuney's Pan-African semiotic.

A Repressed Pan-African Semiotic

One of the key memories that function to remind Avey of her abject condition in the symbolic illustrates her growing awareness of her own death-in-life status, which unconsciously spurs her quest to reclaim Aunt Cuney's semiotic praxis in order to access an alternate system of meaning with which to rewrite her subjectivity. Deciding to leave the cruise ship she is on, Avey is reminded of a trip to the Laurentians, when, looking at the snow-covered mountains, she almost cried for no reason: *"The mood had passed as mysteriously as it had come, and she had gone on to enjoy their brief stay. Nevertheless, for months afterwards, she would find herself thinking—again for no apparent reason—of the practice among the Eskimos long ago of banishing their old people out on the ice to die"* (81, original italics). As she becomes aware of her abject condition, Avey unconsciously relates to the woman as a figure for the abject, condemned to live a death-in-life on the "snowy wastes" of the symbolic, which disconnects the individual from the wider community. Following Kristeva and adapting her theory to the postcolonial context, McClintock has suggested that "[u]nder imperialism certain groups are expelled and obliged to inhabit the edges of modernity: the slum, the ghetto" (72). These people, transformed into figures of the abject, are "those whom industrial imperialism rejects but cannot do without: slaves, prostitutes, the colonized, domestic workers," who return "to haunt modernity as its constitutive, inner repudiation" (72). Her remarks resonate with Avey's subconscious perception of the abject condition to which she is condemned by *homo economicus's* symbolic order, based upon the violent exclusion of those it deems "unworthy" of living or "less than human."

As her subsequent memories and ghostly encounters make clear, having precipitated into this symbolic terrain, Avey has repressed the semiotic praxis that can sustain her by connecting her to a Pan-African community of othermothers. This leaves her vulnerable to the violence of racial terror, but the journey spurred by her great-aunt Cuney's appearance in a dream and the semiotic rupture within the symbolic that this generates triggers Avey's reconnection to a nourishing Pan-African semiotic, offering her a way to escape the death-in-life condition imposed by the symbolic.

When asked for an explanation of her sudden resolution to leave the cruise, Avey cannot provide one: "It was nothing she could put her finger on. She had simply awakened in the middle of the night and decided she would prefer to spend the rest of her vacation at home. It didn't make any sense, she knew, but her mind was made up" (*Praisesong* 20). Avey does not mention what spurred her decision, i.e., the parfait she had for dinner and her dream of her aunt, because "[t]hey sounded too illogical and absurd. [Her friend] Thomasina Moore would have been quick to use them as proof positive that she had indeed lost her mind" (30). But "the two things were linked, she sensed, in some obscure but profound way, with her decision to leave" (31). What links these two occurrences that set her out for a journey of rebirth is the semiotic ruptures within *homo economicus's* symbolic order that they represent.

According to Kristeva, once in the symbolic order, the connection with the semiotic can be perceived only "as contradictions, meaninglessness, disruption, silences, and absences in the symbolic" (89). Avey begins to experience such disruptions in the symbolic order dominated by *homo economicus's* Logos. Trying to rationally explain her strange feelings, she uses "the very logic of the symbolic—arguments, demonstrations, proofs, etc." (Kristeva 15). But the semiotic, understood as "any cultural effort to displace the Logos, which represents the univocal signifier, the law of identity" for the "heterogeneity and dependency characteristic of the maternal terrain" (Kristeva 67), has already started to rupture the symbolic.

Aunt Cuney's appearance functions as a catalyst, creating the condition of possibility for the repressed semiotic to resurface into Avey's consciousness. As Aunt Cuney's role as a griot and her retelling of the legend of the flying Africans reveal, while the semiotic that the novel retrieves is related to Kristeva's conception of it as the realm of indeterminacy and ambivalences opposed to the Logos of the symbolic, it goes beyond her definition as it relates to a Black diasporic epistemology that connects the individual to a wider community. This constitutes a Pan-African semiotic based upon ancestral rituals and forms of knowledge like conjure or hoodoo, which in the symbolic terrain dominated by Logos can only be dismissed as meaningless or "primitive superstitions."

Aunt Cuney's connection to this Pan-African semiotic enables her to reimagine the signification process beyond the constraints of an imperial symbolic as she welcomes its heterogeneity. She acts as a mediating figure that opens a portal to this repressed semiotic and its own alternate praxis of signification, which in the end, Avey herself will be able to embrace: in her role as a griot, Aunt Cuney functions as a pre-Oedipal othermother performing the role of a Signifyin(g) Monkey or Eshu figure.[4]

Dreaming about her great-aunt, Avey remembers her summers on Tatem Island, South Carolina, and the walk "that had been a ritual with them" every August (32). As the past intrudes upon the present, Avey is brought back to that time and space when Aunt Cuney would prepare for their walk as if it were a solemn ceremony, donning a "field hat" and an additional warriorlike belt. Like *Song of Solomon*'s Pilate, Aunt Cuney used to wear both male and female garments: with "headtie and braids," a "belt like the one for a sword or gun holster," she forged ahead "in her dead husband's old brogans, which on her feet turned into seven-league boots" (33–34).

When they reached the Landing, Aunt Cuney, like a West African griot, would recount "some far-fetched story of people walking on water which she in her childish faith had believed till the age of ten" (42), i.e., a version of the Ibo Landing legend passed on to her by her grandmother. She seemed to be talking with a "voice that possessed her" (38) as if her grandmother were speaking through her: "the minute those Ibos was brought on shore they just stopped, my gran' said, and taken a look around. A good long look. Not saying a word. Just studying the place real good" (37). Endowed with the capacity to see both the past and the future, those Africans saw "things [. . .] you and me don't have the power-to see. 'Cause those pure-born Africans was peoples my gran' said could see in more ways than one. The kind can tell you 'bout things happened long before they was born and things to come long after they's dead" (37–38). Hence, they knew what was to come: "The slavery time and the war my gran' always talked about, the 'mancipation and everything after that right on up to the hard times today [. . .] Even seen you and me standing here talking about 'em" (38). After the Ibos had seen all this, "iron on they ankles and they wrists and fastened 'round they necks," they walked back on the water singing: "The way my gran' tol' it (other folks in Tatem said it wasn't so and that she was crazy but she never paid 'em no mind) 'cording to her they just kept on walking like the water was solid ground [. . .] and they was singing by then, so my gran' said" (39). Since they seemed "they were having such a good time," Cuney's grandmother followed them "[i]n her mind. Her body she always usta say might be in Tatem but her mind, her mind was long gone with the Ibos" (39).

As Barbara Christian has noted, the story of the Ibo landing "is a touchstone of New World Black folklore. Through this story, peoples of African descent emphasized their own power to determine their freedom though their bodies might be enslaved. They recalled Africa as the source of their being" (76). Much like the praxis of maroonage in the Caribbean, this oral form of storytelling, passed on by Aunt Cuney, belongs to "that tradition of resistance science that establishes an alternative psychic space both within and beyond the boundaries of the enslaving plantation" (Cooper 4). Linked to Cuney's grandmother's struggle against slavery, this legend becomes an example not only of wisdom and strength but also of a maternal connection to a Pan-African semiotic where people can fly and walk on water. As Brown has argued, with each retelling of the myth, the living are able to revitalize its creation of a portal to the spirits of Africa (121). Through her storytelling, Aunt Cuney enacts a form of othermothering, passing on the ability to access a maternal gateway to a Pan-African semiotic that can give access to an alternate order of meaning and praxis of signification with which to reinvent subjectivity and create an otherworld.

Avey has lost touch with this maternal connection as she is determined not to follow her aunt, refusing to believe in this maternal story of struggle so that she can neither draw support from it (Rogers 80) nor access the power of its semiotic. In her role as an othermother figure connected to a matrilineal heritage, Aunt Cuney represents the maternal semiotic that Avey has learned to repress in order to gain access to the symbolic or dominant order of meaning. Consequently, her aunt reappears to her in a visionary dream to remind her of her connection to a resilient Pan-African semiotic maternal, rooted in the communal links with a broader Pan-African community, that can provide her with an alternate system of meanings. Aunt Cuney displays a function analogous to that of the Signifyin(g) Monkey as she acts as a mediator between two realms: the dominant one and the one fostered by the Pan-African semiotic she cultivates. She provides the means through which to access an alternate world where the heterogeneity of the maternal can be embraced and an alternative signifying praxis performed so as to reimagine being.

Aunt Cuney's retelling of the Ibo Landing legend puts her in touch with a communal semiotic, a connection expressed also through her appearance. Much like Eshu, and its African American heir, the Signifyin(g) Monkey, she embodies ambiguity, displaying contradictory features and a protean ability to defy *homo economicus's* taxonomies of being: like them, she "dwells at the margins of discourse [. . .] embodying the ambiguities of language" (Gates 57). She becomes a figure of the abject as "the in-between, the ambiguous, the composite," that which "disturbs identity, system, order:" in spite of her age, she is still very strong, appearing "unmarked by the grave in the field hat and the dress with the double belts, beckoning to her with a hand that should have been fleshless bone by now" (40). When she grasps her wrist with an iron grip, Avey is surprised by her strong and familiar touch: "How could her flesh still be so warm and her smell the same homey mix of brown washing soap and the asafetida she wore in a sac pinned to her undershirt to ward off sickness? How could she still be so strong?" (43). Attesting to her strength, the day after the dream, Avey is still troubled, even physically, by her oneiric encounter and feels her body aching: "that morning her body had felt as sore when she awoke as if she had actually been fighting [. . .] she had sensed her great-aunt still struggling to haul her off up the road. Even now her left wrist retained something of the pressure of the old woman's iron grip" (47). In spite of this, her aunt is unusually silent as "her voice, unlike her body, had apparently not been able to outfox the grave" (41) so that in her anguished and disappointed eyes "was reflected [. . .] the mute plea: *'Come/Won't you come'*" (44).

Like *Song of Solomon's* Pilate, Aunt Cuney displays a protean quality. Not only do the trees speak for her but she even resembles them "in her straight, large-boned mass and height," and she charges toward Avey "like one of those August storms she remembered would whirl up without warning" (43). She is then "transformed into a preacher in a Holiness church imploring the sinners and backsliders to come forward to the mercy seat. *'Come/O will you come . . . ?'*" (42). Since Avey, all dressed up "in a new spring suit" and with "a fur stole draped over her arm," remains unwilling to follow her aunt, digging "her shoe heels into the dirt and loose stones at her feet," Aunt Cuney resumes the motherly role she had played for her and keeps "coaxing her forward, gently urging her, the way a mother would a one-year-old who hangs back from walking on its own" (40–41). Like Lebert and Rosalie, Aunt Cuney displays the heterogeneity characteristic of the semiotic since she is able to take on multiple roles, personas, and different appearances, defying distinctions and categorizations. Resisting "all discrete and univocal signification" (Kristeva 89), she is both dead and alive, male and female, young and old. This "undecidability [. . .] suggests a dissolution of the coherent, signifying subject into the primary continuity which is the maternal body" (45). Manifesting even physically, through her appearance, her deep connection with the maternal and its semiotic, fluid praxis, Aunt Cuney takes on a pre-Oedipal othermotherly role, teaching her not only to performatively reconnect with the semiotic but also to rebuild the links with a Pan-African community of othermothers. Through Aunt Cuney, the novel connects Kristeva's notion of the semiotic to a Pan-African epistemology that withstood racial terror and created a resilient Black diasporic community of othermothers, whose praxis is a source of an alternate system of signification which Avey must learn to perform if she is to survive racial terror.

Treated "like a year-old baby who needed to be coaxed," Avey muses: "Couldn't she see she was no longer the child in scratchy wool stockings and ugly high-top shoes scrambling along at her side over the wrecked fields? No longer the Avey (or Avatara as she insisted on calling her) she had laid claim to for a month each summer" (42). Even before she was born, Aunt Cuney had exercised her influence on her as she was the one who chose her name, which testifies to the maternal connections she has forgotten: "There was the story of how she had sent word months before her birth that it would be a girl and she was to be called after her grandmother who had come to her in a dream with the news: 'It's my gran' done sent her. She's her little girl'" (42).

Avey's maternal legacy is underlined even before she is born but she has now rejected it; however, the dream and the memories it spurred have opened up for Avey the possibility to access again a Pan-African semiotic, allowing her not only to change perspective but also to expand her vision and, like Aunt Cuney, "see in more ways than one" (41). Aunt Cuney's Pan-African semiotic gradually enables her to perceive an alternate system of meaning that, erased by the violence of *homo economicus,* slowly resurfaces and troubles her conception of both her external and internal world. But, before she can access the maternal otherworld of Carriacou, she must unveil the separations that sustain the dominant order of *homo economicus* and its racial terror, symbolized by the cruise ship.

As her great-aunt manifests to her, Avey's experiences are reminiscent of Kristeva's theorization of abjection as she has a series of strange occurrences that make her aware of a deep sense of separation that troubles her. During the evening meal in the cruise's aptly named Versailles Room, filled with "gilt-framed mirrors," her daughter's words resurface in her mind: "'*Do you know how many treaties were signed there, in that infamous Hall of Mirrors, divvying up India, the West Indies, the world? Versailles'—repeating it with a hopeless shake of her head*" (46–47, original emphasis). The tables are transformed into an archipelago: they look to Avey "like islands [. . .] and she felt oddly chilled; each table an island separated from the others on the sea of Persian carpeting" (47). Avey senses the violent separations artificially inflicted by the symbolic: there disconnections thrive, as opposed to the embodied interconnectedness of the semiotic inhabited and embodied by her aunt.

Through her processual and gradual reconnection to Aunt Cuney's semiotic, Avey becomes attuned to the separations that characterize the symbolic and how they affect her own sense of her subjectivity so that she can acknowledge her need for a Pan-African maternal network of support. She starts perceiving herself as split into two incompatible parts, internalizing and embodying the deep sense of disconnections that she has just discerned in the room's exterior. Looking at her reflection in the mirrors, Avey is unable to recognize her own figure, and she talks about herself in the third person: "for a long confused moment Avey Johnson could not place the woman in beige crepe de Chine and pearls seated with them [her friends Thomasina and Clarice]" (48). Avey's experience of alienation in the symbolic recalls W.E.B. Du Bois's concept of "double consciousness" or self-dissociation. In *The Souls of Black Folk*, he describes it as a "sense of always looking at one's self through the eyes of others, of measuring one's soul through by the tape of a world that looks on in amused contempt and pity. One ever feels his twoness—an American, a Negro; two souls, two thoughts, two unreconciled strivings" (9). Because of racial terror, the Black subject has been constructed—to borrow Gilroy's words—as in, but not of, the dominant order. Hence, in this dominant order, Avey's sense of her own subjectivity can only be alienating as she experiences the paradoxical sensation of both being and nonbeing. She gradually unveils her relegation to an abject status, slowly becoming conscious of her internalization of the symbolic order's enforced separations and their repercussions on her own sense of self. This alienating experience of doubleness, of being other to herself, makes her reflect on similar occurrences when, not recognizing herself, she perceived herself as alien: "On occasion, shopping in her favorite department store she would notice a black woman with a full-figured and compact body [. . .] And in the way she always did she would quickly note the stranger's clothes" (48). Even at home, Avey sometimes failed to recognize her own face, becoming, in Du Bois's terms, a stranger in her own house and mind, thinking and referring to herself in the third person: "she even accosted Avey Johnson in her bathroom mirror as she raised up from washing her face" (49).

These psychic disconnections find a bodily instantiation, as they start to manifest corporeal effects, leaving her feeling increasingly uneasy and out of control of her own bodily drives. When she tries to eat the dessert, "*Peach Parfait à la Versailles* was the name given it on the menu" (49), she cannot move her hand, which, "as if stricken with a sudden paralysis, come[s] to a stop" (50). Unable to control her movements, she feels "a peculiar sensation, troubling" and worrying her: "without her having anything to do with it, her hand suddenly came alive again with a jerk, and she found herself firmly placing the spoon back down on the table. Her heart was beating thickly. Her stomach, her entire midsection felt odd" (50). Avey cannot pin down the causes of the "mysterious clogged and swollen feeling which differed in intensity and came and went at will" (52), and she is at pains to find the words to explain her strange uneasiness and bodily discomfort: "At its mildest it felt to be nothing more than a little trapped gas. At its worst, it seemed as though she had foolishly gone ahead and not only eaten the parfait but all the things she had omitted earlier in the meal"; however, "[o]ddly enough there was no nausea or pain" (51). The feeling of uneasiness and repulsion Avey feels towards the peach parfait and its ambiguity as neither solid nor liquid constitutes an experience of abjection: as Kristeva has noted, "food loathing is the most elementary and most archaic form of abjection" (25). Avey's experiences start to unveil the dynamics through which her abject status is constructed by the dominant symbolic order, and how these result in both psychic *and* physical, embodied effects.

For Avey, Aunt Cuney's semiotic unleashes a process of discovery of her own sense of self, her body, and the world as constructed by the dominant system of meanings based upon violent forms of abjection. Avey keeps experiencing bizarre events "as if her eyes were playing tricks on her" (56): these can all be related to experiences of abjection that slowly make her aware of the racial terror that underpins *homo economicus*'s symbolic order. She starts perceiving the cruise ship, called the *Bianca Pride* (white pride), as an unsafe and violent symbolic underworld dominated by racial violence, where she feels "as exposed and vulnerable, as fated even, as the balls the golfers [. . .] were slashing into the sea from their practice range at the port railing" (56). As Eugenia C. DeLamotte has pointed out, the "power of vision the dream bestows on Avey leads, correspondingly, to a visionary stripping away of the trappings of luxury on the *Bianca Pride* that reveals them as masks for death, isolation, and a violence specifically directed at Avey as an African American" (90). After her re-encounter with Aunt Cuney and her semiotic, Avey cannot ignore the separations of the symbolic and the abject condition to which it relegates her. In Tatem, the Pan-African semiotic of Aunt Cuney made available for her the resilient ancestral rituals of African people who found life in death. Here, by contrast, the visionary power Aunt Cuney and her Pan-African semiotic have bestowed upon her results in experiences of abjection, revealing the racial terror upon which the symbolic is built; apparently, innocent games disclose a horrific violence and people become figures of the walking death.

From her location above the sports deck, Avey sees the numerous shuffleboard games turning "into a spectacular brawl, with the players flailing away at each other with their cue sticks [. . .] the padded Neanderthal men clubbing at each other with the murderous sticks while the crowd cheered" (56). These games acquire a brutal, homicidal violence that shocks Avey and transfigures even the noise into "the sound of some blunt instrument repeatedly striking human flesh and bone" (56) as if the players were violently killing each other. This scene reminds her of "the hockey games she sometimes glimpsed on her television screen" but a more ominous and frightening memory of racial violence comes to life as the past intrudes upon the present. Avey vividly recalls in all its gory details one night long ago when she and her now deceased husband watched in horror a Black man being brutally beaten to death by the police for a minor traffic violation: *"Under the rain of blows the man finally sank screaming to his knees, his blood a lurid red against his blackness in the light of the streetlamp overhead [. . .] Unable either of them to go back to sleep afterwards, she and Jay had sat up the rest of the night till dawn, like two people holding a wake"* (56). After having been reconnected to the semiotic in her encounter with Aunt Cuney, Avey can see beyond the trappings of luxury on the *Bianca Pride,* unveiling the symbolic underworld of forceful separations, death, and racial terror upon which it depends. Perceiving past and present not as distinct and stable categories but as complexly intertwined, she is unmasking the ongoing racial violence against those "deselected others" (Wynter 264) who are reduced to life devoid of value: the figures of abjection from which one does not part. This recollection spurs Avey's unconscious meditation on the violent nature of the ordered hierarchy of the symbolic based upon a severance of connections.

Avey identifies with a clay pigeon in a game of trapshooting, which takes on a human appearance: "It struck her as being somehow alive despite the stiffness—as something human and alive—and she felt a sudden empathy with it" (57). When the pigeon is shot "she recoiled as violently as if the old woman with the gun had [. . .] fired at her" (57). Her identification with the clay pigeon reveals her own vulnerability to such random and unmotivated acts of violence against lives that are not recognized as such and can be violated without punishment. Recalling Paul D's fleeting moment of identification with a rooster in Morrison's *Beloved*, this scene shows the extent to which Avey's being has been warped by *homo economicus's* symbolic order. Now able to perceive such distortions of being, she has "the look of someone hallucinating" and wanders "the decks in a dazed, shaken state" for the rest of the morning (57). The semiotic ruptures her perception of her surroundings, unveiling a frightening picture. Re-experiencing Aunt Cuney's semiotic terrain, Avey has gained the ability to see differently as her eyes "retained the look of someone in the grip of a powerful hallucinogen—something that had dramatically expanded her vision, offering her a glimpse of things that were beyond her comprehension, and therefore frightening" (59).

The passengers on the cruise, herself included, are revealed to be figures of the living dead as the words from her daughter Marion again resurface in her mind: "*Don't you know that practically everyone who goes on these cruises is at least a hundred years old! Moribund, Mother!*" (58). The alienation, death, and racial violence that lie beneath the façade of elegant leisure reach a climax when an old man appears as a figure of the living dead: "[i]n a swift, subliminal flash, all the man's wrinkled sunbaked skin fell away, his thinned-out flesh disappeared, and the only thing to be seen on the deck chair was a skeleton in a pair of skimpy red-and-white striped trunks and a blue visored cap" (59). This image of death-in-life is a reminder for Avey of her own descent into the symbolic underworld of *homo economicus*, ruled by materialistic concerns and based upon the banishment of those abject or deselected others. For Kristeva, corpses represent "the outmost of abjection" (73). As figures of violence, they have the potential to destabilize the symbolic: "refuse and corpses show me what I permanently thrust aside in order to live" in the symbolic order of *homo economicus*. With the visionary semiotic powers Aunt Cuney has bestowed upon her, Avey can no longer ignore the figures of violent abjection upon which the symbolic is based, acknowledging her own condition and linking it to episodes of racial terror. The material seductions of the cruise ship and its horrific racial violence entrap Avey in a death-in-life condition, relegating her to an abject status.

When Avey steps ashore, on the island of Grenada, she finds herself unwillingly following "a crowd of perhaps two hundred men, women and children" wearing clothes of "bright colors and prints:" "curious, the taxi forgotten for the moment, she followed their movement past her" (65). Realizing they are speaking in patois, she is overwhelmed by the musicality of their foreign speech: "She had been so busy examining them she had failed to take in their speech [. . .] But reaching her clearly now was the flood of unintelligible words and the peculiar cadence and lilt of the Patois she had heard for the first time in Martinique three days ago" (67). Musing about it, she notices that, when she heard it for the first time, "it had fleetingly called to mind the way people spoke in Tatem long ago. There had been the same vivid, slightly atonal music underscoring the words. She had heard it and that night out of nowhere her great-aunt had stood waiting in her sleep" (67). Connected to the semiotic, the homely musical quality underlining the speech is linked to the dream and her remembrance of her childhoods in Tatem: "Had that fleeting impression perhaps set off the dream? [. . .] The vaguely familiar sound of the Patois might have resurrected Tatem and the old woman" (67). The islanders and their speech become a communal and embodied instantiation of the relationality that characterizes Aunt Cuney's Pan-African semiotic.

Not only their speech but also their gestures feel familiar to Avey, creating a welcoming atmosphere that troubles her: "[t]here was a familiarity, almost an intimacy, to their gestures of greeting and the unintelligible words they called out which she began to find puzzling, and then even faintly irritating the longer it went on" (69). A woman waves "to her like someone who had known her all her life" (71), and a man mistakes her for "[t]he twin of some woman he knew named Ida" (72). Connections are emphasized as they treat her as if she were one of them, oblivious to the fact that she is a stranger: "from the way they were acting she could have been simply one of them there on the wharf" (69), and "[i]t was as if the moment they caught sight of her standing there, their eyes immediately stripped her of everything she had on and dressed her in one of the homemade cotton prints the women were wearing, whose West Indian colors [. . .] seemed to add to the heat" (70). But, experiencing "that special panic of the traveler who finds himself sealed-off, stranded in a sea of incomprehensible sound" (70), Avey feels uncomfortable and overwhelmed by them and their musical speech.

In contrast to the isolation and sense of separations she felt on the cruise, in Grenada, she experiences a sense of community as they happily welcome her into their group. While on the cruise ship there is an alienating, hostile, and deathly environment where Avey is chased by figures of the walking dead and reminded of racial violence, here images of life and home predominate as she recalls her happy childhood while a musical quality pervades the air. With their musical, poetic quality, heterogeneity, and communality, the language and gestures of the islanders become an instantiation of the Pan-African semiotic that Aunt Cuney's dream enacted. The lively colors and the musicality of their speech create a joyous and communal atmosphere that foreshadows the ending of the novel, when Avey welcomes this Pan-African semiotic that fosters connections, leaving behind the violent separations of the symbolic underworld of *homo economicus* symbolized by the cruise ship.

Descent into the Symbolic Underworld

In this section, I want to suggest that the rich cultural life Avey and Jay used to cultivate is linked to the notion of the Pan-African semiotic that I have established in the previous section. Avey and Jay's cultural life used to be characterized by creative rituals that were based on, and thus kept them in touch with, this Pan-African semiotic as they fostered an acceptance of heterogeneity and a sense of interconnectedness and community. Their semiotic rituals welcomed the multiplicity of meanings characteristic of poetry, which, according to Kristeva, represents, together with maternity, one of the "privileged practices within paternally sanctioned culture which permit a non psychotic experience of the heterogeneity and dependency of the maternal terrain" (52). Their rituals also cultivated nonverbal signifying systems like music, which are based on the semiotic. Tapping into a rich Black heritage, their rituals fostered a sense of a Pan-African community and kept them connected to it, much like the legend of the Ibo landing, part and parcel of Aunt Cuney's Pan-African semiotic. However, to enter the symbolic order of *homo economicus,* they had to repress and forget these rituals. Paradoxically, Avey and Jay's decline into the symbolic underworld is triggered by her experience of maternity. Pregnancy represents the pivotal moment when Jay and Avey are initiated into *homo economicus's* symbolic underworld of death-in-life. This results in their rejection of their semiotic rituals and their cutting off a wider African American community.

Jay's appearance spurs Avey into a remembrance of their married years, back in the 1940s, when they struggled to make ends meet in a small and uncomfortable apartment on Halsey Street in Brooklyn, where they lived among the abject lives of the poor. When he arrived home in the evenings, he would be tired from working "[t]wo jobs for the salary of one" (92) at a shipping room in a small department store in downtown Brooklyn, assisting the man in charge. Jay "had acquired the reputation of being hard-working, efficient, dependable"

(92) since this was the only way to succeed. So "absorbed in what he was do-ing," he would hardly notice anything else as his mind "would all the while be on the sheaf of orders and invoices on his hand" (92). In a situation where maximum output and profit are key, Jay is reduced to and praised for being an efficient machine: with his "highly organized mind and photographic memory which permitted him to keep track of practically every piece of merchandise that came and went," he meticulously ran all the shipping and receiving (92). Dominated by the symbolic logic of *homo economicus*—where productivity and efficiency are praised while instincts, passions, and creativity become unnec-essary distractions—Jay's workplace performs a dehumanizing function. This symbolic order, based upon the Logos, demands the repression of the semiotic, and can only accept activities that are deemed economically productive, sup-pressing "any physical and psychic expenditure not aimed at profit and accu-mulation" and especially the prediscursive libidinal economy of the maternal.

However, at home through little rituals, Jay used to be able to cultivate and keep in touch with a Pan-African semiotic that allowed him to be creative and passionate, fashioning an alternative self that ran counter to the symbolic logic that dominated in his workplace. Alongside his recitations of beloved Langston Hughes's poems on Sundays, there was also the everyday ritual of listening to his favorite jazz music. In spite of his fatigue, both physical and psychological, as soon as he got home, he used "to turn up the volume on the phonograph which would already be playing their favorite records" (93). Jay would solemnly close his eyes and let the songs "work their magic, their special mojo on him. Until gradually, under their ministrations, the fatigue and strain of the long day spent doing the two jobs—his and his boss's—would ease from his face, and his body as he sat up in the chair and stretched would look as if it belonged to him again" (94). Listening to African American music constituted a ritual that sustained him: "In his hands the worn-out album with its many leaves be-came a sacred object, and each record inside an icon [. . .] A careful ritual went into dusting each one off, then gently lowering it onto the turntable, sliding the lever to 'on' and finally, delicately, setting the needle in place," and, as the music filled their apartment, "he would remain standing, head bowed, in front of the phonograph" (94). This creative ritual infused him with life, allowing him to become a different person, more passionate and playful than the one, efficient and absorbed into the tasks, that he had to be at work. Listening to those records shielded Jay from the dehumanization that his job performed day after day, constituting a source of new life. Much like in juke joints, where

Black people, as Robin Kelley has observed, were able to reclaim their bodies as instruments of pleasure rather than labor (84), through this ritual, Jay can recover the sensuous subjectivity his workplace repressed. His ritual nourished him and kept him connected to "the other Jay behind that carefully protected public self," performing a creative transformation of a lifeless being into a lively one: "[t]he Jay who emerged from the music of an evening, the self that would never be seen down at the store, was open, witty, playful, even outrageous at times [. . .] affectionate [. . .] And passionate" (95). His ritual recitation of African American poetry and listening of jazz music allow him to access a special psychological space separated from his ongoing daily duties and requirements, preserving the Pan-African semiotic that he had to repress while at work and shielding him from the death-in-life condition of the symbolic. Much like Aunt Cuney, Jay is performing a maternal praxis, helping to create for Avey and himself a sheltered maternal space through which he can access a Pan-African semiotic that allows him to refashion his being by giving new meanings to it.

Enabling him to accept and welcome his creative and passionate side opposed to his public self and to keep in touch with a powerful community of Black poets and musicians, this ritual enables Jay to access a similar Pan-African semiotic to that passed on by Aunt Cuney, where heterogeneity and connections thrive. If through the retelling of the Ibo Landing legend peoples of African descent were able to determine their freedom despite their bondage and recalled Africa as a source of life, here Jay's enactment of these daily rituals achieves a similar result. Despite the symbolic logic that dominates his dehumanizing working place and that compels him to leave aside his creativity, he manages to preserve the semiotic through these passionate rituals and nurture a different kind of subjectivity, which defies the rules of the symbolic. His cultivation of African American music and poetry form an important part of his maternal praxis, which can withstand the violence of the symbolic and disrupt it: it is through this praxis that the abject other cannot only find a voice but also a different modality of being. But this is a praxis that he shares with Avey as they both engage in communal performances in which both are rebirthed anew.

Avey and Jay used to share these rituals, which helped them cherish a Pan-African semiotic that nurtured creative connections and encouraged a different kind of subjectivity from the one dictated by the logic of the symbolic. The passionate self that Jay transformed into used to stage improvised dances just for Avey, pretending they were infamous Harlem dancehalls, like the Rockland Palace or the Renny (95), underlining their connections to the wider African

American community of Harlem. He would magically conjure up a grand ball-room, asking her: "What's your pleasure this evening, Miss Williams?"—calling her by her maiden name. "Will it be the Savoy, Rockland Palace or the Renny again?" (123), and she would enjoy the fantasy with him. Offering her his arm, he would pretend to clear a way for them "through the imaginary crowd in the make-believe ballroom," leading her to its center (123). They would then dance together with "their bodies fused and swaying" (123) as if they were one.

Then, there was the poetry of their powerful lovemaking, which used to be a sacred ritual as Jay "would lie within her like a man who has suddenly found himself inside a temple of some kind [. . .] sensing around him the invisible forms of the deities who reside there" (127). As Avey was transformed into the goddess presiding over this temple, he used to feel overwhelmed by a spiritual presence: awed, he would fall silent for a while and then resume speaking "with his body," discovering an even "more powerful voice. Another kind of poetry" (127). The novel casts this nonverbal signifying system as connected to the kind of prediscursive libidinal economy Kristeva theorized as a paramount feature of the system of bodily drives and erotic interchanges characteristic of the se-miotic, while also relating it to Aunt Cuney's rituals.

"[H]is scandalous talk" was the ritual which used to precede and accom-pany their lovemaking: "Amid the touching and play at the beginning Jay some-times talked, telling her [. . .] what he thought of her skin, how the rich smooth feel of it had got all up inside him the first time they had met and he had taken her arm to lead her to the dance floor" (126–27). He would be joyful and play-ful, teasing her about "what he was going to do when she finally permitted him in [. . .] Talking that talk until he turned her into a wanton with her nightgown bunched up around her neck like an airy boa she had donned as a fetish to feed his pleasure" (127). The jokes that Avey and Jay were able to enjoy in their bed-room performed a similar function to that of the hoodoo herbs of Aunt Cuney, protecting them from the misery and the death of the symbolic world out-side: they used to sprinkle "Vaudeville-like jokes" as if they were "juju powders around the bed to protect them. Jokes with the power of the Five Finger Grass Avey's great-aunt Cuney used to hang above the door of the house in Tatem to keep trouble away" (107). Functioning like the talismans of hoodoo, their joy-ous lovemaking and jokes form part of that same Pan-African semiotic praxis of Aunt Cuney and have similar protective and regenerative powers that undo the unmaking of their playful subjectivities operated by the symbolic.

The rituals they cultivated at home are linked to Aunt Cuney's semiotic praxis as their regular summer trips South to honor her memory and the legend she passed on confirm. When Avey walked Jay to the Ibo Landing and recounted to him the legend her great-aunt passed on to her, he asserted his firm belief: "I'm with your aunt Cuney and the old woman you were named for. I believe it, Avey. Every word" (115). In touch with the semiotic, Jay embraces Aunt Cuney's ancestral wisdom, believing in the creative possibilities that can be found even under death-in-life conditions.

Enabled by these maternal connections, Avey and Jay's semiotic rituals have the power to withstand the dehumanizing and divisive praxis that characterizes and sustains *homo economicus's* symbolic underworld. Entering a Pan-African semiotic terrain of connections, they can draw nourishment from it and escape the death-in-life condition of the symbolic through a playful refashioning of their subjectivities. These rituals recall enslaved people's creation of a "rival geography:" through clandestine parties, they "animated [. . .] their bodies— flesh regarded as no more than biddable property," reclaiming them from the slaveholder's control (Camp 540). Throwing parties and enjoying themselves on the margins of the plantations, enslaved people in a sense forgot themselves, "having abandoned 'their place' in the plantation spatial and temporal order— and the self they had to be there—in favour of [. . .] their own place" (Camp 553). Similarly, these rituals allow Avey and Jay to forget 'their place' in the symbolic underworld of *homo economicus* and let them access a Pan-African semiotic akin to Aunt Cuney's and permeated by a different sense of time, place, and being, where connections can thrive, and a creative sensuality can be embraced. Leaving behind the Logos or the paternal law that drives the symbolic underworld where there is no room for leisure, playfulness, ambiguity, and a prediscursive libidinal economy, these rituals perform a world-making function, creating an otherworld where they can infuse new life into their bodies and imaginatively rewrite their subjectivities under different terms than those established by the dominant symbolic order of *homo economicus.*

However, despite these powerful semiotic rituals, they succumb to "the ruin and defeat steadily overtaking the block" (89) as Avey and Jay begin "the inevitable long slide down" (97), and their lives become indistinguishable from the other wasted or abject lives that crowd their poor neighborhood. It is the experience of maternity that, rather than bringing them closer to the semiotic, functions instead as the pivotal moment that precipitates their rejection of a Pan-African semiotic and their descent into the symbolic order of Man as *homo economicus.* According to Kristeva, the condition of possibility for the symbolic, or the normative order that governs identity, is the repudiation of the maternal body, closely connected to the semiotic realm. But, as we have seen in the introduction, in Man's dominant system of meanings it is specifically the role of the Black woman as "potential genitrix" of life that is erased: the Black maternal can only be imagined as tethered to death and deviance, becoming the quintessential symbol of abjection. As Doris Witt has demonstrated in her discussion about Black women and food, the Black maternal "has historically been construed as a source of pollution" and, as such, made abject (196). Avey and Jay's horrified refusal of maternity functions to inscribe them in the symbolic order of Man, predicated upon such an erasure: what represents the foundational abjection of this order is the Black maternal, symbolized by Avey's pregnant body. Since in the dominant order, the Black maternal is constructed as "outside cultural legitimacy, still within culture, but culturally 'outlawed'" (Butler, "Body" 118), aspiring to assimilate into the realm of *homo economicus*, they identify with its symbolic order and internalize the concomitant erasure of the Black maternal. Rendering them unable to resignify the Black maternal and untether it from a state of abjection, their entrance into this symbolic domain at the same time functions to relegate them to the abject status of death-in-life. The couple's horrified rejection of Avey's pregnancy triggers the abandonment of their semiotic rituals, initiating them into *homo economicus's* symbolic order and condemning them to a death-in-life, isolated from the wider African American community.

Pregnant again, with Marion, "[f]ar too soon for it to have happened again" (89) and unable to afford another baby, Avey attempts to abort: "She tried everything in the beginning: the scalding hot baths, castor oil, the strong cups of fennel root tea she had learned about from her mother. She bought the unmarked packet of small brown pills in the drugstore and swallowed them all at one time. She douched one day till it seemed her entire insides had been flushed down the bathtub drain" (89–90). Seeing no signs "of the hoped-for blood," she "took and hurled her body down the steep steps and then up again [. . .] until she finally collapsed on the landing outside their door. All to no avail" (90). The disgust at and rejection of Avey's pregnancy is evident in the way Avey and Jay not only avoid speaking about it but divert their gaze, afraid to look at its bodily signs, echoing Kristeva's claim that "the symbolic becomes possible by repudiating the primary relationship to the maternal body" (Butler, "Body" 110). Anxious to enter the symbolic, Avey and Jay repress the maternal, and this manifests in their rejection of Avey's pregnant body: the sight of it is enough to elicit revulsion. As the months pass, Avey avoids looking at herself in the mirror, and Jay's eyes begin "to shy helplessly away from her stomach" (90). Working for longer hours to earn more money and avoid the sight of pregnancy, "his look when he was home became more evasive and closed:" Jay's repression and terror of the maternal body plunge him deeper and deeper into the symbolic terrain.

Having rejected the maternal, he has "the look of someone who carried a weight on his spirit that was as heavy in its way as the child in her womb" (103). It is then that Avey's mind shatters as "the china bowl which held her sanity and trust fell from its shelf in her mind and broke" (91). Contrary to Kristeva's assertion, what engenders a psychotic break for Avey is her and her husband's rejection of the semiotic, which harks back to her contact with the maternal body and her initiation into the symbolic. Growing together with her baby are her suspicions about her husband's infidelity as "another reason for his lateness began to take shape in her thoughts with the same slow and inevitable accretion of detail as the child in her womb" (91). She begins seeing the white salesgirls at the store as they are "intrigued by him," and "[s]he could almost hear them thinking [. . .] in the hopeless Brooklynese they spoke" (92–93). Their nourishing rituals are replaced by her "restless pacing that was a nightly ritual," mechanically wandering from one room to the other following a set path and moving as if possessed, "scarcely conscious of being on her feet" (99). Having rejected the maternal, there is nothing creative about Avey's mechanical and lifeless pacing as she starts to become a figure for the walking dead. Spending every day alone, marginalized from social life, Avey's condition exemplifies the social death that characterized slavery. Living the solitary death-in-life of a phantom, her existence cannot be apprehended as a life worthy of life, and it starts becoming just another of those wasted lives that pepper their poor neighborhood as figures of the abject or what the symbolic order of *homo economicus* needs to cast off.

Refusing to become another "wasted life" left behind by progress (Bauman 74), Jay is eager to enter the symbolic terrain. He transforms into a *homo economicus*, embracing the logic of the symbolic and rejecting the semiotic rituals that used to be a source of life and shielded him from the deadly violence of the symbolic, which takes control of his life and the terms under which his subjectivity is imagined. The semiotic created by those rituals no longer holds its nurturing power as the symbolic requires the repression of its libidinal force, which can only be gratified in ways deemed productive. Adopting *homo eco-*

nomicus's mode of reason and entering the symbolic, Jay takes on another job and begins a correspondence course in accounting, devoting all his spare time to business manuals rather than to semiotic rituals: "He took to reading books on career building, personality improvement, selling techniques, business English and the like. The long trolley ride to and from downtown Brooklyn each day, the time he had to himself on his evening job, and all day Sunday at home were spent immersed in the study manuals for the course or in one of the books [. . .] And these were the first things he reached for—still half asleep—on the night table beside the bed in the mornings" (113). Rather than reading and performing African American poetry with Avey, he solitarily peruses business books: these become the economic narratives that inform his view of the world and himself. Organizing his time to maximize his economic productivity, he has none to dedicate to his rituals, which now look like a waste of time. If he is to succeed in his race for success in the dominant symbolic order, he must abide by *homo economicus's* system of meanings, dominated by an instrumental view of time and the self. He invests in his time and himself, trying to be as efficient as possible, to "sell his person:" he would set out every Monday "wearing the dark suit he had been married in, his mustache carefully trimmed" to look "neat, personable, well-spoken" to find an office job (113). But, because of racial terror, he finds none and goes home silent, letting "his shoulders, collapsed under the jacket or coat, speak for him" (114). Avey and Jay ultimately manage to move out of Halsey Street to a big house in North White Plains. But, while the specters of those abject others of Halsey Street have seemingly been left behind, other frightening phantoms of abjection loom large over their new-found richness.

Absorbed in his race for material well-being, Jay leaves behind their rituals and lets himself have no distractions to arrive first in the imaginary competition he is having with others: "[h]e went about those years like a runner in the heat of a long and punishing marathon, his every muscle tensed and straining, his body being pushed to its limits" (115). Running "as though he had put on blinders to shut out anything around him that might prove distracting [. . .] things that had once been important to him, that he needed, such as the music, the old blues records that had restored him at the end of the day, found themselves abandoned on the sidelines" (115). Their dancing rituals, their regular trips to Tatem, and their visits to their friends in Harlem are "supplanted by the study manuals, the self-improvement books" (116). Since Jay's priorities change and his powerful rituals are "out of his line of vision" (115), they can no longer perform their life-restoring magic. As with Avey's lone and mechanical pacing, there is nothing creative about these activities that now fill Jay's days. The music, dancing, and poetry are all replaced with accounting books and courses, his passion with his obsession for efficiency and time management: the poetic language of such rituals is substituted with the language of Logos or of "univocally signifying signs" (34). Becoming, to use Du Bois's terms, a stranger in his own house, Jay loses every source of nourishment: no longer protected against the violence of the symbolic, he enters a death-in-life condition.

Even the seemingly inviolable and sacred lovemaking "as with everything else, [. . .] gradually felt victim to the strains [. . .] and to the punishing years that followed" (129). Absorbed in his race for money, Jay loses his poetic touch as it "increasingly became that of a man whose thoughts were elsewhere, and whose body, even while merged with her, felt impatient to leave and join them" (129). His outrageous talk, which Avey needs, disappears and sex is reduced, as is the case for Macon and Luther, to "a burden he wanted rid of. Like a leg-iron which slowed him in the course he had set for himself" (129). Having assimilated a materialistic outlook, he considers love-making a waste of time: his creative energy is distorted and rechanneled towards material pursuits and economic success. He loses the sustenance of his rituals and the connection with the semiotic they provided, descending into a symbolic underworld populated with figures of the walking dead. With nothing to protect him against such deadly violence, he succumbs to it and becomes one of them.

As the libidinal economy that characterized their rituals fades away, repressed by the symbolic norms to which Jay adheres, nothing remains of his affectionate, joyous, witty, and playful nature. Since this Pan-African semiotic used to be his source of vitality and creativity, he no longer has access to its (re) generative powers: "the man Jay used to become at home, who was given to his wry jokes and banter, whose arms used to surprise her [Avey] as they circled around her from behind, gradually went into eclipse" (116). With his collapsing shoulders and bloodshot eyes, Jay loses his exuberance, and his face becomes expressionless and lifeless: "on his face a clenched and dogged look that was to become almost his sole expression over the years" (115). Avey has the sensation that Jay "had lost a necessary shield" and that "the last trace of everything that was distinctive and special about him had vanished" (130–31) as he starts leading a death-in-life, no longer protected by their rituals. Entering the symbolic and abiding by its logic, he is transformed into an abject other.

As Jay loses his connection with the semiotic, Avey experiences a frightening sensation, which recalls Ellison's narrator's feeling right after the artificial maternal displacement, that "I had been talking beyond myself, had used words and expressed attitudes not my own, that I was in the grip of some alien personality lodged deep within me" (240). She senses Jay's transformation into a living corpse: "[o]n occasion, glancing at him, she would surprise what almost looked like the vague, pale outline of another face superimposed on his, as in a double exposure" (131). This superimposed face is a lifeless, "strange pallid face," "hovering pale and shadowy over his" (131). Disfiguring "his familiar features" (131), it makes him appear not only a stranger to Avey but also a ghost. His existence absorbed by the economic calculations and preoccupations of the symbolic, he can no longer be enlivened by the semiotic: he slowly dies while living.

While he has raised himself from the appalling conditions of poverty that characterized the wasted lives of Halsey Street, he continues to inhabit the liminal condition of the slave, who "appears as the perfect figure of a shadow" dwelling in "a phantomlike world of horrors" (Mbembe 21). While Jay lives in twentieth-century America, his existence comes nonetheless close to the form of death-in-life that Mbembe has theorized as constitutive of slave life. His remarks about the treatment of the slave as "no longer existing except as a mere tool and instrument of production" resonate with Jay's devotion of his entire existence to the enhancement of his productivity and marketability. What has reduced Jay to such a death-in-life condition is not the violent dehumanization of slavery but that of the symbolic terrain of *homo economicus* and its rejection of the semiotic, which has cut him off from his source of renewed life and reduced him to a living corpse. Marshall establishes the link between Jay's condition and that of enslaved Africans via the figure of the zombie or living dead, which, according to Kaiama Glover, "represents the lowest being on the social scale: a thingified no-person reduced to its productive capacity" (93). As Morales-Franceschini has noted, in the Afro-Caribbean imaginary, the corpse is not the only figure of violence that destabilizes the symbolic. Haitian writers deploy the figure of the zombie or the living death, whose closest historical kin is the enslaved African, as a literary metaphor for an enslaved consciousness. Describing Jay's descent into the symbolic, Marshall uses this figure of the living dead, tapping into the rich literary sources of Haiti.

Jay starts talking as if he were possessed: "the voice was clearly his, but the tone and, more important, the things he said were so unlike him they might have come from someone "(perhaps the stranger she thought she spied now and again) who had slipped in when he wasn't looking and taken up residency behind his dark skin" (131). Jay's body appears inhabited by somebody who views "the world and his fellow man according to a harsh and joyless ethic" and talks with an "unsparing, puritanical tone" (131). His subjectivity is remade by the strict economic norms of the symbolic: there is no room for the refashioning of his being through the Pan-African semiotic as he represses its interconnectedness and playfulness. While he used to love music, poetry, dancing, and performing his dance rituals with Avey, he now deplores ballrooms and rejects his connection with the wider African American community: "'If it was left to me I'd close down every dancehall in Harlem and burn every drum! That's the only way these Negroes out here'll begin making any progress!'" (132). His comments reflect his misplaced resentment and economic aspirations, which alienate him, erasing the communal links he was able to maintain through the semiotic.

Avey "gradually found herself referring to him as Jerome Johnson in her thoughts" as it becomes impossible for her "to *think* the name Jay" (132). At his funeral, she is afraid to look at his face because "of what she might find there" (133). When she finally has the courage to look, she finds "that other face with the tight joyless look. Jerome Johnson was dead, but it was still alive; in the midst of his immutable silence, the sound of its mirthless, triumphant laughter could be heard ringing through the high nave of the church" (133). Jay's new name signals the undoing of his subjectivity performed by the symbolic and his transformation into a living corpse. This process recalls that of enslavement whereby people are similarly zombified through the severance of maternal and communal ties and the changing of their names.

Looking back at their marriage, Avey can now mourn their losses and recognize the importance of their semiotic rituals: as the narrative comes back to the present time and space, Jay's ghost vanishes, and Avey starts to cry, "sobbing wildly" as for the first time "she was mourning him, finally shedding the tears that had eluded her even on the day of his funeral" (134–35). But what she is mourning is "not his death so much, but his life" since she realizes that he lived a death-in-life and had been dead even though alive: "Jay's death had taken place long before Jerome Johnson's," and "[t]here had been nothing to mark his passing. No well-dressed corpse, no satin-lined coffin, no funeral wreaths and flowers. Jay had simply ceased to be. He had vanished without making his leaving known" (135–36). Without a corpse and a proper ceremony, hers "was a much larger grief, a far greater loss:" "the plaintive voice of the sea" rises in order to mourn with her (135) the unrecognized loss of a life and remember the rituals that nourished their lives. If "[a]n ungrievable life is one that cannot be mourned because it has never lived, that is, it has never counted as a life at all" (Butler, *Precarious* 38), grieving the loss of her husband for the first time, Avey is affirming the value of her husband's life against its erasure enacted by the symbolic. Reminiscent of Willa's mourning practice, in Avey's grieving process, Avey is giving him new life.

She mourns the loss of their life-sustaining semiotic rituals that connected them to a Pan-African semiotic, but that had vanished with him: "in leaving he had taken with him the little private rituals and pleasures, the playfulness and wit of those early years, the host of feelings and passions that had defined them in a special way back then, and the music which had been their nourishment" (136). She recognizes that those small semiotic rituals that nurtured their lives had been "[n]ot important in themselves so much as in the larger meaning they held and in the qualities which imbued them," which revealed the presence of "[s]omething vivid and affirming and charged with feeling" (137) that made them feel fully alive: the semiotic and the life-sustaining connections it provided. Those rituals were a source of life because of "an ethos they held in common," which joined "them to the vast unknown lineage that had made their being possible" (137). These life-sustaining maternal connections, which thrive in this Pan-African semiotic, "had both protected them and put them in possession of a kind of power" (137), enabling them to escape the limited form of subjectivity available within the symbolic. But "running with the blinders on" they let the semiotic "slip out of the living room" unnoticed (137), forgetting and rejecting its life-giving power. Much like Aunt Cuney's semiotic praxis, those rituals fostered a Pan-African semiotic that kept connections alive through a passing of cultural traditions like legends, music, songs, dances, and poems. Together with Jay, such powerful semiotic connections had vanished, condemning them to live as figures of the abject, becoming mere shadows of themselves living a death-in-life that recalls that of enslaved Africans.

Avey acknowledges her own descent into the symbolic underworld as she asks herself: "Hadn't she, in the same formal way, also started referring to herself as Avey Johnson? Hadn't she found it extremely difficult as the years passed to think of herself as "Avey" or even "Avatara"?" (141). As is the case with her husband, Avey is living a death-in-life: the "names 'Avey' or 'Avatara' were those of someone who was no longer present" since the "woman to whom those names belonged had gone away, had been banished along with her feelings and passions to some far-off place" like the woman in Avey's troubling and recurring vision "who had been cast out to await her death alone in the snow" (141). Avey's name changing, like Jay's, symbolizes the processual undoing of her being following her descent into *homo economicus's* symbolic underworld, where she is reduced to a death-in-life status.

She recognizes that her life is starting to resemble that of a zombie, as she has been leading a death-in-life akin to that of Jay, slowly dying while still alive. Disconnecting herself from their semiotic rituals and their generative maternal powers, she has lost her individuality transforming herself into Jay's twin, a mere copy and extension of her husband, even taking on his aspirations. This results in a lack of recognition from their community. She recalls how their friends noticed that they "were getting to look, even to sound alike [. . .] the same little mannerisms, the same facial expression almost, the rather formal way they held themselves. They could almost pass for twins!" (141). Her transformation signals "the inscription of the gender roles of the dominant culture on Avey" as she has subsumed her specific identity into her husband's (DeLamotte 89). Seeking inclusion into *homo economicus's* symbolic underworld, they inscribe themselves into the dominant gender roles, resulting in a further erasure of Avey's being: descending into the symbolic and entering its realm while leaving aside the semiotic results in her double abjection as a Black woman. As Wynter has argued, the enactment of specific gender roles is a function of the enacting of a specific genre of being human: disengaging in the performance of their semiotic rituals and their attendant relational ontologies, Avey and Jay instead reenact the gender roles inscribed in the dominant symbolic order that sustains a hierarchical understanding of the human as Man. Their relationship, far from empowering and nourishing, becomes cold and sterile, undoing their subjectivities. In a Mephistophelean drama, Avey and Jay trade their precious semiotic rituals in exchange for the material riches promised by access into *homo economicus's* symbolic. Deprived of the maternal connections those semiotic rituals fostered, they become mere shadows, hollow and vulnerable zombies, wandering the waste lands of the affluent neighborhood of North White Plains.

As Collins has observed, as African Americans experience social mobility and assimilation, communal networks such as those nurtured by othermothering become increasingly difficult to maintain: "new residential, school, and work settings [. . .] tested this enduring theme of bloodmothers, othermothers, and woman-centered networks" (Collins 182). Recalling a dynamic found also in *Linden Hills*, as they climb the social ladder, Avey and Jay find themselves increasingly isolated, unable to draw support from a wider community. Moving into the middle class, they encounter a different value system and slowly adopt the dominant lifestyle, in which "family life is based upon privatization" (Collins 182) and an atomization of the individual. This results in their abandoning of their nurturing semiotic rituals and the severing of the communal connections they fostered because in the dominant symbolic order, they are regarded as "anathema to the ethos of [individual] achievement" (182), which finds its representation in the Logos of the symbolic. This terrain is predicated upon violent forms of abjection that uphold racial terror, as Jay's and Avey's ghostly transmutations attest.

Becoming aware of this progressive undoing of her subjectivity, Avey experiences herself dying, feeling so old and feeble that she senses "in her bones the old woman she had become hobbling off to her grave" (143). Her perception of time changes: "Time might have played a trick on her while she was on the balcony, and brought her to the senile end of her days in the space of a few hours. The years telescoping, she might have lived out the rest of her life in a single evening" (143). Not long afterwards, she collapses on the bed. She needs to let go of the zombified Avey Johnson created by the Logos of the symbolic and experience the death of this constructed subjectivity to rebirth herself anew, refashioning her being through her contact with a nurturing Pan-African semiotic.

Preparing for a New Birth

Smelling a "faint but familiar" odor that reminds her that "somewhere a baby needed changing," Avey realizes that "[t]he baby smell was nothing more than the staleness of her own flesh in the slept-in clothes" (149–50). With "a spent face" and "a curiously blank expression in her eyes," she stares at her hat, gloves, and shoes with no signs of recognition as if her mind "had been emptied of the contents of the past thirty years during the night, so that she had awakened with it like a slate that had been wiped clean, a *tabula rasa* upon which a whole new history could be written" (151). As Carissa Turner Smith has observed, "[l]ike the postcolonial subject, she must un-remember or dismantle the histories narrated by the oppressor (including [. . .] the false narratives about economics that Avey told herself in order to survive in a white-dominated world)" (723). Taking off the rumpled clothes, Avey is "as slow and clumsy as a two-year-old just learning how to undress itself" (151). Looking around "with a child's curiosity and awe" (154), she is learning how to relate to the world anew. It is Lebert Joseph who, performing a similar function to that of Aunt Cuney, will guide her through this process of reimagining the world and herself, aiding her rebirth.

Like Aunt Cuney and Pilate, Lebert can change his appearance, gender, and age: one moment, he seems old and weak and the next, he is suddenly young and strong. Part and parcel of the "changing same" nature of his improvised vernacular performances, his appearance is always different, unstable, and changing. Limping and with a "slight, winnowed frame scarcely [. . .] able to support the clothes he had on," Lebert first appears to Avey as a very old man "close to ninety perhaps, his eyes as shadowed as the light in the rum shop and the lines etched over his face like the scarification marks of a thousand tribes" (161). But the vigor and celerity with which he crosses the room "denied both his age and infirmity" (161–62). His "large, tough-skinned, sinewy" hands suddenly seem "powerful enough to pick up Avey Johnson still clinging to the chair and deposit her outside" (161). However, after a while, the oversized "hands that had looked capable of depositing her bodily outdoors lay slack on the table," and the "white shirt he had on suddenly appeared sizes too big for his shrunken frame" (169).

Recalling Aunt Cuney and embodying ambiguities, Lebert performs the role of a Signifyin(g) Monkey as he troubles the symbolic order's system of meanings, which is based on univocal signifiers. When dancing and singing the Juba, he is young again, and takes on feminine qualities: his voice "sounded more youthful" and "had taken on a noticeably feminine tone" as had his gestures, which "were the movements of a woman" (179). Later on, when he joins Avey and his daughter on the way to the ceremony in Carriacou, Avey for a moment "failed to recognize him [. . .] because the man suddenly appeared older (if such a thing were possible!), of an age beyond reckoning, his body more misshapen and infirm than ever before" (232–33). He resembles a ghost who has just come right out of a tomb to wander in the woods: "the weight of those added years had bent him almost double over the stick and turned him into an apparition that had come hobbling out of Shad Dawson's wood to frighten a child on a dark country road" (233). However, the next moment, "the crippled figure [. . .] pulled his body as far upright as it would go (throwing off at least a thousand years as he did), and was hurrying forward with his brisk limp to take her arm" (233). Having reached the place of the Big Drum ceremony, Lebert "had abandoned the stick and was down on his knees inside the clear space at the center of the yard," joining the dances and singing as "an indefatigable host, appearing to be everywhere at once" (243). He makes and unmakes his being according to the situation: "what of the crippled dwarf of a thousand years she had seen or perhaps not seen at the crossroads earlier? [. . .] He had been packed away for another time in the trunk containing the man's endless array of personas. Another self had been chosen for the fete" (243).

Performing the Bongo, which "tells what happened to a Carriacou man and his wife during the slave time," Lebert begins to sing in Creole, "transformed in voice and person into the grief-stricken mother" (176). He recounts the terrible events as if he had witnessed them himself: "From the anguish in the man's voice, in his face, in his far-seeing gaze, it didn't seem that the story was just something he had heard, but an event he had been witness to. He might have been present, might have seen with his own eyes the husband bound in chains for Trinidad, the wife [. . .] sold off to Haiti, and the children, Zabette and Ti Walter (he even knew the names), left orphaned behind" (177). Representing the semiotic Avey repressed, Lebert can connect to different times, places, and subjectivities: perceiving no separations, he can inhabit a state that eschews those brutally imposed by *homo economicus's* realm. Marking him as belonging to Eshu's terrain, his gaze penetrates Avey's thoughts and can interpret them with no difficulty: "There was no thought or image, no hidden turn of her mind he did not have access to. Those events of the past three days which she withheld or overlooked, the feelings she sought to mask, the meanings that were beyond her—he saw and understood them all from the look he bent on her" (171). The old man's "penetrating look [. . .] marked him as someone who possessed ways of seeing that went beyond mere sight and ways of knowing that outstripped ordinary intelligence (*Li gain connaissance*)" (172). He taps into forms of knowledge unavailable in the dominant symbolic order unless one is initiated into a Pan-African semiotic.

Lebert has godlike qualities, and his characterization recalls that of Eshu-Elegba or "the God without boundaries" (Falola 3), a divine messenger central in Yoruba religion in Africa and "in related [. . .] cultural traditions in the African diaspora" (Borgatti 165). Able to metamorphose, he is regarded as the Yoruba trickster: "[l]arge and small, powerful and gentle, high and low, swift and immobile, present and absent," he is a figure of sharp "contrasts and reversals, and apparent contradictions" (25). Lebert has similar characteristics, which make him impossible to neatly categorize: neither dead nor alive, neither old nor young, neither male nor female, he inhabits a semiotic heterogeneity outside the symbolic.

As is the case with Aunt Cuney, Lebert's semiotic praxis slowly begins to affect Avey as she acquires the ability to connect with the past and thus uncover the links between the distinct but related forms of death-in-life of antebellum and neoliberal America. When onboard the ship to Carriacou, lying down in the deckhouse, Avey, even though certain of being alone, has the strong and vivid impression "of other bodies lying crowded in with her in the hot, airless dark. A multitude it felt like lay packed around her in the filth and stench of themselves [. . .] Their moans, rising and falling with each rise and plunge of the schooner, enlarged upon the one filling her head. Their suffering—the depth of it, the weight of it in the cramped space—made hers of no consequence" (209). Avey is re-experiencing the sufferings and violence of the Middle Passage—when African people, crammed into ships, were transported to the Americas—a symbolically crucial experience in their transformation from humans to slaves (Kokontis 4). She conjures the presence of her enslaved ancestors with an embodied immediacy that recalls Lebert's performance of the Bongo. Through her journey, Avey is becoming more and more aware of the violent processes that undo subjectivities: from her alienation on the cruise ship, to Jay's and her ghostly metamorphosis, to those of enslaved people. While in their efforts to assimilate into the neoliberal order Avey and Jay reenacted the dominant gender roles, the racial terror of the Middle Passage violently reduced people to "genderless flesh:" under slavery "one is neither female, nor male, as both subjects are taken into 'account' as *quantities*" (Spillers, "Mama's Baby" 72). But the novel also links these distinct undoings of subjectivities under neoliberalism and slavery as they both result in the creation of figures of the living dead. It thus posits the process of enslavement and its violent praxis aimed at ontological annihilation as an important antecedent to neoliberalism. Linking these different but related types of ontological violence, the novel underscores the futility of Avey's and Jay's attempts to assimilate into the dominant symbolic order, where they are still relegated to an abject status that undoes their efforts at inclusion.

However, through the description of Avey's journey and her reconnection to a Pan-African semiotic praxis, the text also performs an ontological resistance to racial violence, reimagining an alternate praxis of being human. Avey's reverie happens when she is on a journey that symbolically reverses the Middle Passage and the location of the promised land, which now, "rather than being the United States as represented in the prosperity of the plantations or, today, the Fulton Street of Jerome's success, becomes Africa as represented by

Carriacou," the closest, among the Caribbean islands, to Africa (qtd. in Rogers 91). Her journey seeks to reverse the concomitant transformation from human into a figure of the walking dead as Avey, with the help of pre-Oedipal othermothers, embarks on a process of remaking her subjectivity through the performance of Pan-African semiotic rituals. Reconnecting with her ancestral heritage, she is ready for the final stage in her rebirth when she will reclaim the maternal links that enslavement and then *homo economicus's* praxis sought to brutally erase.

Reanimating the Flesh

In Carriacou, awakening in Rosalie Parvay's house, Avey's body feels "numb, emptied-out" (214). As she meets Rosalie's "far-seeing, knowing, compassionate" gaze she recognizes that her resemblance to Lebert is more than physical: "he had also passed on to her his special powers of seeing and knowing. *Li gain connaissance*" (218). Rosalie has the same protean abilities as Lebert since they both share the same qualities that mark them as connected to the semiotic. While Avey is in bed half-asleep, she "repeatedly come[s] to stand like a votary beside the bed," being "any number of different people over the course of the night: her mother holding in her hands a bottle of medicine and a spoon, the nurse in the hospital where she had had her children [. . .]; the figure had even grown to twice its height at one point to become her great-aunt beckoning to her in the dream" (217). Another pre-Oedipal othermother aiding her rebirth, Rosalie performs multiple caring roles at once, embodying the maternal.

As Rosalie washes her body as if performing a sacred baptismal ritual, Avey feels her powerful touch, which brings out the same magical quality she sensed in Lebert's rum shop: "she felt the small hands from last night come to rest on her arm, on top of the sheet covering it. And they remained there, their light touch calling to mind the current of cool air that had come to rest on her head when she had staggered into the rum shop yesterday. A laying on of hands" (217). While carefully bathing Avey's body, Rosalie starts to sing "what sounded like a plainsong or a chant—a long string of half-spoken, half-sung words in Patois," which helps to ease Avey's tension (220), allowing her to welcome through her body pleasant memories of her past. Activating an embodied memory through a ritual of embodied nurturing, singing, bathing, and massaging Avey, Rosalie, like Pilate, acts as a midwife, and aids her (re)birth through the ancient ritual of the laying on of hands. Channeling an embodied form of love and nurturance through the powerful medium of touch, this healing praxis, which is given particular emphasis in African American Christianity, is connected to the art of midwifery as the hands of midwives were "regarded as particular sites of power" (Wardi 204).

Feeling the embodied power of Rosalie's touch, Avey recalls her childhood in Tatem: "Hadn't there been a tub like it out in back of the house in Tatem? It suddenly came to her that there had been [. . .] It had been her bathtub during those August visits. While her great-aunt rigorously administered the weekly scrubbing, she would sit drawn up in the tub" (221). Her recollection is so vivid that she becomes a child again: "The memory took over and for long minutes she was the child in the washtub again" (221). Rubbing her skin with lime-scented oil, Rosalie's praxis reminds Avey of her own maternal rituals: "It was the way Avey Johnson used to stretch the limbs of her children after giving them their baths when they were infants. To see to it that their bones grew straight [. . .] she would repeatedly stroke and pull on them in the same gentle yet firm manner—stretching, straightening the small limbs" (222–23). Rosalie's massages activate embodied memories that attest to "a continuity of nurturing and support" and to the importance of "a person's existence in a context which affirms and sustains them" rather than the individual's economic success (Rogers 89). Reinfusing her body with the vitality it had lost, these memories testify to a community of maternal care that comprises a whole array of different othermothers: nurses, midwives, aunts, and mothers. Triggering such memories, Rosalie's massage reclaims the maternal Avey rejected, infusing her with new life and reanimating her lifeless flesh.

Experiencing an orgasm-like sensation "that was both pleasure and pain," Avey feels a warmth that encompasses all of her body. This reaches her heart and provokes a sensation akin to that "of a chord being struck," awakening her flesh as "the reverberations could be heard in the remotest corners of her body" (224). Through Rosalie's maternal praxis, Avey's flesh is reconnected to that prediscursive embodied and libidinal economy that characterized her and her husband's rituals and that, according to Kristeva, is a signature feature of the semiotic. The reduction to flesh, one of the "primary narratives" that for Spillers enabled the "thingification" of captive bodies (67), is reimagined: the flesh, understood as the genderless antecedent to the body and the product of racial terror, is reanimated and reclaimed as a "relational vestibule to alternate ways of being" (Weheliye, *Habeas Viscus* 35).

As a result of her bodily reawakening, Avey, now dressed and sitting at the dining table, changes her perception of "the candle and the innocent ear of corn" that are set up for the ancestors. Previously, when Lebert mentioned this custom to her, she had thought it was "senile [. . .] even slightly demented" (224). But now, going back with her thoughts to her childhood, "she found nothing odd or disconcerting about them [the candle and corn]. They were no more strange than the plate of food that used to be placed beside the coffins at funerals in Tatem" (225). She also connects these ancestral rituals to her great-aunt: as "[a]nother long-forgotten fragment drift[s] up to imprint itself with the sharpness and immediacy of something that might have happened only moments ago on the empty slate of her mind," Avey suddenly recalls "the funeral of an old man her great-aunt had taken her to" (225). Avey rebuilds her links with her great-aunt, reconnecting with the semiotic as she learns to welcome what might be perceived as "nonsense" by the Logos, governed as it is by discrete signification and admitting no contradictions: entering a realm of heterogeneity, she starts to embrace Aunt Cuney's praxis.

When the celebrations start, there is music, singing, and dancing with "rum kegs that served as drums" (240) against the background of "a large de-nuded dirt yard," a lone and leafless calabash tree, and the remains of a "dilapi-dated house, which seemed about to collapse in a heap of dust and gray rotted boards" (234). The dark, bare, lifeless, and ghastly background suddenly alerts Avey to the fact that the ceremony of "The Big Drum—Lebert Joseph's much vaunted Big Drum—was the bare bones of a fete. The burnt out ends. A fete in keeping with the depleted-looking slopes she had seen from the dining window earlier, the leafless tree and the wreck of a house before her now, and the faces of most of the guests which attested to the long trial by fire" (240). Rather than being disappointed, Avey finds herself "drawn more and more to the scene in the yard" as "[i]t was the essence of something rather than the thing itself she was witnessing" (240). She starts to feel a strong admiration and a willingness to emulate them: "All that was left were a few names of what they called na-tions which they could no longer even pronounce properly, the fragments of a dozen or so songs, the shadowy forms of long-ago dances and rum kegs for drums [. . .] And they clung to them with a tenacity she suddenly loved in them and longed for in herself" (240). Embracing a Pan-African semiotic, Avey starts to realize its potential: it can and does bring into being a whole complex system of signification that is founded on a relational acceptance of the semiotic rather than on its repression. Through these rituals, these people have been able to reimagine their being.

With their determination, these people bring such "bare bones" and "burnt out ends" to life, changing them. Emphasizing communal ties, they draw upon ancestral traditions going back to Africa and adapt them to their specific New World context, creating a culture that, while looking back to Africa as a principal source and point of origin, is also something else. While their dances and music display a desire to reunite with and claim Mother Africa as a source of being, at the same time, they reveal the impossibility of doing so as the journey to the New World forced them to refashion their subjectivities and their traditions in light of a different context. While these display the traces of their ancestral origins from Africa, they remain distinct from and unassimilable to them; connections endure but are not binding. The desire to reunite with the pre-Oedipal mother transmutes into a desire to reunite with Mother Africa, worked through a recognition that, while total reunification might be impossible, this regenerative connection is still there and needs to be cultivated through the performance of rituals such as the Big Drum ceremony.

Through her reclamation and reenactment of this semiotic praxis, a transformative process is underway also for Avey's being. Inhabiting a Pan-African semiotic terrain, Avey acquires the protean qualities of Aunt Cuney and Lebert Joseph. She impersonates her great-aunt as she walks eagerly towards the dancers with a stride that is that "of her great-aunt striking out across the fields toward the Landing [. . .] A stride designed to cover an entire continent in a day" (242). Different timeframes and places fuse as she is transported back again to her Tatem childhood: "it was a score of hot August nights again in her memory, and she was standing beside her great-aunt on the dark road across from the church that doubled as school," even the "strangers [. . .] had become one and the same with people in Tatem" (248–50). Her hips, like her feet, begin to respond to the music, "weaving from side to side on their own," so that Avey finds herself dancing "with a vigor and passion she hadn't felt in years" (249). Reminded of "the Saturday night pretend dances" with Jay (250), she reclaims the nurturance of those semiotic rituals that used to sustain them. Her participation in the dances results in her renaming and reclamation of semiotic connections against the separations that the symbolic imposed in an effort to relegate her to a status of abjection and social death.

An "old woman who was at once an old man," "Tiresias of the dried dugs," enquires about her name, reminding her of Aunt Cuney's admonition: "The old woman used to insist, on pain of a switching, that whenever anyone in Tatem, even another child, asked her her name she was not to say simply 'Avey,' or even 'Avey Williams.' But always 'Avey, short for Avatara'" (251). Avatara is the name of her grandmother, and it is derived from "avatar," meaning an incarnation of a deity: through this reclamation of her name, Avey reforges her maternal connections and transforms herself into a maternal goddess. Via this transformation-possession, Avey-Avatara is both self and other, the same and different: she acquires the powers of Lebert and rewrites her abject status, transforming her body into a "signifier waiting to receive its meaning from a relational experience" (Benedicty-Kokken 36). As happens in spirit possession, this process relieves a sense of "displacement and desubjectification" (34). While the signifier, her external appearance, seems to remain the same, her sense of subjectivity has changed: she retains the body of Avey but has become a maternal goddess that can take up an array of personas, internalizing Aunt Cuney's maternal praxis. Hence, Aunt Cuney's Pan-African semiotic praxis is revealed to be a signifyin(g) praxis of repetition with a difference that does not require univocal signification or maternal abjection, underscoring the arbitrariness of the process of signification.

Avey's final transformation-possession can be perceived and thus become legible only by those initiated and attuned to this Pan-African semiotic through a performative reimagination of maternal praxis. Requiring the mutual recognition of a like-minded community that engages in such performance, this process is communal and relational. The reinscription of her subjectivity is recognized when the crowd suddenly bows in front of her as if they were paying tribute to a divine creature: this acknowledgment from the community allows her to reclaim the social life that the dominant symbolic order sought to deny her, giving her life new meaning through the creation and recognition of a parallel system of signification. Echoing a similar dynamic in Lorde's text, reclaiming her name allows Avey to undo the erasure of her subjectivity performed by *homo economicus's* symbolic. She resocializes and re-subjectifies herself into a Pan-African community through the performance of semiotic rituals that are revealed as constituting a maternal signifyin(g) praxis passed down through a maternal continuum. Reclaiming the social death of the dominant system of meaning and rewriting it as social life, this praxis (re)signifies what Calvin Warren has termed "Black being" (*Ontological* 26). It transforms "Black" from a signifier of ontological lack to one of ontological fullness: "Black being," infusing it with a renewed sense of aliveness.

Engulfed by the dancers, "what seemed an arm made up of many arms reached out from the circle to draw her in, and she found herself walking amid the elderly," slipping "without being conscious of it into a step that was something more than just walking" as her feet move "of their own accord" (248). Avey feels a strong sense of community and belonging, reclaiming a long-lost social life as she senses "the threads streaming out from the old people around her in Lebert Joseph's yard. From their seared eyes. From their navels and their cast-iron hearts. And their brightness as they entered her spoke of possibilities and becoming even in the face of the bare bones and the burnt-out ends" (249). This is the same sense of maternal community that engulfed her during her childhood boat rides up the Hudson River, when she felt an umbilical cord linking her to all the people there. When she stood beside her great-aunt outside the church in Tatem, watching the elderly perform a dance called the Ring Shout, her experience is described similarly: "she would feel what seemed to be hundreds of slender threads streaming out from her navel and from the place where her heart was to enter those around her" (190). These joyous subconscious memories that suddenly resurface link her present experience of Caribbean dances, and the annual expedition to Carriacou, with other rituals she used to perform during her childhood in New York and South Carolina, which enabled her to feel connected to a sustaining maternal community. Avey perceives the connections between not only different times, past and present, but also the different geographical spaces of the Black diaspora, creating a relational Pan-African continuum: the North and South of the United States and the Caribbean. The reversing of the process of "thingification"—requiring name changing and social alienation—is complete as she reclaims her name and a nurturing maternal community. If the slave is introduced as nonperson into the enslaver's household, here Avey is reintroduced into a Pan-African community and resignified as a maternal deity: enabled by her reconnection to a Pan-African semiotic, her signifyin(g) praxis results in a redesignation of the meaning of both her "self" and her surroundings.

When Avey leaves Carriacou, she has the sensation of having lived a dream as the island seems more unreal than ever: "Everything fleeting and ephemeral. The island more a mirage rather than an actual place. Something conjured up perhaps to satisfy a longing and need. She was leaving Carriacou without having really seen it" (254). While the "rival geography" she and Jay conjured up in the living room of Halsey Street was, much like the secret gatherings of slaves, precarious and fleeting, always doomed to be destroyed by the violence of racial terror, Carriacou attains an idyllic status, constituting a secluded and safe maternal place away from racial violence, where Avey can rebuild her connection to the maternal undisturbed.[5] It constitutes a narrative recreation of what bell hooks termed a "homeplace" or a "safe place" created by Black women "where black people could affirm one another and [. . .] heal many of the wounds inflicted by racist domination" (*Yearning* 42). The island's Pan-African semiotic can create and sustain its own order of meaning, in which the semiotic is embraced rather than rejected so as to reforge a social life and engage in an alternate praxis of signification that can reimagine the meaning of Black being. While this belies Kristeva's claim that the symbolic always prevails upon the semiotic, it points toward a maternal subversion that remains confined to the creation of a dreamlike, almost utopian terrain.

However, the novel's ending suggests that the dynamic that brought about this utopian-like Caribbean otherworld can be transposed to New York. Avey's experience of semiotic disturbances and its subsequent reconnection with a Pan-African semiotic is not without consequences in "the canyon streets and office buildings of Manhattan," where "[s]he would haunt the entranceways of the skyscrapers" (255). Returning from a utopian-like place, Avey is determined to keep alive her great-aunt's Pan-African semiotic and testify to its disruptive power. She would tell people about her journey towards rebirth and "about the living room floor in Halsey Street: of how when she would put on the records after coming in from work, the hardwood floor, reverberating with the music, used to feel like rich and solid ground under her" (254), bearing witness to the semiotic that sustained her and her husband. She is determined to take up an othermotherly role, cultivating the semiotic rituals that, according to Kristeva, are "privileged practices" within the terms of the symbolic (43).

Among these semiotic rituals there is her great-aunt's storytelling, as Avey will recount the legend she had passed on to her to keep her maternal connections alive: "It was here that they brought them," she would begin—as had been ordained. "They took them out of the boats right here where we are standing . . ." (256). Much like Milkman at the end of *Song*, Avey assumes the maternal role of her great-aunt: a matrilineal heiress, she becomes not only a griot but a Signifyin(g) Monkey herself, who can mediate between two realms of signification and whose duty it is to pass on the semiotic that can offer a portal to an otherworld.

Through its deployment of literary and historical sources from various African diasporic cultures, the novel itself attests to and draws from the generative force of a Pan-African semiotic and its resilience, seeking, like Aunt Cuney's retelling of the Ibo Landing legend, to revitalize the portal to a maternal otherworld. As it posits the figure of the Signifyin(g) Monkey as a maternal figure, the novel not only operates on the edge of speech and writing, at the cross-roads between the semiotic and the symbolic order, performing a maternal mediating role between two different realms. It also attempts to initiate the readers into the parallel system of meanings that the maternal praxis of signi-fyin(g) can conjure up and where a Pan-African semiotic is embraced rather than repressed. Against the patriarchal and imperialist symbolic of *homo eco-nomicus,* which rejects and represses this semiotic, it offers a reclamation of an ancestral maternal wisdom that can bring about an otherworld based upon an alternate signifying praxis. The novel suggests that this praxis can provide a dif-ferent meaning for the term "human" as it empties the signifier "of its received concepts" and fills it with its own, upending the dominant order's system of meanings and its reliance on the law of noncontradiction. For this semantic process of repetition with a difference to take place, the maternal itself must be reclaimed and imaginatively reinterpreted: signifyin(g) is based upon a creative act of maternal revision.

4

Erotically Rewriting
Maternal Connections

Luce Irigaray has observed that "our society and our culture operate on the basis of an original matricide" (11). It is this maternal abjection, upon which Western culture is based, that Audre Lorde's "biomythography" *Zami* confronts, challenging a dominant way of thinking about motherhood and identity: only by undoing an imposed maternal rejection can Lorde rewrite herself into being. Her narrative questions the premise that a break from the mother must happen for individuation to occur; what *Zami* offers is a non-matricidal praxis to imagine a more relational model of subjectivity that, while allowing some degree of autonomy in its cultivation of new relations, at the same time admits strong maternal connections in an erotic rewriting of the maternal.

To describe her text, Lorde coins the term "biomythography," positioning it not as autobiography—i.e., a narrative of her own life—but as a processual "re-narrativization" of the human itself. According to Wynter, our "human eusocial systems are [. . .] *hybrid languaging cum storytelling (if biologically implemented) living systems,*" or "*bios/mythoi*" systems governed by humanly crafted laws, codified in our hegemonic narratives (Wynter and McKittrick 28). Since the human is a hybrid being that employs narratives to implement its own culturally specific mode of being, Lorde's lexical choice presents her text as an ambitious project of rewriting the human through a rewriting of its narratives. But how does Lorde's text characterize this "biomythographical" rewriting of the human? Informed by Lorde's own theoretical elaborations on erotic and poetic epistemologies, this chapter argues that *Zami* represents this rewriting of being human as an erotic (re)embracement of the maternal, with the figure of the Black mother positioned as both the ends and the means of this processual reclamation.

In her essays, Lorde offers a useful theoretical lens with which to approach her biomythography as a rewriting of Western accounts of the process of subjectivation, which form part of the narrative construction of the human as Man. In "Poetry Makes Something Happen," she notes how poetry "coins the language to express and charter the implementation of [. . .] freedom" (185). But for Lorde, as well as for Walker and Marshall, this liberatory potential of poetic knowledge is connected to the maternal since it is the figure of the Black mother that represents the poet. Chiming in with Marshall's identification of her mother as a poet in the "wordshop" of her kitchen and the main influence for her own work, Lorde identifies the figure of the Black mother as the source of poetry's creative impulse, noting how "the Black mother within each of us, the poet within each of us, whispers in our dreams: I feel, therefore I can be free" ("Poetry" 38). In a rebuke to the white father's assertion that "I think, therefore I am" (38), the Black mother offers an alternate understanding of subjectivity that privileges affect rather than reason as a way to freedom. The Black mother, as Lorde's writing characterizes it, becomes the source of a poetic knowledge with a creative and liberatory potential.

In "Uses of the Erotic," she then connects this potentially transformative poetic-maternal knowledge to the erotic, a link that she further explores in *Zami.* Defining the erotic as a poetic and non-rational knowledge that lies deep "within each of us" (87), Lorde draws a connection between the poetic, the erotic, and the maternal: being a poetic form of knowledge the erotic is similarly enabled via a connection to the Black maternal. For her, the erotic is a powerful, spiritual, and creative life force that can infuse life with new meaning and that arises in the sharing of joy: forming "a bridge between the sharers, it lessens the threat of their difference" (89). While in the dominant order, it has been distorted and misconceived as pertaining only to the sexual, the erotic can pervade any daily activity: it can be found in any practice founded not upon an (ab)use of the other, but on a relational sharing of affect. Rooted in feeling and a source of power, the erotic arises from a relational creative process connected to the figure of the mother, who, as enabler of this lifegiving force, can produce a poetically infused onto-epistemology: the erotic is a maternal praxis that has a creative and transformative potential.

In the same essay, Lorde tracks how in "a system which defines the good in terms of profit rather than in terms of human need," such as the dominant Euro-American one, this erotic praxis has been misnamed, devalued, and co-opted to abuse women for the interests of men, robbing it of its lifegiving power

(88). But this power can be accessed, as she suggests in *Zami*, through an erotic (re)embracement of the mother within one's own self. In order to tap into a revolutionary potential for change, one must reconnect to the erotic's creative force—a reclamation that, as *Zami* shows, corresponds to a parallel reclamation of the maternal.

As we shall see, erotically (re)embracing the Black mother and its poetic language, *Zami* offers a comprehensive reenactment of the process of subjectivization as a reclamation of the eroticized figure of the Black mother. Her text traces how an erotic maternal praxis, passed on through the mother but then co-opted by the dominant order, must be relearned via the reenactment of an erotically infused maternal relationality. Through a creative reframing of the process of subjectivization, Lorde's writing offers a reappraisal of the human, untethering it from the matricidal praxes that permeate many narratives of the Euro-American order, which brought about the current understanding of the human as Man. But what are these dominant matricidal narratives of the process of subjectivization to which my reading of *Zami* offers a counterpoint?

Western psychoanalytical theories often posit a break from the maternal as a requisite for the attainment of an independent and free subjectivity: both the Freudian and Lacanian psychoanalytic traditions as well as object relations theory not only postulate the hetero-patriarchal family as the norm but are also founded on the premise of maternal abjection. Many Western scholars, such as Donald Winnicott, have long maintained the necessity of a gradual maternal withdrawal that will enable the child to develop their own separate identity (24). Even some feminist rereadings of these theories, while providing much-needed correctives to their heteropatriarchal biases, remain unable to move beyond this premise. Following Jacques Lacan, Kristeva postulates the Oedipal phase as the moment in which separation from the mother is achieved and the subject enters the symbolic order and language (by contrast to the pre-Oedipal, maternal space of undifferentiation, which she calls *chora*). From then on, the maternal semiotic will be repressed (more or less successfully) and can only be perceived as contradictions and silences in the symbolic, where the paternal law remains hegemonic. Kristeva's work, while very different from Winnicott's and under many aspects challenging of received notions of the self, displays a tendency to think about identity as separation from the mother: ultimately, she does not challenge the assumption that maternal separation is foundational to the process of subjectivization, and culture itself. While she believes that the maternal should be reevaluated so that it is not seen as a threat, she claims that "[f]or man and for woman the loss of the mother is a biological and psychic necessity, the first step on the way to autonomy. Matricide is our vital necessity, the *sine qua non* condition of our individuation" (38). What Kristeva, Lacan, Freud, and other scholars like Winnicott do not question is the necessity and inevitability of this process of separation from and radical rejection of the maternal.

Rooted in Black diasporic cultural traditions, Lorde's autobiography unsettles these psychoanalytic approaches to individuation. As the *Prologue* makes clear, the Freudian triangle of the heteropatriarchal family is replaced with a powerful maternal female triad: "*I have felt the age-old triangle of mother father and child, with the 'I' at its eternal core, elongate and flatten out into the elegantly strong triad of grandmother mother daughter, with the 'I' moving back and forth flowing in either or both directions as needed*" (5, original emphasis). Reclaiming Lorde's maternal genealogy, the *Epilogue* further celebrates her reunion with an extended family of othermothers as she enumerates all the women she has loved and states that "[t]heir names, selves, faces feed me like corn before labor. I live each of them as a piece of me" (304).

However, her narrative does not only problematize and rewrite the Freudian triangle of the heteropatriarchal family, substituting it with a female lineage. It also refutes the maternal abjection postulated by psychoanalytic theories, reimagining the dynamics of the process of subjectivization as deeply maternal and relational. Among all the women she loved, two particularly stand out: her mother Linda and her maternal lover Afrekete. They appear at two pivotal and connected moments in her biomythography: the beginning, when she introduces her mother, and the ending, when she recounts her relationship with Afrekete, nicknamed Kitty, through poetic descriptions which recall those used to describe her mother. Ending where it began, Lorde's narrative positions the maternal as both a departure and an arrival point, so that her final coming of age corresponds to a maternal reunion rather than a separation from and a rejection of it: "it is said that the desire to lie with other women is a drive from the mother's blood" (304).

Unlike some autobiographies and *bildungsromans* of the Euro-American tradition, in *Zami*, the circular structure that highlights the return of the maternal constitutes an enabling force that drives Lorde's rebirth, rather than an impediment: the recurrence of the maternal is not seen as a failure of development but as necessary for a new definition of the self. The maternal is both the means and the end of the narrative process of individuation, resulting in a circular pattern that does not hinder either her personal or narrative development but rather facilitates an alternative understanding of subjectivity based upon maternal relationality.

In Lorde's narrative, individual development can only take place through a maternal reclamation since the violent rejection of the maternal is shown to be a hindrance to individual development rather than a necessary step towards it. Matricide, reenacted through abjections, is hardly a "vital necessity" but the starting point of Lorde's downward climb towards a death-in-life condition that recalls the one experienced by enslaved people on their arrival in the nonworld of America: as slave narratives and the accounts of historians suggest, a break from the maternal enabled the process that unmade them as persons and made them into slaves or "living corpses."

After her break with her mother and an abortion, both related in the same chapter, Lorde, like Avey in *Praisesong,* forgets the maternal and descends into a nightmarish underworld of death that unveils the damaging effects of the violent break from the maternal postulated by psychoanalytic theories: "It didn't occur to me that I wasn't totally free from any aftermath of that grueling affair" (133). Even the language loses the poetic rhythms of her mother's. But reclaiming an eroticized maternal will enable Lorde to rewrite herself into a new being: through Afrekete's maternal loving, which will teach her new definitions of the female body, she will be able to (re)embrace the maternal and find new life in the Caribbean otherworld cherished by her mother.

Being her attempt at "recreating in words the women who helped give me substance" (303), Lorde's narrative, like Jacobs's, constitutes an account of a maternal search, which challenges dominant models of subjectivation based upon maternal abjection. Much like Jacobs rewrites herself as a free individual through a return to the maternal, Lorde's final reclamation of her new "*Carriacou name for women who work together as friends and lovers*" (303) corresponds to a retrieval of a maternal knowledge and its poetic language, where she can find new definitions of being human and new ways of living: "new living the old in a new way" (303). For Lorde, as for other African American writers like Jacobs, maternal recuperation rather than matricide becomes "our vital necessity," the *sine qua non* of living.

Maternal (Im)possibilities?

In her reconceptualization and reevaluation of the term "erotic," Lorde notes that "[i]n order to perpetuate itself, every oppression must corrupt or distort those various sources of power within the culture of the oppressed which can provide energy for change" (87). While in her essay she focuses on the distortion, devaluation, and co-optation of the erotic in the Euro-American order, in *Zami*, she connects this degradation and misuse to the maternal abjection that also pervades this order. This becomes evident especially in chapter fifteen, which links her abortion and maternal separation to an inability to draw from the creative and poetic knowledge that, for her, characterizes the erotic: maternal abjection is connected to erotic abjection.

In what follows, I trace Lorde's descent into a hellish, motherless underworld of death, precipitated by her estrangement with her mother and her abortion, two important events that Lorde links by placing them in the same pivotal chapter as emblems of her thwarted womanhood and sexuality. While she oddly does not dwell on her break with her mother, she gives more details about her abortion. However, she remains quite matter-of-fact and indirect about her suffering, and her language becomes more objective and scientific. But her feelings, in particular her pain and frustration, which this language strives to obliterate, still transpire from her descriptions of the bleak atmosphere of death that surrounds her and her memories of a dream. These reveal a quite different account of her abortion: rather than the "[v]ery safe and clean" procedure reported by the nurse, it is a "grueling affair" that uncovers the death-in-life condition to which Black women are condemned in America. If Lorde is to escape this situation, she must find a way back to the maternal.

Chapter fifteen, where Lorde recounts her abortion through images suggestive of death, sterility, and Kristeva's maternal abjection, is also the one where she very briefly relates her losing touch with her mother. Her account of their estrangement is made up of gaps and silences in the narration since she does not give many details about her fight with her mother and her decision to suddenly leave home: when a confrontation ensues with her sister "[m]y mother threatened to call the police and I left" (119). While she dwells at length on other episodes of her life, here, Lorde is oddly succinct and matter-of-fact about what must have been a very painful decision, given how close she used to be with her mother. Her account of her abortion fills in these gaps, symbolizing her painful rejection of the maternal.

Not long after she leaves her mother, Lorde finds herself pregnant and is determined to abort: "I walked to the subway from the doctor's office, knowing I could not have a baby and knowing it with a certainty that galvanized me far beyond anything I knew to do [. . .] Whatever was going to be done I had to do. And fast" (124). Her account remains incomplete and vague as she does not explain her reasons for her sheer determination to end her pregnancy and does not dwell long on her sadness. She feels "[t]rapped" and desperate: "No one else can take care of this. What am I going to do?" (123). But, rather than her pregnancy, what entraps her is the sterile underworld of America, which leaves her alone and with no alternative: "Black babies were not adopted. They were absorbed into families, abandoned, or 'given up.' But not adopted" (128). Despite this, she tries to reassure herself that it was "a shift from safety towards self-preservation," "a choice of pains," but nonetheless still a choice because "[t]hat's what living was all about. I clung to that and tried to feel only proud" (128).

However, the memory of a dream suddenly erupts to remind her of the difficulties she faces as a Black woman in America: she might not have been as free to choose as she might think. Retelling the dream she had when still in her mother's house allows Lorde to indirectly and allusively describe her sadness and frustration for having been denied motherhood: "I woke up in my mother's house to the smell of bacon frying in the kitchen, and the abrupt realization as I opened my eyes that the dream I had been having of giving birth to a baby girl was in fact only a dream. I sat upright in my bed, facing the little window onto the air shaft, and cried and cried and cried from disappointment until my mother came into the room to see what was wrong" (127). Her dream and her following sadness underline the difficulties for a Black woman to fully claim the maternal role: for Lorde having a baby remains, at least for now, only a dream she cannot realize. This reveals her painful awareness of the obstacles she would face as a Black mother: as she observes in her essay "Man Child," "raising black children—male and female—in the mouth of a racist, sexist, suicidal dragon is perilous and chancy. If they cannot love and resist at the same time, they will probably not survive" (74).

Echoing the dynamics of slavery, racial terror seeks to make Black mothering a practice that has as its primary aim the production of forms of death-in-life, with the result that, as scholars have pointed out, Black women continue to be denied control over their reproductive abilities and their bodies. In an antiblack world where racial terror seeks to relegate Black people to a space and state of death, those contemplating having children find themselves questioning the possibility and even desirability of mothering: "One may contemplate whether one should or could mother children under such dangerously oppressive conditions" (Césaire 519). As Rogers and others have argued, this is "another attack against their reproductive rights" (521). These attempts at controlling Black women's reproduction with the aim to "weaken the possibility that Black life would carry on into the future" perform a specific kind of necropolitics, what Césaire, Melonas, and Jones have named "Black maternal necropolitics" (522), which echoes and extends the erasure and co-optation of the maternal at work during slavery. In the case of Lorde, against this brutal legacy of racial and maternal violence, it will take a return to the mother and her erotic-poetic knowledge to reimagine mothering as a life-giving and life-sustaining praxis.

After numerous desperate attempts to end her pregnancy, from castor oil and bromo quinine pills to mustard baths and jumping off a table, which all fail, Lorde is left with no choice but to get a clandestine abortion, which she later describes as a "grueling affair" (133). Here, however, the language becomes objective and scientific, at odds with the poetic rhythms of her mother's. This is evident when she takes on the voice of the nurse who carries out the abortion: the procedure, performed through a Foley catheter, is related in an impersonal and cold, matter-of-fact way at odds with the lyrical style dominant in other parts of her autobiography. As Lorde reports the nurse's explanation of the procedure, allegedly "[v]ery safe and clean," the language becomes medical and objective: "The narrow hard-rubber tube, used in post-operative cases to keep various body canals open, softened when sterilized. When passed through the cervix into the uterus while soft, it coiled, all fifteen inches, neatly into the womb. Once hardened, its angular turns ruptured the bloody lining and began the uterine contractions that eventually expelled the implanted fetus, along with the membrane. If it wasn't expelled too soon. If it did not also puncture the uterus" (125). Scientific terms such as *cervix, uterus/uterine, fetus, membrane,* and *lining* contrast with her mother's creative use of Caribbean words and, later on, Afrekete's own special erotic language, which will teach Lorde "new definitions of our women's bodies" (297). The language here momentarily loses the poetic, sensuous and strongly evocative tone rich in metaphorical and suggestive expressions, evident in the opening and final chapters as well as in the numerous brief sections in italics that recur throughout Lorde's narrative. This creative language, linked to the maternal and its erotic-poetic knowledge, is replaced by the nurse's emotionless medical language that erases any trace of subjectivity: maternal abjection also performs an erotic abjection, leaving Lorde unable to draw sustenance from them. The highly impersonal tone of the passage reduces a woman to being just a 'uterus' or 'cervix,' stripped of any subjectivity that would register her suffering, disregarding the relationship between her embodiment and her subjectivity. This scientific language reduces Lorde to the solely biological, transforming her from body to "flesh," which Spillers has defined as "that zero degree of social conceptualization" ("Mama's" 67). Commenting on an advertisement for a slave, Spillers observes that, through an "atomizing" of the captive body, its technical and scientific language achieves a "total objectification": "we lose any hint or suggestion of a dimension of ethics, or relatedness between human personality and its anatomical features, between one human personality and another" (68). The passage above reflects a similar dynamic as it employs technical language to enforce an erasure of subjectivity, or of "social and human differentiation" (78). Echoing slavery's processual transformation of "*personality* into *property*," the nurse's language performs a "theft of the body" that disconnects it from its motive will and turns it into flesh, "a territory of cultural and political manoeuvre" (Spillers 67). This ontological annihilation is similarly enabled via a process of maternal abjection through the erasure of the erotic-poetic knowledge of her mother's creative use of language.

This scientific account, reminiscent of Evelyn's impersonal recipes in *Linden Hills*, is devoid of any human presence since even the performer of the operation is effaced: the tube just softens when sterilized and is then passed through the cervix as if by magic. Borne of scientific knowledge, this impersonal language "enumerates, measures, classifies and kills," and employing it means that "mankind *depersonalized* itself, *deindividualized* itself" (Césaire 19, original italics). Pregnancy is divested of all emotional significance, and a difficult and traumatic experience like an abortion loses all traces of pain, becoming merely another mechanical, impersonal procedure to be carried out as efficiently as possible, not unlike in a factory. It is only through this perspective and language that such a procedure can be deemed "[v]ery safe and clean" (125).

The description of the surrounding landscape challenges such a claim, creating a deadly atmosphere and exposing the maternal violence done to her body by the procedure. While Lorde walks to the nurse's apartment, her description of the greyness and coldness of New York stands in stark contrast to her earlier characterization of the lushness and greenness of the Caribbean: "even though it was only 1:00 P.M., the sun had no warmth," and she walks through "[t]he winter grey of mid-February and the darker patches of dirty Upper-East-Side snow" (125). Grey is as dominant in New York as green, the color of fertility, is in the Caribbean. After the procedure, waiting for the train "over the bleak edge of south Brooklyn," she notices that "[t]he Coney Island parachute jump steeple and a huge grey gas storage tank were the only breaks in the leaden skyline" (127). In this motherless and sterile landscape, the lush natural vegetation of the Caribbean is replaced by gas storage tanks and parachute jump steeples, which stand out against a colorless sky. When, later on, she goes out for a walk "in the crisp February darkness" there is "no moon" (128). With no source of light, New York becomes dark as hell.

The spectre of death looms large throughout Lorde's recollection of her illegal abortion and her fears about it, both before and after the procedure, which refutes the nurse's description of the procedure as "[v]ery safe and clean," unveiling the pain and death that the scientific language tried to conceal under its apparent objectivity. What transpires is a quite different account of the abortion as a "grueling affair" with long-lasting consequences for Lorde. Remembering the friends who died as a result of "too many" botched abortions on "bloody gurneys," she is "terrified by the stories [. . .] about the butchers and the abortion mills [. . .] These horrors were not just stories, nor infrequent" (123). The magical Caribbean otherworld summoned up by her mother through her stories, tropical fruits, and spices is replaced by a terrifying hellish underworld of death populated by all too real and scary butchers, bloody gurneys, and horrible abortions mills. These horrific metaphors give the lie to the nurse's naïve assurances that everything will be fine as Lorde's suffering intensifies and seems "interminable:" "Now all I had to do was hurt" (126–27).

Her memories bear witness to the maternal violence marked on the flesh: a few hours after the procedure, like Anna Morgan in Jean Rhys's *Voyage in the Dark,* Lorde has "stabbing pains" in her groin, keeps losing huge amounts of blood, and feels "afraid" that she "might be bleeding to death" (129). This is blood from the soul: "a decimation of the deepest and most soulful aspects of one's creative life" (Estés 55). The bleeding caused by the rejection of the fetus is connected to Kristeva's theory of maternal abjection as the body expels that which it considers as "other." The blood from Lorde's fetus is akin to the waste that drops "so that I might live," representing the other, the not-me that must be cast off in the process of subjectivation (3). But what is the price to pay for this rejection? Feeling more and more uneasy, Lorde tries to reassure herself that everything is going to be alright, but "watching clots of blood fall out of my body into the toilet" she cannot help but wonder whether "I was all right, after all [. . .] They scared me" (129). Lorde escapes Anna's tragic fate and survives, but her abortion precipitates her descent into a motherless underworld that undoes creativity, subjectivity, and even life itself. Until she learns to embrace the maternal and find a way back to the mother through her loving of Afrekete, she is condemned to a death-in-life.

The bleak and hellish atmosphere of death, dirtiness, and despair New York revealed after Lorde's abortion is the same one she finds when working at Keystone Electronics in Stamford: "The two floors of the plant rang with the whine of huge cutting and refining machines. Mud used by the cutting crew was all over everything, cemented by the heavy oil that the diamond-grit blades were mounted in. Thirty-two mud saws were always running. The air was heavy and acrid with the sickly fumes of carbon tetrachloride used to clean the crystals. Entering the plant after 8:00 A.M. was like entering Dante's Inferno. It was offensive to every sense, too cold and too hot, gritty, noisy, ugly, sticky, stinking, and dangerous" (145). Dirt is everywhere and machines dominate the scene, which seems devoid of human presence, and it is as dirty, grey, and colorless as New York was after Lorde's abortion. Likened to Dante's *Inferno*, the factory can be both too cold (for the ice) and too hot (for the fire). But while in Dante's *Inferno*, the noises came from the suffering souls trapped in hell; here, the noises emanate from the machines. Exuding deadly fumes of carbon tet, the factory constitutes hell on earth, where human presence can be inferred only from the instruments of their labor (as was the case in the nurse's description of the abortion). The workers are reduced to mere economic tools to be used, exploited, and then discarded. In contrast to the maternal Caribbean otherworld summoned up by her mother, the factory creates a sterile and hellish underworld where creativity and life cannot thrive: a microcosm that mirrors the larger one of New York. The appalling conditions together with the dullness and monotony of the job make Lorde question how she "could get through eight hours of stink and dirt and din and boredom," so much so that she thinks she "would slit my throat" had she "to work under such conditions for the rest of my life" (147).

The threat to life itself is even more direct as carbon tetrachloride is a highly toxic and carcinogenic substance.[1] But this is never mentioned either to Lorde or to the many Black women who, underpaid, do the work nobody else wants to, violently reduced to economic resources to be exploited: "Nobody mentioned that carbon tet destroys the liver and causes cancer of the kidneys. Nobody mentioned that the X-ray machines, when used unshielded, delivered doses of constant low radiation far in excess of what was considered safe even in those days" (146). Imbued with toxins, even the air they breathe becomes an instrument of death rather than life. Forced to take up such jobs in order to find the means to live, Black women are silently condemned to death: this is the underworld of America, where the troubling recurrence of slavery manifests itself in "skewed life chances, limited access to health and education, premature death, incarceration, and impoverishment" (Hartman 6). Black people live "under sentence of death" as they were during slavery and the Middle Passage (Glissant 6). Black lives continue to be fungible and disposable, much as they were on slave ships when they were sometimes thrown overboard in order to lighten the cargo. In recent historiography on the Middle Passage, the slave ship is likened to a "factory," a space where "the commodity called 'slave'" is created "to advance the 'accumulation of capital" (Rediker 45), transforming African captives into Atlantic commodities (Smallwood 36).[2] As the slave ship remade African people into slaves, here, factory work remakes Lorde's and Black women's lives into disposable ones, condemning them to death. The word "factory" itself, is derived from the Portuguese word *feitoria*, meaning a merchant's company trade outpost. First used in the slave-trading forts of West Africa (Hartman 111), it exposes the links between the industrial system and slavery.

Alone, motherless, and childless, Lorde slowly comes to realize her closeness to her mother as her own strength "was after all not so very different from my mother's" (120), acknowledging the maternal as a source of empowerment. Like Jacobs after the death of her mother, Lorde unconsciously searches for maternal surrogates and finds them in the various women she loves, who join a community formed by her othermothers: "I found other women who sustained me and from whom I learned other loving. How to cook the foods I had never tasted in my mother's house [. . .] *Their shapes join Linda and Gran'Ma Liz and Gran'Aunt Anni in my dreaming, where they dance with swords in their hands, stately forceful steps, to mark the time when they were all warriors*" (120, original emphasis).

Maternal Beginnings

The first chapters establish the Caribbean as a magical presence linked to the maternal. Her mother's deep connection to the island is manifested even physically as she is described in terms reminiscent of its lush landscape. Linda's connection to a Caribbean otherworld shields her from the American underworld of death-in-life. Cultivating her links to her maternal foremothers, whose knowledge helps her survive in the grey and sterile New York, Lorde's mother is able to draw on their alternative epistemology, devalued in the West. Recalling a similar dynamic in *Praisesong*, she summons up a Caribbean otherworld in the US, where Lorde can find sustenance: she is described as a strong woman with the powers "to change reality" (17).

Lorde needs to reconnect to her mother's alternative way of knowing and describing the world, derived from her connection to the Caribbean and conveyed by her creative expressions. From the very first paragraph, the Caribbean is established as a strong presence connected to the maternal: before plunging into her family history as would be customary when writing an autobiography, Lorde begins her biomythography by paying tribute to the Caribbean and to Grenadian women, who are her "forebearing mothers" and "the root of my mother's powers" (7). The opening chapter is particularly rich in poetic evocations of the Caribbean and its lush vegetation: the island is described multiple times as a sensuous, fertile, and green "home" (17). The description of her mother's longings also results in a summoning up of the island's fertile landscape and joyous atmosphere: "She missed the swift-flying bananaquits and the trees and the rank smell of the tree-ferns lining the road downhill into Grenville Town" (9). As we shall see, such descriptions will reappear at the end, when Lorde recounts her relationship with Afrekete, who shares many characteristics with her mother.

Much as the island is associated with a green, lush landscape and other images of abundance and fertility, so too Lorde's mother is described as linked to natural elements: she is born "amid the heavy smells of limes" and knows "the peaceful, healing qualities of water" and that "green things were precious" (11). The Caribbean's florid landscape, abundant with plants and trees, emanates from her mother. Her links to the island's natural landscape are so profound that she is described as the Caribbean itself. She exudes its sensuous smells directly from her mouth with scents so powerful that they conjure up the island's vegetation, transforming the darkness of Lorde's Harlem room and making it tolerable: "She breathed exuded hummed the fruit smell of Noel's Hill morning fresh and noon hot, and I spun visions of sapodilla and mango as a net over my Harlem tenement cot in the snoring darkness rank with nightmare sweat. Made bearable because it was not all. This now, here, was a space, some temporary abode, never to be considered forever nor totally binding nor defining, no matter how much it commanded in energy and attention. [. . .] then someday we would arrive back in the sweet place, back *home*." (11, original emphasis)

Even though Lorde has never set foot on the island, she knows it "well out of my mother's mouth:" through her storytelling, the island magically exudes from her. Lorde's mother and her connection to her homeland infuses her childhood with the hope to reach the otherworld represented by the island. This other-world stands in stark opposition to the sterility, gloom, sadness, and greyness of her descriptions of New York after her abortion.

The Caribbean, for Lorde, represents not only home, but also "a magic place," "a far way off," "a place I had never been to but knew well out of my mother's mouth" (11–13). As a child, unable to locate it on the books and atlases in the library, Lorde believes that "my mother's geography was a fantasy or crazy or at least too old-fashioned" (13). Eluding definitions and categorizations, it is characterized as a secluded and idyllic refuge full of tropical fruits, but her mother's Caribbean is more than a geographical place. Her mother's storytell-ing has transformed it into a fugitive maternal topography of the mind: "a sweet place somewhere else which they had not yet managed to capture on paper. It was our own, my truly private paradise of blugoe and breadfruit hanging from the trees, of nutmeg and lime and sapodilla, of tonka beans and red and yellow Paradise Plums" (13). Fertile, sensuous, and maternal, her mother's Caribbean becomes "a magic name like cinnamon, nutmeg, mace, the delectable little squares of guava jelly each lovingly wrapped in tiny bits of crazy-quilt wax-paper" (12). It is this maternal otherworld that she will be able to recreate through her lovemaking with Afrekete.

Directly opposed to the US, depicted as the "cold and raucous" place (10) "of my mother's exile" (120) or as "the stranger's country" where she remains "[t]rapped" (8), this maternal Caribbean offers a dreamlike refuge from such a grim reality. While "there was no black-elm tree in Harlem, no black oak leaves to be had in New York City" (10) with its "winter-dim streets" (124), her mother, keeping her connection to the island, is able to recreate the magic and fertile atmosphere of the Caribbean in such a hostile country: "Little se-cret sparks of it [the island] were kept alive for years by my mother's search for tropical fruits 'under the bridge,' and her burning of kerosene lamps, by her thread-machine and her fried bananas and her love of fish and the sea" (8). Telling her children stories about the Caribbean, Linda seeks to transmit to them her knowledge of and connection to this maternal otherworld. Her cre-ative accounts summon up its lush and sensuous landscape with all its trees and plants: "She told us stories about Carriacou, where she had been born, amid the heavy smell of limes. She told us about plants that healed and about plants that drove you crazy [. . .] And she told us about the trees and fruits and flowers that grew outside the door of the house where she grew up and lived until she was married" (11). Her storytelling becomes the source of this maternal other-world based on an alternative oral knowledge, devalued by Western thought, that Linda passes on to her children as the women on the island did with her.

Even though "there was so little she [Linda] really knew about the stranger's country," she possesses an alternative knowledge rooted in her maternal Caribbean otherworld and its culture. Lorde spends pages and pages enumerating all the ways in which her mother "knew how to make virtues out of necessities": "She knew about Paradise Plums—hard, oval candies, cherry-red on one side, pineapple-yellow on the other. She knew which West Indian markets along Lenox Avenue carried them in tilt-back glass jars on the countertops. She knew how desirable Paradise Plums were to sweet-starved little children [. . .] She knew about mixing oils for bruises and rashes [. . .] About burning candles before All Souls Day to keep the soucoyants away, lest they suck the blood of her babies" (8–9). The incessant repetition of the verb to know, which appears more than ten times, emphasizes her mother's skills and alternative knowledge, while the references to tropical fruits, West Indian markets, and soucoyants connect this knowledge to the Caribbean and the maternal. It is the women on the island who taught Linda all she knows: "Ma-Mariah, her root-woman grandmother, had taught her well under the trees on Noel's Hill in Grenville, Grenada, overlooking the sea. Aunt Anni and MA-Liz, Linda's mother, had carried it on" (10). They display a strength, resourcefulness, and connection to nature that they pass on to her: they "tended the goats and groundnuts, planted grain and poured rum upon the earth to strengthen the corn's growing, [. . .] harvested the limes" (12). In contrast to the heteronormative patriarchal family prevalent in the US, these women cultivate a strong othermotherly community of women, building strong ties with their offspring as they "wove their lives and the lives of their children together" and "came to love each other" (12). Linda grows up sustained by a community of foremothers, learning about conjure and the healing properties of different plants and trees as they initiate her into their alternative forms of knowing the world. However, in America "there was no call for this type of knowledge now" (10–11). So it is her mother's teaching that enables Lorde's survival: "thanks to what she did know and could teach me, I survived [. . .] better than I could have imagined" (120).

What her mother misses the most about the Caribbean is "the music that did not have to be listened to because it was always around" since "[e]verybody in Grenada had a song for everything" (9). Music there becomes the carrier of an alternative type of knowledge based on orality: "[t]here was a song for the tobacco shop," a "jingle serving to identify the store for those who could not read TOBACCO" (9). In opposition to Western tradition, the ear displaces the eye as the receiver of knowledge since the tobacconist is not identified through a written sign. Such a symbol is replaced by a sung jingle, connected to Kristeva's maternal semiotic: according to her, "non-verbal signifying systems," such as music, "are constructed exclusively on the basis of the semiotic," which is linked to processes that are predominantly oral (93). Rather than seen through the written word, knowledge in the Caribbean is heard through the spoken word: the written archive of the West is replaced by an oral one made up of songs and dances, but also stories and recipes transmitted orally. It is this oral archive of ancestral wisdom and knowledge that her mother is passing on to her, much like Aunt Cuney did with Avey.

It is not only through her stories, memories, and cooking that Linda nurtures her and her children's connection to the Caribbean and its alternative sources of knowledge. Part and parcel of this maternal remaking of the world, to which Afrekete will reconnect Lorde, is also her mother's own creative language, full of Caribbean-derived words and expressions that recall the lush landscape of the island. Such a maternal language, which repeatedly ruptures the narrative through poetic paragraphs in italics, consists of sensuous, colorful, and rhythmical expressions at odds with the objectivity of the scientific language used to describe her abortion.

This maternal language is fundamental in Lorde's development as a poet. In a brief section of chapter three, entitled "How I Became a Poet," she relates her first days of school. Reminiscent of Marshall's essay "From the Poets in the Kitchen," Lorde directly links her mother's poetic language "full of picaresque constructions and surreal scenes" and her "special and secret relationship with words" (32–33) to her becoming a poet, reclaiming her maternal links: "*I am a reflection of my mother's secret poetry*" (34): as she does in her essays, Lorde here posits the maternal as a source of poetic knowledge. When she ventriloquizes her mother, such a language makes her reflect on words and meanings: "*When the strongest words for what I have to offer come out of me sounding like words I remember from my mother's mouth, then I either have to reassess the meaning of everything I have to say now, or re-examine the worth of her old words*" (32). It is only when she becomes a poet that Lorde can grasp the meaning of her mother's expressions, which always baffled her as a child: "Impassable and impossible distances were measured by the distance 'from Hog to Kick 'em Jenny.' *Hog?* *Kick 'em Jenny?* Who knew until I was sane and grown a poet with a mouthful of stars, that these were two little reefs in the Grenadines, between Grenada and Carriacou" (33). Much like her other maternal practices, her mother's rich and poetic language mirrors and recreates the lush fertility of the Caribbean.

In this new maternal language, body parts are given creative and "puzzling, if no less colorful" names: the bottom becomes "bamsy" or "bam-bam" and "anything between your hipbones and upper thighs" is referred to as "*l'oregión*" (33). The pelvis region is "bam-bam-coo" and "on the infrequent but magical occasions when mother performed her delicious laying on of hands for a crick in the neck or a pulled muscle, she didn't massage your backbone, she 'raised your zandalee,'" an expression Lorde herself will use when making love to a woman. This is a very different way of describing the body than the nurse's: rather than scientific and apparently objective, it is richly allusive, metaphoric, and poetic. Initiating Lorde's into the "new definitions of our women's bodies" that Afrekete will teach her, her mother finds alternative words to describe their anatomy.

Like Creole writers, such as Patrick Chamoiseau, Linda, knowing different languages, is able to construct her own. If, as one character in Ntozake Shange's novel *Liliane* (1994) put it, "there is no word in any one of those damn languages in which we are simply alive [. . .] There's no word for us [. . .] but what we say to each other that nobody can interpret" (66), then Linda creates her own words to imagine a world in which Black people can live. The dominant order does not provide a language with which to express Black aliveness, attempting to erase and silence Black life. Lorde's text suggests that a language to transform this enforced "silence into language" can be found in the creative and poetic force of the maternal. Linda's maternal language constitutes not only an alternative way to describe, and thus understand, the world but also a creative praxis that can bring about onto-epistemological changes and thus create an otherworld. Establishing maternal relations, her idiosyncratic relational practice, which Lorde will mirror in the end by renaming herself Zami, is reminiscent of Glissant's technique of repeatedly destabilizing "'standard' French in order to decategorize understandings and establish new relations" (xii).

As the works of Aimé Césaire, Édouard Glissant, and Derek Walcott demonstrate, Caribbean thought has often insisted on "the transformative powers of poetic knowledges" (405), while the works of Black women such as Alice Walker and Paule Marshall, among others, have linked poetry to the maternal.

Drawing upon these rich traditions, Lorde's narrative links the transformative potential of poetic knowledges to the maternal, foregrounding it as the primary source of a creativity that has the power to conjure up not only another language but also an otherworld. Lorde's narrative specifically ties the maternal to poetry, positioning maternal knowledge as a type of poetic knowledge that can bring about onto-epistemological metamorphoses. As we have seen, in her essay "Poetry is Not a Luxury," Lorde explicitly compares the figure of the Black mother to that of the poet, highlighting the creative potential of poetry and thus, by extension, the maternal: "[t]he white fathers have told us: I think, therefore I am. But the Black mother within each of us, the poet within each of us, whispers in our dreams: I feel, therefore I can be free. Poetry coins the language to express and charter the implementation of that freedom" ("Poetry" 186). Recalling Jacobs's understanding of freedom as a return to the mother, Lorde's writing positions the maternal as a locus of liberatory possibilities—an opening into an alternative understanding of subjectivity and the world.

But the creative force of this maternal language and otherworld can only be accessed through an erotic (re)embracement of the Black mother: the maternal is both the means and the ends of this process. It is the eroticization of the maternal that initiates Lorde, and the reader, to this alternative language and its praxis—embodied, sensual, and erotic. Describing her coming of age in her mother's kitchen, Lorde explicitly connects this maternal otherworld to the erotic or that "resource within each of us rooted in the power of our unexpressed or unrecognized feeling" ("Uses" 89).

Eroticizing the Mother

Lorde's coming of age corresponds to her menstruation and her initiation into the pleasures of eros. However, rather than describing her first sexual intercourse, Lorde relates the orgasmic sensations she has while pounding spices with her mother's West Indian pestle and mortar, whose shape reminds her of an avocado. While her description of her abortion is characterized by narrative gaps and the use of scientific language, this episode is related in all its sensuous details and with highly allusive and metaphoric language, as the act of pounding spices for her mother's souse is connected to Lorde's budding womanhood and sexuality. Through such a language and the episode's explicit links to the Caribbean and Lorde's mother, the eroticization of the maternal is shown to be an enabling and indispensable force towards a new way of experiencing subjectivity.

In chapter eleven, Lorde's initiation into womanhood corresponds with the first time she menstruates and the last time she pounds spices for souse, her mother's "special and unforgettable" Caribbean dish, with her mother's West Indian mortar (80). Such a mortar has a special significance for Lorde as it comes from "that amorphous and mystically perfect place called 'home.' And whatever came from home was bound to be special" (81). Associated with her mother and the Caribbean, the mortar acquires the magical power to summon up a homely atmosphere of security and images of abundant meals: "The heavy sturdiness of this useful wooden object always made me feel secure and somewhat full; as if it conjured up from all the many different flavors pounded into the inside wall, visions of delicious feasts both once enjoyed and still to come" (82).

Made of a "mysterious rose-deep wood," "foreign and fragrant" that "fitted into the hand almost casually, familiarly," (82) the mortar has a strangely familiar quality. With its shape suggestive of an avocado, a fruit which will reappear in the descriptions of Afrekete's lovemaking, and its "intricate and most enticing" carvings of fruits like bananas, plums, and cherries, it exerts a strong alluring power on Lorde, who longs to use it. Every time her mother lets her choose a meal, she asks for souse, knowing that her mother will not have time to pound the herbs and spices and she will get to use the mortar. She yearns for the tactile and sonorous pleasures the mortar arouses in her as well as for the fragrant smells it emanates. Just touching it gives her an erotic pleasure as she "loved to finger the hard roundness of the carved fruit" and "the anticipated taste of the soft spicy meat had become inseparable in my mind from the tactile pleasures of using my mother's mortar" (83). Lorde loves "caressing the wooden fruit with my aromatic fingers" (84), starting a sensuous rhythm with the pestle going up and down the mortar: "Up again, down, around, and up—so the rhythm began. The *thud push rub rotate up* repeated over and over" (84). In a scene full of sensory details and pleasures, which will recur in her account of Afrekete's loving, Lorde describes how the fragrances and feelings evoked by the magical mortar have the power to transport her into a powerfully sensual otherworld that reinvigorates her: "The mingling fragrances rising from the bowl of the mortar [. . .] The feeling of the pestle held between my curving fingers [. . .] [a]ll these transported me into a world of scent and rhythm and movement and sound that grew more and more exciting as the ingredients liquefied" (84). Exuding a sense of erotic excitement and the sensuous lushness of the Caribbean, the mortar becomes a maternal tool that enables her to access an erotic maternal otherworld.

On her fifteenth birthday, pounding spices for the last time, Lorde menstruates and feels her body as "new and special and unfamiliar and suspect all at the same time" (88). Right before she starts pounding, she perceives "the delicate breadfruit smell rising up from the front of my print blouse that was my own womansmell, warm, shameful, but secretly utterly delicious" (88), connecting her odor of womanhood to that of a Caribbean fruit, and, hence, to her mother. Whenever she thinks back to that odor, she has an erotic fantasy that reveals her longing to unite with her as she imagines them together, intimately "touching and caressing each other's most secret places" (88). Becoming a woman and discovering sexuality are linked back to the mother as an enabling and essential force in this process. It is not surprising, therefore, that her initiation into the pleasures of eros takes place in her mother's kitchen. Rather than having her first sexual intercourse, it is pounding spices for her mother's Caribbean dish that gives Lorde orgasm-like sensations and functions as a pivotal moment in her growing awareness of the bodily pleasures of eros. Unlike some biographies or *bildungsromans* of the Western canon, Lorde's narrative substitutes the heteronormative narrative of romantic love with an erotic embrace of the maternal. Using the mortar, she experiences an orgasmic feeling of connection that joins her womanly smells to those of the spices and herbs of her mother's kitchen: an "invisible thread, taut and sensitive as a clitoris exposed, stretched through my curled fingers up my round brown arm into the moist reality of my armpits, whose warm sharp odor with a strange new overlay mixed with the ripe garlic smells from the mortar and the genera; sweat-heavy aromas of high summer" (89). The pestle and mortar link her budding womanhood and sexuality to the lush landscape of the Caribbean and to her mother: the maternal is both the means and the end of Lorde's narrative process of self-creation and its attendant rewriting of the subjectivization process.

Lorde's mother, who has a long-lasting impact in her life, shares many qualities with Lorde's maternal lover, Afrekete: among these is her strong association with the Caribbean, and its lush and fertile landscape and fruits, since both have the power to summon up its presence in the underworld of New York as an antidote to its greyness, sadness, coldness, and sterility. They are also both connected to an alternative epistemology manifested in their poetic maternal language, which Lorde expresses through her final renaming of herself: like her mother, Afrekete teaches Lorde a new erotic language, embodied and sensuous, rooted in the musical rhythms of their bodies. Able to re-embrace an eroticized maternal and give a new meaning to her womanhood and sexuality, Lorde re-names herself Zami, a Carriacou name for women who love other women.

Reimagining Maternal Connections

In the last chapter, Lorde recounts her relationship with Afrekete, often de-scribed in terms reminiscent of her mother. Like Lorde's mother, Afrekete has a strong connection to the island and to its exotic fruits. She shops in the West Indian markets, where she buys bananas, plantains, avocados, and pippins: "*She brought me live things from the bush, and from her farm set out in cocoyams and cassava*—those magical fruit which Kitty bought in the West Indian markets" (296). In her flat full of plants and tropical fruits, Afrekete recreates a fertile landscape reminiscent of the Caribbean. The final impressions and memo-ries of Afrekete's apartment mirror the narrative's opening descriptions of her mother's birthplace and her power to summon it up. Much like her mother conjured up a maternal Caribbean in their Harlem tenement, so too, Afrekete's flat with its warm sunlight, green mass of plants, magical fish tank, and trop-ical fruits strongly recalls the lushness of the Caribbean as described in the first chapter. Both her mother's recreation of the Caribbean and Afrekete's flat sharply contrast with and offer a maternal refuge from the bleak, dirty, grey, sterile, and hellish underworld of New York's streets and the factory in Stam-ford where Lorde works for a short period of time.

The sunlight and the greenness of the "mass of plants" in Afrekete's apart-ment are stressed multiple times throughout the chapter: always associated with her flat they stand in stark opposition to the cold and grey sterility of the streets of New York and to the deadly atmosphere in the factory. Her apartment is closer to the maternal landscape of the Caribbean that Lorde's mother cher-ished and recreated in Harlem: from the shelves "tossed and frothed, hung and leaned and stood, pot after clay pot of green and tousled large and small-leaved plants of all shapes and conditions" that "filtered the southern exposure sun through the room" (295). The walls are "always warm to the touch" but "chance breezes [. . .] rustled her plants" (297). There is a "glowing magical tank of exotic fish" that seems to come alive as it "murmured softly, like a quiet jewel, standing on its wrought-iron legs, glowing and mysterious," while at the bottom of the tank, "the colored gravels and stone tunnels and bridges" create a "marvelous world" (295). Life is everywhere as the flat exudes a powerful creative force from every corner: even the lifeless tank is reanimated by it.

Full of bright plants and suffused with "green sunlight," Afrekete's apartment mirrors many of her qualities. Recalling Lorde's mother, she is often referred to as a goddess and a *"mischievous linguist"* (303), and Lorde has the impression that, with her collarbones reminiscent of wings, she "came out of a dream" (296). Sensuous imagery is linked to Afrekete as her skin has "a deep shiny richness:" she has a "spicy herb-like odor" that "anointed the car," "coconut-spicy hands," and "great lidded luminescent eyes" that create a "calmly erotic gaze" and make Lorde's body sing (288–92), reanimating it, like Rosalie in *Praisesong*. She is described through water imagery as Lorde remembers "dreaming the roll of this woman's sea into and around me:" "her lips moved like surf upon the water's edge" (295). Central in Derek Walcott's poetry, the sea, "a receptacle of the history of the Middle Passage" (Farrier 25), carries images and memories of the dead, representing "the book of the dead [. . .] with countless [. . .] buried at the bottom" (Hartman 136). However, Lorde's description of Afrekete's body as sea overturns its deadly connection to the Middle Passage and its necropolitics, linking it instead to the eros, plenitude, and fertility of a maternal Caribbean. As she passionately makes love to her with a green avocado kept liquid by "the oil and sweat of our bodies" (298), they become alive and shine like lights. The avocado—linked to her mother's West Indian mortar, whose shape reminds Lorde of one—connects Afrekete to the erotic, the maternal, and the lushness of the Caribbean.

Through this image, the text links their lovemaking to Lorde's sexual initiation in her mother's kitchen: if maternal abjection is connected to erotic abjection, then maternal reclamation also corresponds to a reclamation of the erotic in a final erotic (re)embracement of the Black mother. In sensuous scenes reminiscent of her pounding of spices in her mother's kitchen, Lorde makes love to Afrekete using green plantains, a ripe banana and a green avocado that melt and become one with her lover's body: *"the deep undulations and tidal motions of your strong body slowly mashed ripe banana into a beige cream that mixed with the juices of your electric flesh [. . .] and locked into our own wild rhythms, we rode each other across the thundering space"* (296). This rhythmical movement of her body, akin to that of tides, is the new maternal language Afrekete teaches Lorde, a language that in its musicality harks back to the oral and embodied maternal archive of the Caribbean preserved by Lorde's mother.

Right after her abortion, while Lorde walks into a dark and moonless New York, making love to Afrekete on her flat's roof under "the Midsummer Eve's Moon," she sees "the silver hard sweetness of the full moon, reflected in the shiny mirrors of our sweat-slippery dark bodies, sacred as the ocean at high tide" competing with "the ghostly vague light drifting upward from the street" (300). The moon finally wins over "*the discarded evils, abandoned at all cross-roads*" (300) and becomes one with Afrekete: "I remember the full moon rising [. . .] *I remember the full moon like white pupils in the center of your wide irises*" (300). References to the moon abound in just a few short paragraphs: since the moon is a powerful symbol of femininity and fertility, these images underline Afrekete's maternal powers.

Linked to Caribbean fruits and the poetic rhythms of the maternal, Afrekete's loving constitutes a ritual of rebirth that undoes the death-in-life condition that resulted from Lorde's maternal rejection, through a reclamation of her maternal bonds and the relationality and sensuality of her body. This ritual of maternal reconnection constitutes a reversal of that undergone by African captives in their transformation from persons to slaves. Remarking that the slave trade established a maternal loss since "[T]o lose your mother was to be denied your kin, country, and identity" (85), Hartman reports that in North Africa, alongside ceremonial baths and the singing of incantations, herbal medicines were also used to transform "able-bodied men and women into vacuous and tractable slaves. The plant *Crotalaria arenaria*, a leguminous undershrub found in the savanna, was called *manta uwa*, which means 'forget mother' in Hausa" (157). This plant was able to turn people into slaves by making them not only forget their kin but also "cease to think of freedom:" "[n]o longer anyone's child, the slave had no choice but to [. . .] accept a new identity in the household of the owner" (157), thus entering the liminal death-in-life status of the slave. Similarly, Lorde entered a hellish underworld of death-in-life following her rejection of the maternal. However, thanks to Afrekete's maternal ritual she reclaims the maternal and with that also a new being for herself in a maternal Caribbean otherworld.

Much like her mother passed down to Lorde the maternal knowledge of her Caribbean foremothers and her poetic language, Afrekete "taught me roots, new definitions of our women's bodies—definitions for which I had only been in training to learn before" (297). Afrekete leaves a permanent mark on Lorde's life; even though their relationship ends, and Lorde will never see her again, "her print remains upon my life with the resonance and power of an emotional tattoo" (301). Through Afrekete's maternal praxis of lovemaking, Lorde has reenacted her eroticization of the maternal as she was coming of age in her mother's kitchen, allowing her to reclaim an erotically embodied maternal language with which to reimagine the process of subjectivation.

As a result, a processual rewriting of being can take place, one that also rewrites a different point of origin. Lorde can now rewrite her woman's body as "*a living representation of other life older longer wiser*" connected to her foremothers and to the natural landscape of the Caribbean: "*The mountains and valleys, trees, rocks. Sand and flower and water and stone. Made in earth*" (5). Afrekete's teachings complement Linda's and allow Lorde to claim a new being, a creative praxis represented by her renaming herself Zami, a name that celebrates her (re)connection to the maternal: "in those years my life had become increasingly a bridge and field of women. *Zami. Zami. A Carriacou name for women who work together as friends and lovers*" (303). If, as we have seen, the second stage in the ritual of enslavement was the changing of the slave's name, Lorde's renaming, much like Avey's, is the final step in her reclamation of a new being, one that enables her to reverse this undoing of subjectivity. In a move reminiscent of newly freed slaves, Lorde refashions and "renew[s]" herself by taking on a new name, Zami, that celebrates her maternal relations and (re)introduces her into an ancestral community of othermothers, allowing her to claim a new life by returning to the mother.

According to the Caribbean writer and philosopher Édouard Glissant, for many African captives, the arrival on the American shores as slaves constituted a rebirth into a "nonworld" that constituted "a reverse image of all that had been left behind" (7). During the Middle Passage, they "fell into the belly of the boat," which "is your womb, a matrix, and yet it expels you. This boat: pregnant with as many dead as living under sentence of death" (Glissant 6). With no written records attesting to their birth or names, the slave ship's sole acknowledgment of enslaved people's lives could be found on account books: "The only written thing on slave ships was the account book listing the exchange value of slaves" (5). Thus, for enslaved people, who lost their mothers as their communal links were violently severed, the slave ship assumed the status of a new point of origin, not to a new life but to a death-in-life condition. The womb of the boat rebirthed them to the nonworld of America, in which they occupied a liminal status between life and death. What Lorde's narrative accomplishes is a rewriting of this point of origin as she searches and finds another maternal womb that rebirths her into a new life in the Caribbean otherworld created by her maternal foremothers.

5

Maternally Reimagining
the Urban Landscape

In Toni Cade Bambara's short story "The War of the Wall," set in a Southern town but inspired by her memories of growing up in Harlem, the only "recreational facility" Black children are left with is a wall on the street. Feeling that "[t]his wall belongs to us kids of Talbro Street," the children become upset when an artist starts painting a mural on the wall and spend the entire weekend trying "to scheme up ways to take our wall back" (Bambara, *Deep Sightings* 123). But the mural is an homage to their community and their struggles to create spaces where children can play:

> Mama tapped us on the shoulder and pointed to a high section of the wall. There was a fierce-looking man with his arms crossed against his chest guarding a bunch of children. [. . .] One kid was looking at a row of books. Lou hunched me 'cause the kid looked like me. The one that looked like Lou was spinning a globe on the tip of his finger like a basketball. There were other kids there with microscopes and compasses. And the more I looked, the more it looked like the fierce man was not so much guarding the kids as defending their right to do what they were doing. (59)

The mural makes clear its function: much like the fierce-looking man, it performs a maternal role, building a sense of community and ensuring the kids get the necessary space "to do what they were doing," i.e., fashioning their being in the act of creative playing. Even though the ending does not clarify whether the children continue to play, the mural's function is highlighted throughout since it spurs the kids' engagement in creative play as they try "to scheme up ways to take the wall back." The very process of the mural's creation makes it possible for both the artist and the children to engage in a playful reclamation of space. In this chapter, I want to argue that Bambara's novel, *The Salt Eaters*, generates a similar dynamic while it frames playing as a maternal praxis of being: the text posits Minnie's maternal ritual as a reclamation of play that, engendering a corollary transformation of subjectivities, mirrors its writing process.

Against an enforced prohibition of play, Bambara's writing foregrounds the resilience of Black playfulness, which results in a reimagination of the city that goes hand in hand with a reinvention of subjectivity. Set in the fictional town of Claybourne, Georgia, where "[r]ates of unemployment, nonemployment, homicide, drug traffic were so high, the city administrator had asked the editor to soft pedal it" (211), *The Salt Eaters* juxtaposes an urban environment constructed as playless with a resilient creativity, evident in Minnie's maternal praxis and in the novel's language. Conjuring up the space for playing that the urban landscape seeks to erase, her novel frames such a creative praxis of reclamation of space and subjectivity as a maternal praxis, and the denial of play as an act of maternal erasure.

In opposition to the Latin term *ludus*, which denotes a system of rules, "play" is derived from the Greek word *paideia*, which emphasizes "spontaneity as well as the absence of constraint, precise aim and setting," and a lack of a predetermined outcome (Lenormand 96). With its emphasis on a lack of restrictions, play starkly contrasts "to work, the keystone of slavery" (King 108). Regarding playing as an essential creative practice of self-making, Winnicott understands it as a spontaneous, creative, and relational process, which generates the possibility for a new experience of the self and the world. Focusing not so much on the content of play but on "playing as a thing in itself," he understands it as a relational process in which the mother has a fundamental role as facilitator and preserver of this space: it takes place in "the potential space between mother and child" (71). Existing in this maternal space sheltered by the mother's presence, where paradoxes are welcomed, playing is a maternal praxis that can refashion subjectivities and generate an otherworld. Drawing upon Winnicott's insights, Perry understands playing as a free and experimental practice that must be guarded from external threats. It exists "in the space sheltered by the mother's eyes, hands, and voice," which enables the development of "the individual's sense of an independent inner reality not always synchronized with external circumstances" (5). Adult creativity grows out of this childhood experimentation with play, and, while art and play are different kinds of activities, Perry recognizes that each takes place in a liminal place whose extraordinary spatial and temporal status is enabled by a mother figure (7–9). While Perry's theorization of play and art assume the existence and even availability of this maternal "protected space" separated "from the ongoing events of daily life," Bambara's novel highlights not only the obstacles to create such a space in the face of racial and maternal violence but also the impossibility to disentangle such a space from the "events of daily life" (Perry 5). Even when attained, this maternal space of play remains precarious and linked to the realities of racial terror, which remain ever present and felt in spite of a maternal rewriting of the city and Black life.

In what follows, I trace how Bambara's text foregrounds playing as a maternal praxis sustained through the creation of a maternal space. In so doing, I argue that her novel both confirms and pushes against sociocultural constructions of the ghetto as solely or primarily a carceral space of death, not dissimilar to the plantation, where the maternal is erased. As we shall see, the novel, echoing Minnie's praxis, performs the maternal in an attempt to reclaim an otherworld. While racial terror seeks to deny such a maternal space through the infrastructural deterioration of the ghetto, the text's maternal practice rewrites Black subjectivities into the urban landscape, resisting racial terror's ontological erasure of Black childhood. Bambara's writing posits playing as a creative maternal praxis that can reimagine Black being against its denial in an antiblack society. Conjuring up a maternal space where to play and be anew, it reframes the ghetto as a space potentially geared towards life rather than death.

Her descriptions of a bleak urban landscape that does not register the needs of Black children contrast sharply with her playful use, in *The Salt Eaters*, of a music-like language, connected to the buried maternal knowledge of which Minnie is a repository. Responding to the absence of recreational facilities for Black children, evident in the urban landscape, Bambara's writing manages to conjure up a maternal space in which to play. Through its use of a maternal imaginary drawn from different mythologies, humor, wordplay, the play of voices, and the musical rhythms of its language, the novel engages in an act of play that involves reader, writer, and characters.[1] Rather than imagining alternative Caribbean topographies of the mind, such as those of Marshall and Lorde, Bambara's text unleashes the maternal potential buried underneath the urban landscape: for her, this is the only alternative. Informed by the creative energy of hip hop culture, her text superimposes creativity directly onto an urban landscape that has been constructed as playless and dangerous, rewriting

Black being into the city. While her words denote a grim space, they also infuse it with a musical playfulness.

Some critics have read *The Salt Eaters* as a healing narrative. Drawing from Mervyn Alleyne's notion of the magical power of the word in Afro-Jamaican culture, Gay Wilentz regards the novel as a "wellness narrative" or "healing text" and Bambara as an "authorial healer" (73). Focusing on its use of African-based traditions, and its blending of science and the traditional healing arts, she interprets the novel as performing a "linguistic laying on of hands" on the readers (73). Commenting on Bambara's skillful use of humor and the vernacular, she argues that "language, in addition to touch, is the medium in which healing occurs" (74–75). But, offering "an epiphany of creation and community" (Gregory 764), through its language, the novel not only heals Velma and the community of readers. It also enacts a more radically transformative process, directly engaging in a maternal praxis that recalls Minnie's, which catalyzes the rebirth of Velma and the entire community. Towards the end of the novel Velma, like Avey in *Praisesong*, not only heals but rebirths herself anew with the help of Minnie: she lets her shawl fall, as if shedding old skin. The title itself alludes to regeneration: in Haiti, the only way to bring a zombie back to life is with salt. The apocalyptic imagery and the violent storm suggest the end of the world and the beginning of a new era, recalling the apocalyptic Afrofuturism of *Linden Hills*. All these observations indicate a process more radical and transformative than a healing, which implies the retainment of the old, if only in an improved way.

As we shall see, through the playfulness of its language Bambara's text unsettles the construction of poor inner-city neighborhoods as merely dangerous and grim "spaces without," recording a communal quest for a maternal place and offering an alternative maternal language with which to reimagine Black subjectivity. Like the unnamed speaker in Brooks' poem "my dreams, my works must wait till after hell," who meticulously stores away bread and honey in hope of a better future (79), Bambara encapsulates and safeguards a joyful (and forbidden) playfulness in and through her writing, seeking to preserve a maternal space to play against a hostile world based upon racial violence. This space where playfulness can be performed becomes an otherworld in which Black being can be refashioned.

In the first section, I will provide a sociohistorical overview of the development and deterioration of the New York territories where Bambara lived, worked, and raised a family, as well as the concomitant reclamation of urban space that Black people performed. Against the denial of play that aims to construct childless landscapes, Bambara's work taps into the creative energy of the then-emerging hip-hop culture. In the second section, I will show how *The Salt Eaters* not only draws attention to the erasure of Black being scripted into the urban environment, linking it to a widespread state of childlessness and motherlessness. It also foregrounds how these ontological erasures are unsettled by a repressed and buried maternal energy that erupts at various points in the novel. In the third section, I will demonstrate how the novel resurrects suppressed mythologies of fertility that the reader is invited to explore through the reading of the text as if engaged in a treasure hunt. In the final section, I will argue that the writing of the novel, enacting Minnie's maternal praxis, provides access to a maternal language that can offer a playful counterpoint to the playless urban landscape. Blending different voices and timeframes, the writing itself performs an act of play that draws the reader in, as it entices them to unpack its intricate web of allusions and play along.

(Un)imaginable Childhoods

In some of her short stories, Bambara tackles the pressing issue of the lack of recreational facilities for Black children: in "Broken Field Running," anthologized in her short story collection *The Sea Birds Are Still Alive* (1977), the coldness and darkness of the streets are emphasized, and the numerous images suggestive of sterility prefigure the erasure of Black childhood evident in the built environment, which fails to meet the needs of Black children and mothers. Similar to the poor Black neighborhood in Naylor's *The Women of Brewster Place* (1982), the Lawndale Homes are designed by people who "didn't have kids in mind:" "quite naturally the designers of Lawndale have not installed a bathroom on the ground floor . . . there's no bathroom in the play area either, cause there is no play area for the sixty families averaging three kids apiece" (*The Sea Birds Are Still Alive* 47–61). There are also no windows from which the parents can watch their kids, but there are "bushes planted special for rapists and muggers" (56). The dominant order constructs the urban environment as devoid of a maternal space for playing, seeking to erase Black life. This landscape is generated and sustained by a lack of a sociocultural imaginary for Black childhood: in the dominant order, there is no space, either symbolically or literally, to imagine Black life.

The characterization of the Bronx as a lawless territory in Tom Wolfe's *Bonfire of the Vanities* (1989) and newspaper articles that construct it as the epitome of "America's Woes,"[2] where "Mr. Death is always looming" (qtd. in Holloway 143), exemplify how the ghetto often tends to be portrayed as an abject space of crisis, ruin, and decay. As a result, in the popular imagination, the children who inhabit such a space are imagined as always in the proximity of death. The resilient and alternative forms of being they perform through playing are erased, becoming legible only in terms of "lack." Their experiences and those of their mothers are criminalized and constructed as always deviant and pathological against the normalizing grid of white childhood and motherhood. As we have seen in the case of the "crack epidemic," this failure to imagine Black childhood and motherhood as other than pathological and in need of intervention engenders an attempt to regulate maternal praxis. Noting how "the fun of playing" is "something unknown to some children,"[3] a 1972 *New York Times* article comments on the significance of The Mother Child Project, which it casts as an important federal plan aimed at fostering children's development through the improvement of their home environment, framed as "lacking."

Reiterating the ontological erasure of Black praxes of being, such accounts of the ghetto testify to what Michael J. Dumas and Joseph Derrick Nelson have called a "broader *unimaginability*" of Black childhood (31). According to them, Black childhood has "been rendered both unimagined and unimaginable" since Black boys have been subjected to "an adultification that erases even their right to childhood and their status as *still* children": "we have created a world in which Black boys [and girls] cannot *be*" (36). But, as Bambara's work suggests, they cannot be because they cannot play: the erasure of playing as a maternal praxis is foundational to this lack of a cultural imaginary that can register Black childhood. Such imaginary cannot exist without the rewriting of a space for maternal praxis, i.e., for playing.

Bambara's writing insists that this erasure of childhood is processual and happens through the denial of play, an erasure scripted in an urban environment that denies the maternal. But it also foregrounds the alternative ways through which Black children manage to keep playing and thus engage in maternal praxis to rewrite the urban landscape as a space geared towards new life. With its emphasis on the wall's function for Black children, "The War of the Wall," quoted at the opening of this chapter, posits the wall as a fundamental coping mechanism against racial violence that allows them to keep playing. Because of gratuitous acts of racial terror, Black children rely on the wall as their sole means to create their being through playing: "It was our wall. We'd been pitching pennies against the barbershop since we were very little kids. We'd played handball and pop fly against that wall since so-called integration when the crazies cross town shut the park down and poured cement in the swimming pool so we couldn't use it" (*Deep Sightings* 123). As we have seen, the painting of the mural on the wall highlights its important maternal role and ensures the preservation of such a space for the continuing performance of maternal praxis.

As Bambara's writing reminds us, in spite of racial terror, Black people devise alternative ways to play and develop informal community networks of care to create the necessary maternal space to play that an antiblack world violently denies. In his book *There Are No Children Here* (1992), about two boys struggling to survive in a public housing complex in 1980s Chicago, journalist Alex Kotlowitz describes how, in a neighborhood with no movie theatres, skating rinks, or bowling alleys, "[o]ne mother moved aside her living room furniture to make an open and safe place where her children could frolic" (29). Drawing from his personal experiences, Baldwin's only children's book *Little Man, Little Man. A Story of Childhood* (1976) focuses on a day in the life of three children as they roam the streets of Harlem. Told through a child's perspective but labeled "a child's story for adults," its narrative follows them as they play improvised ballgames aided by various members of the community, who help them navigate the perilous streets, juxtaposing danger and play. While acknowledging the precariousness of Black children's games, always vulnerable to racial terror, his writing also emphasizes the creative resilience of Black children's forms of play and the communal ties that both foster and are fostered by such practices.

Gordon Parks's photograph of African American children captures their exclusion from recreational sites: his 1956 photograph "Outside Looking In" shows a group of Black children gaping into a gated playground, out of their reach. However, another untitled 1948 shot of Harlem portrays Black children playing makeshift water games with the help of an adult who breaks the water pipes on the street: through their creative communal practice, they are able to reimagine the city as a swimming pool. Commenting on Mel Rosenthal's shot of kids playing among ruins, Berman has observed: "These children won't be robbed of their childhoods: They won't stop playing just because their playground has been destroyed" (218). While their creative reinvention of playing is often erased in popular accounts of the ghetto that have shaped the cultural fantasy of what David Roediger has called the "black, antineighborly, and uninhabitable city," Black children have imagined alternative ways to play that seek to preserve a symbiotic relationship with their communities against the progressive dearth of recreational facilities in Black inner-city neighborhoods that aim to violently erase maternal and communal links.

As historian Victoria W. Wolcott has documented, African Americans' access to recreational facilities remained extremely limited throughout the twentieth century, and even when they did approach these spaces, they were confronted with racial violence. In the era of Jim Crow, segregation barred them from freely accessing these spaces, and many children, excluded from segregated swimming pools and beaches, died in rivers and ponds. Growing up in 1920s Pittsburgh, educator and activist Dorothy Height remembers how, eager to learn to swim, she approached YMCA's front desk only to be told that "Negro girls [cannot] swim in the YMCA pool" (56). Height never learned to swim, but this experience inspired her to work for the desegregation of all YMCA facilities. Many other Black children had similar recollections that spurred their passion for racial justice: 1960s activist Livingston Johnson, for instance, was thrown out of a roller-skating rink, an incident that inspired him in his later struggle for civil rights.

Even after the 1964 Civil Rights Act was passed, "owners of pools and parks used a variety of subterfuges, particularly privatization, to subvert the law. And many municipalities closed down public facilities rather than comply with the courts" (Wolcott 7–8). In Birmingham, white officials closed public parks and drained pools to forestall desegregation. Gratuitous acts of racial terror were by no means isolated incidents: in the early 1970s, in Stonewall, the town leaders buried the local swimming pool rather than allow Black people in. Many owners let urban amusement parks deteriorate, selling the land to developers: by the late 1960s and early 1970s, most had closed. One young Black woman wrote to the *Chicago Defender* that the closing of Riverview Park "just seems to be part of a horrid thing that is happening in Chicago. There are so many vacant lots where places, not all of them run-down, have been demolished. Then nothing is erected in the vacant areas. Riverview was a children's paradise. Now that is gone too" (qtd. in Wolcott 220). A similar loss was experienced by African American communities in Newark, New Jersey, Washington, DC, and Louisville, Kentucky: across the country, the urban amusement parks Black people had fought hard to gain access to either fell into disrepair or closed. Most of them were now being built in the suburbs, inaccessible by public transportation: "this was a public accommodations' version of the 'color-blind meritocracy' historians have found in public discourses around housing and education.

Those who could afford to go to the theme park in their private cars belonged there. Those who could not were relegated to the city with few recreational options" (Wolcott 9).

Part and parcel of the process of ghettoization, this denial of play went hand in hand with that of "urbicide." First coined by Marshall Berman, the term urbicide refers to "the murder of the city" (8). This process of "deliberate denial or killing" of the city (Graham 38) is made possible by "practices of place annihilation," which, by constructing and designating some densely populated and stable communities as "slums," enables their destruction in the name of "urban renewal" policies. Reflecting on Robert Moses's Slum Clearance project, Berman observes how "[m]iles of streets alongside the riad were choked with dust and fumes and deafening noise [. . .] Apartments that had been settled and stable for over twenty years emptied out, often virtually overnight; large and impoverished black and Hispanic families, fleeing even worse slums, were moved wholesale" (290–92). The late 1960s and early 1970s witnessed many such "slum clearance" projects, which disproportionately affected Black and Puerto Rican communities, not only in New York, where Moses's plans for the Cross-Bronx Expressway required the demolition of entire communities, but also in other major metropolis, such as San Francisco, Los Angeles, and Boston.[4]

Alongside these practices of literal erasure of neighborhoods and the displacement of their inhabitants, urbicidal praxes are also enacted through the deliberate neglect of the needs of inner-city communities, through which their presence is denied: "blackness in the Americas is deeply connected to sites of environmental, social, and infrastructural decay," which are constructed as "spaces 'without'/spaces of exclusion, even as those who have *always* struggled against racial violence and containment populated them" (McKittrick 951, original emphasis). Connecting urbicide to Mbembe's "necropolitics" and envisioning the plantation as a "*blueprint* for the modern city," McKittrick interprets the "plantation logic" as anticipating "the empirical decay and death of a very complex black sense of place" and being: the displaced bodies created by urbicide are "reminiscent of those working to death for a plantation economy" (953, original italics).[5]

The construction of the urban space of the ghetto through violent discriminatory practices of urban planning underscores "slavery's mark on the now" (Davis). Loïc Wacquant, among others, has underlined how the ghetto remains closely related to the plantation and the prison, positing their "functional equivalency, structural homology, and cultural fusion," which creates a "*carceral*

continuum" (85, original emphasis). The ghetto becomes a space for the management and control of those "deselected" others borne of late capitalism. Now
serving a negative economic function, this "surplus population devoid of market utility" (87) cannot be incorporated into a neoliberal marketplace and thus
needs to be confined to a space of death. Such a space attempts to efface any
sense of freedom and subjectivity through the erasure of communal links of
support. Much like the plantation and the prison, the ghetto attempts to create
a space of social death where people are transformed into "walking corpses"
living a death-in-life via the removal of informal networks of social support.
Through the infrastructural decay that characterizes processes of urbicide,
rendered imaginable by a plantation logic, the construction of the ghetto as
a carceral space of death-in-life displaces and erases maternal praxes of play
and their related insurgent modes of Black social life: via a matricidal process,
urbicide strives to perform the "onticide" of Black being, enforcing a dynamic
redolent of slavery.

Moses is one among many white officials whose view of the city exemplifies this process of urbicide and its concomitant efforts to erase Black childhood through the withholding of the maternal praxis of play scripted in the
infrastructural deterioration of the ghetto and its construction as a motherless
death-world not dissimilar to that of the plantation. A *New York Amsterdam
News* article dated March, 4, 1939 quotes passages from a letter directed to him:
"The Bedford-Stuyvesant area [a Brooklyn neighborhood known as 'Brooklyn's
Little Harlem'], in which our school is located, is singularly devoid of the bar-
est provision for recreation for young people . . . there is practically no place
where young people may spend their leisure time profitably, without danger,
and without unnecessary temptation"[6] (11). In another letter published in a
1965 *New York Amsterdam News* article, Benjamin F. McLaurin, a co-founder of
the Negro American Labor Council, attacked Moses's social myopia, observing
that his "lack of understanding of and lack of sympathy for children from economically deprived environments: Negroes, Puerto Ricans and all other ethnic
origins, is gross"[7] (9). Other articles published in the 1950s and 1960s testify
to the Black community's growing discontent because of a lack of adequate
recreational facilities.[8]

In *The Power Broker*, Robert A. Caro has noted how Moses opposed the construction of parks for the Black community, even though "the need for new sites
for recreation was acute in black neighborhoods" where "parks, playgrounds,
athletic fields, and recreation centers were scarce and swimming pools did

not exist" (148). Even after a building program had tripled the city's supply of playgrounds, Black neighborhoods remained affected by an alarming lack of adequate recreational facilities:

> 'We have to work all day and we have no place to send the children,' one Harlem mother had written before Robert Moses became Park Commissioner. 'There are kids here who have never played anyplace but in the gutter.' She could have written the same words after he had been Park Commissioner for five years. There was still almost no place for approximately 200,000 of the city's children—the 200,000 with black skin—to play in their own neighborhoods except the streets or abandoned, crumbling, filthy, looted tenements stinking of urine and vomit. (1505–6)

Social surveys linked a lack of play to "the high rates of disease, illiteracy, and delinquency among black youth," casting Black children as violent and dangerous and thus in need of intervention and policing (162). This construction of the city demonstrates that, through a denial of a maternal safe place where to play, the urbicidal process of ghettoization not only sought to enforce a physical and spatial containment of Black people but also attempted to erase Black subjectivities. Constructing the ghetto as a space that creates what is regarded in the dominant order as a form of deviant childhood (and, as we have seen, deviant motherhood and adulthood in general) always lacking or in crisis and thus in need of regulation, urbicidal praxes enabled via maternal erasure aim to foster the construction of forms of death-in-life that pave the way for the civil death of the prison. In this order, not only the maternal but also alternate forms of being human and inhabiting space are erased and displaced.

Moses's plans for New York well illustrate the urbicide that constructed what St. Clair Drake and Horace Cayton termed a "Black Ghetto," or "Black Belt," a space of subordination and marginalization created by whites for Black people, where the latter are contained and displaced through practices of antiblack violence and where housing is substandard, schools are subpar, and recreational facilities are lacking. This view chimes in with the Kerner Commission's conception of the ghetto as a contained place with deteriorating facilities, where "segregation and poverty converge on the young to destroy opportunity and enforce failure" (229).

However, according to Drake and Cayton, alongside this violent space of racial terror exists another one—what they call "Bronzeville," "Black Metropolis," or "the South Side"—which spatially denotes the same space after Black people creatively transform it as a space of sociality and leisure. Upon the grim realities of the Black Ghetto, Black people superimpose a space of cultural richness and social vitality characterized by a "tenacious clinging to life," a "struggle for liberty," and a "quest for happiness" (396). An "object of pride," Bronzeville is *their* city within a city," a world within a world (115, original italics). While Drake and Cayton refer specifically to 1940s Chicago, their analysis effectively captures the simultaneous suffering and resilience of Black people confined in urban neighborhoods where a rich social life endures despite poverty and crime.

As the twentieth century progresses, however, such social ties are put under enormous strain: Wacquant calls the late twentieth-century ghetto a "hyperghetto," which, in contrast to earlier forms, is characterized by a complete breakdown of social relations, alienating each inhabitant. Much like the plantation and the prison, the hyperghetto creates a space of social isolation, where the informal networks of social support that characterized Drake and Cayton's Bronzeville have all but disappeared. While Wacquant is right in noting how the strong communal links and vitality of what Drake and Cayton referred to as Black Metropolis have been progressively eroded during the 1980s as a result of urbicide, Bambara's writing shows how such "tenacious clinging to life" can and has become rechanneled through different outlets. With rampant "urban renewal" projects and other urbicidal praxes, the only alternative to create a "city within a city" remains that of superimposing creativity directly onto a grim urban environment that seeks to erase a Black sense of place and being. The city is transformed into a canvas to be reimagined through playfulness: upon its ruins, another space is superimposed to allow a creative rewriting of place and being.

In the late twentieth century, hip-hop culture originated out of this attempt, and Bambara's writing takes up its creative praxis, reframing it as maternal. Being all about "tak[ing] something that may be scraps and turn[ing] them into jewels" (qtd. in Gates xxxii), hip-hop culture has emerged as a set of praxes—such as graffiti, breakdancing, and rapping—that involved playful forms "of re-invention and self-definition" like self-naming, which for young people have constituted a source "of alternative identity formation and social status in a community whose older local support institutions had been all but demolished along with large sectors of the built environment" (Rose 34–35). In such a culture, improvised playing has been a fundamental element as its practitioners, many of whom were as young as fifteen years old, conjured up makeshift equipment and locales: connecting their turntables to any electrical source available, even streetlights, early DJs turned "streets into impromptu parties and community centers" (Rose 51). While the ghetto has been constructed as a dark place of social death, Black people have always engaged in creative ways to reimagine it, even though the dominant order of Man has provided no means through which to conceive or even render imaginable such Bronzevilles. As Bambara's novel demonstrates, only via a reappraisal of maternal praxis can such a (re)imagination take place. But, however ripe with fugitive possibilities, such neighborhoods remain places borne out of the violent coercive measures of antiblack terror. Can the bleakness of the Black Ghetto and the creative possibilities of Bronzeville, as reclaimed via maternal praxis, ever be unyoked? This is the question Bambara's writing explores.

If in the American urban landscape as well as in its cultural imaginary there is no place for Black being as a result of a denial of a maternal space, Bambara's novel tries to conjure up such a space by tapping into the creative energy unleashed by hip-hop culture. Her work tackles a violent denial of play and thus of being, but she offers more than a bleak portrayal of the urban environment that erases Black childhood. Much like hip hop artists, who made art with the scant materials they were left with, against the brutal setting of the ghetto created by urbicidal-onticidal acts, Bambara holds on to the life and creativity found in the Bronzeville of Drake and Cayton's sociological study: for her, this is the only alternative. Bambara's writing manages to capture both the violence of the ghetto and the creativity of Bronzeville as it transposes the imaginative processes of hip-hop culture from the streets directly onto the written page, performing a literary translation of their playful reclamation of the city and linking it to the maternal.

Even though the wintry landscape and the childless architecture portrayed in "Broken Field Running" seem not to leave room for hope, one of its protagonists, Jason, is convinced that "a whole new era [is] coming, Lacey. A whole new world. A new age" when "we won't mind the snow and the wind" because, as one of the children says, "every sister will be my mother" (51–69). It is this hope for a new age that Bambara's novel, *The Salt Eaters*, written while she was in Atlanta, fleshes out through the narration of Minnie's musical ritual and the community's quest for the maternal. In its eschatological vision of "[t]hem four horses galloping already, the seven trumpets blasting" (46), *The Salt Eaters* celebrates the arrival of "another way to be in the world" (104), which can provide a maternal nurturing space in which Black children can play. Against an antipastoral and apocalyptic urban backdrop, Bambara's novel locates in the destruction of the world a possibility or, to use Bennett's words, "a *revelation, or opening*" (*Being,* original italics) wherein Black life can thrive and a different future can be imagined. Hence, apocalypticism becomes a form of Afrofuturism.

This new "way to be in the world," heralded by thunder and a torrential rain that restores fertility to the land and the whole community, is set in motion by the language of the novel. Mirroring Minnie's, its musicality offers an alternative maternal language, heralding Velma's rebirth and Nadeen's labor. Through its allusions, its use of wordplay, the playful intermingling of standard and African American English to the point that the two become almost impossible to distinguish, and the musicality of its language that recalls a jazz suite, Bambara's writing engages in an imaginary narrative act of play, drawing writer, reader, and characters together and offering a much-needed maternal space to play and (re)imagine subjectivities. Not only the characters but also the readers, as they engage in such playfulness, are rebirthed anew. In so doing, her text's maternal praxis and that of Minnie draw from the transformative playfulness of the emerging hip-hop culture, reframing such a reclamation of space and being as a maternal quest.

Motherless Landscapes?

Emblematic of Velma's and the community's motherless state is the episode where a woman has lost her mother and wants "to be Miz Ransom's baby and her mama's mama all at the same time" (110). Yearning for the maternal, she crawls back into Minnie's lap, which functions as a surrogate maternal womb, and tries to rebirth her mother: "she says 'My mama died and I feel so bad, I can't go on' [. . .] Climbed right into my lap" (8) while "yelling about give her some magic pill. Wanted to swallow her mother and grief with the pill, drink down sorrow and keep her inside, as though a daughter could give birth to her own mother" (110). Against this maternal loss, Minnie steps in as a surrogate mother to replenish the painful void left by the biological one. Calling the grieving woman *daughter,* she rocks her "like the mothers of all times hold and rock however large the load, never asking whose baby or how old or is it deserving, only that it's a baby and not a stone" (110).

As is the case in *Those Bones,* where a missing child's shoe connects the personal loss to the larger tragedy that plagues Atlanta, the woman's grief for the loss of the maternal represents that of the entire community, whose orphan-ages are full of babies: "all them babies; all them babies inside all them places waiting on us to bring'm on home" (119). Connectedness is a central motif in the novel as its complex structure links Velma's story to that of the other members of the community. Velma's husband, James Lee, also called Obie, suffers from maternal deprivation and longs for motherly care, which he momentarily finds in his masseuse Ahiro: "'You sound just like my mama.' For a split second when Ahiro came around the table with his arms outstretched Obie thought he was going to follow through on the mother act and gather him up in his arms" (165). Doctor Meadows daydreams about "a family he'd never had: a mother who ran a boardinghouse and who treated the roomers as kin" (176). All these characters long for the maternal, and through them, the novel epitomizes the motherless state of Velma and the entire community.

Nadeen, the pregnant teenage girl present at Velma's healing, has signed "the papers giving consent for the baby to be taken care of," succumbing to the pressure of the nurses who view her as a "silly child": "Babies having babies" (105–6). Buster, her boyfriend, questions her pregnancy and casts doubt on their baby's survival: "if she was really pregnant and not just trying to fuck with his mind, and if the sucker did manage to grow to anything, well then he guessed it would be cool for the old lady [Minnie] to be in the delivery room when the time came" (113). Both he and his mother want Nadeen to get an abortion and maintain that the baby is not his. Despite Buster's refusal to accept paternity, his appearance gives him the lie. When Ruby's friend remarks that he "looks pregnant," she replies: "You're sharp. He is. His body's taken on the weight his mind still refuses to accept. Very young the girl" (237). Nadeen's maternal experience effaced, her pregnancy is displaced onto a male body.

Not only mothers but children too are missing: racial violence can provide neither a maternal nor a childhood imaginary with which to render legible their being. After his son has gone to prison, the bus driver Fred Holt is incapable of perceiving him as real: "Fred was glad he didn't have a kid anymore. He didn't seem to have a son anymore either when it got right down to it" (154). His situation is emblematic of the entire community, whose "little children [are] brought into the place burned, beaten, stabbed, stomped, starved, dropped, flung, dumped in boiling water. It was a sign of the times" (110). Sons are either "going to jail every time" they turn around, like Fred Holt's, or being murdered, like Sophie Heywood's, whose son Smitty was killed during a protest: "The child Sophie grieved for took another form altogether [. . .] a boy face down in the street, his book bag flattened. The police running the statue like a tank. The package up under Smitty's arm. The other flung across the hind of the first brass horse. The blow that caught him in the shins [. . .] The boy gagging on his own blood face down in the street. The cameras on him [. . .] The blow that caught him in the groin." (14)

Velma's husband believes that all the women he loved "kept killing his babies. Junk food addicts, toxemic pregnancies, miscarriages. Excited mothers-to-be, suddenly sullen and unreachable, terror-stricken, abortions. Pills and foams and curses and shouts and long harangues [. . .] The pattern is clear" (99). Through Obie, the text voices the mother-bashing rhetoric that goes back to slavery when, as Genovese has shown, enslavers were afraid that enslaved women might commit infanticide or use abortifacients (496–97). A similar anxiety around Black women's maternal choices has persisted in the twentieth century as exemplified in Reagan's welfare queen myth and the campaign against crack mothers. As Witt has argued, "African American women have never been 'trusted not to' harm or kill their fetuses" (251). But Velma questions her husband: "What kind of poor, abused sistuh would want to kill your baby, James?" (99).

After having a miscarriage, Velma and James adopt a child, whom they name Lil James, but neither has time to mother him, wondering whether they should "hire help to do the 'mother act'" (139). The night before her attempted suicide, Velma has a strange and troubling nightmare in which her son takes on the semblance of Sophie's dead son: "I think it was Smitty. It looked like Lil James, but I seemed to understand in the dream that it was your son, looking like my son" (219). After he is taken to a yard next to the city's power plant, "[a] shot rang," and she is killed to save him (218–19). Velma's dream symbolizes the plight of the community. Here, there are either childless mothers or motherless children: mothers die or are forced to abdicate their role, and children die or get incarcerated.

Bambara's descriptions of Claybourne chime in with contemporary accounts of poor inner-city neighborhoods where community life was being eroded by institutional neglect and crack cocaine: "African-American children and youth often formed the casualties of this expanding market for drugs, from the increasing number of black children in foster care (Nightingale 1993), to children threatened by violence (Canada 1995), to those killed" (Collins 181). Anthropologist Leith Mullings observes that "[t]he depth of worry about children growing up in these conditions is difficult to convey" (qtd. in Collins 181). If we understand reproductive justice more broadly as the right to rear children in safe and stable communities, then these are all attacks on reproductive freedom (Rogers 15) and instances of "Black maternal necropolitics" (522). According to Césaire, Melonas, and Jones, "Black maternal necropolitics is constituted [. . .] by attacks on the children of Black mothers and by direct attacks on Black mothers themselves, their identities as mothers, which relegates them to zones of nonbeing" (527). Bambara's construction of a landscape characterized by maternal loss underscores Holloway's argument about Black mothers' "cultural familiarity" with grief: "The violent absence of our children [. . .] whether buried in urban cemeteries or interred in rural prisons, forced a consistent reckoning" (56). Bambara's text portrays a world that seeks to relegate Black mothers and children to spaces and states of nonlife, and links this "Black maternal necropolitics" to urbicidal acts of racial terror.

As if unconsciously performing a forgetting of the maternal that mirrors the maternal erasure scripted in the urban landscape, Velma finds herself constantly unprepared for her menstrual cycle: showing up unannounced at her sister's house, she starts "rummaging among sheets, pillowcases, fabric, shoe boxes in search of a tampon or a sanitary pad" (142). At a rally she has no tampons with her and cannot find any either: "She felt uncomfortable, damp. There'd been nothing in the machines—no tampons, no napkins, no paper towels, no roll of tissue she could unravel and stuff her panties with" (26). The vending machines are constructed with uninhabited ghost towns in mind: displaying a refusal to acknowledge Velma's fertility, they cannot register her maternal potential, prompting her to search for a bathroom.

Exhausted and "raking of wasted blood and rage" with "a syrupy clot [. . .] oozing down her left leg," Velma searches for "some water to wash up" (35). Spotting the Gulf sign, she "knew beforehand that the rest room would be nasty [. . .] that she would squat over a reeking, smeared toilet bowl stuffed with everything that ever was" so she prays "through clenched teeth for rain" (35). However, with no better place to go, she finds herself "in a nasty bathroom with no stall doors, and in a Gulf station too, to add to the outrage," "[m]ounting a raggedy tampon fished from the bottom of her bag, paper unraveled, stuffing coming loose" (34). Velma has to do with "no soap. No towels. No tissue. No machine. Just a spurt then a trickle of rusty water in the clogged sink then no water at all" as she is forced to wash herself like an animal: "like a cat she'd had to lick herself clean of grit, salt, blood and rage" (36). The sterile environment of such a bathroom, the result of processes of urbicide, writes her out of existence as a human being, negating her human existence or *bios* and reducing her to mere biological life or *zoe*, thus echoing slavery's erasure of *bios* (Weheliye 36–37). Constructed as an uninhabitable place devoid of human presence, the bathroom forces her reduction to what Spillers has theorized as the "flesh," a process that erased gender difference and enabled the transformation of personality into property during the Middle Passage (67). Reducing Velma to genderless flesh, her erasure of subjectivity throws into crisis the language of motherhood. Much as the apartment complexes in "Broken Field Running" were not planned with kids in mind, the vending machines together with the dirty, waterless bathroom enable a denial of Velma's human subjectivity through an erasure of the maternal and its lexis, echoing and extending slavery's dynamics.

As is the case for Black children, who are scripted as nonexistent by the playless urban environment, Velma's being is erased through the negation of her maternal potential inscribed by processes of urbicide in the decayed urban infrastructures represented by the machines and bathroom, which produce a socially constructed vulnerability. Bambara sets the novel in a bleak urban landscape that seeks to erase the needs of Black women and children through urbicide. Describing this urban landscape, her writing creates a textual microcosm in which we find echoes of racial terror's processes of dehumanization as they become apparent in practices of urbicide that construct human-less urban landscapes.

Through the character of Fred, the novel further connects this erasure of Black childhood and motherhood to the urbicidal processes of racial terror. His visions of ghost towns, rendered uninhabitable, testify to an enforced invisibility that rhymes with that created by parkless housing complexes and waterless bathrooms: "Home one minute, a crater the next [. . .] A gaping hole, a grave, a pit. Nothing to even pass by in a car with the grandchildren on a Sunday drive and point to and say . . . nothing. Nothing [. . .] Eleven dead bodies [. . .] Everything ruined and wrecked, made old and garbage before its time" (73). Recalling race massacres, such as that of Tulsa in 1921, and foreseeing the 1985 MOVE bombings in Philadelphia, which raided an entire Black neighborhood and killed eleven people, five of whom were children, this description also evokes the urbicidal practices described by Berman in his reflections on the devastating impacts of Moses's project of slum clearance. Connecting such praxis to racial violence, Velma's experiences and Fred's visions not only testify to "the material consequences of urbicide in the Americas—burned up, bombed out, flooded, crumbling buildings, and infrastructural decomposition" (McKittrick 952), but they also foreground the human toll of this practice as the erasure of place is linked to a denial of being: urbicide enables the onticide of Black being.

Fred's visions of urbicidal-onticidal acts trigger his memories of his dead friend, Porter. As he watches a young boy carrying a basket of snakes, he thinks about Porter's remarks: "'Can you live? Can a nigger live?'" (78). Here, Porter highlights the death-in-life condition to which racial violence condemns Black subjects.[9] Porter's poignant questions make Fred aware of the precariousness of Black life as he recognizes his bus as "unsafe": the white boys look to him as "just like the ones in the lynch mob pictures" (78). Remembering how Porter was killed for no apparent reason by a mysterious woman who stuck two needles in his neck and of whom "no single witness could offer a description [. . .] no one could say whether she was Black, white, blond, fat or a bear in a wig or a moose in a dress," he concludes that "[l]ife was a danger and every minute" (78). The text's description of Porter's senseless, surreal, and absurd death as well as the "wasting disease [that] was eating him up" (80) foreground the fungibility of Black life, established through the process of enslavement and the gratuitousness of acts of racial terror: "You're minding your business, staying off the streets [. . .] [a]nd some asshole expert releases radioactive fumes in the air and wipes you out in your chair reading the funnies" (79). This makes Fred aware of his own descent into death-in-life as a result of environmental racism: "Knitting needles, snakes, can you manage that? [. . .] 'As we sit here,' Porter used to say, grabbing the edge of the counter, 'we are dying from overexposure to some kind of wasting shit—the radioactive crap, asbestos particles, noise, smog, lies. And Fred would nod'" (79). Through Fred's vivid recollections of Porter, set in motion by his visions of urbicide, the text highlights the death-in-life status superimposed upon Black subjects through practices of racial violence. Linking onticide to acts of urbicide and other practices of racial terror, such as bombings, lynchings, and environmental racism, the descriptions of Fred's recollections foreground the processual nature of this erasure of being.

This racial violence unconsciously engenders a maternal quest through which to rewrite an alternative praxis to remake subjectivities. Bambara peppers this bleak landscape with scattered traces of the maternal that her characters will need to retrieve, suggesting this might be a way to counteract racial terror. Despite the onticide and urbicide of the vending machine and waterless bathroom, which fail to register Velma's presence and deny her creative powers, the force of the maternal erupts: the absence of tampons forces Velma not only to be chronically unprepared for her menstrual cycle but also to acquire some corporeality against the vending machine that would not recognize her. "[C]ertain that she was leaving a red-brown smear on the chair" (36), Velma unconsciously asserts not only her presence but also her fertility and procreative abilities.

Infrastructural decay forces Velma to leave her blood traces in an assertion of subjectivity and visibility against urbicidal and onticidal violence that results in a form of maternal graffiti writing. Such traces or maternal tags function as signposts for the community to retrieve the maternal, but no one can read such creative maternal language as not even her sister or her son knows where to find her. As a result, her sister's maternal potential is thwarted as her period stops abruptly: Black childhood and motherhood remain unimaginable in a context dominated by racial terror unless a maternal recuperation takes place to enable the decoding of such signs.

A Maternal Quest

Through its references to the Grail legend, the novel recounts the characters' quest to restore fertility to the land and its inhabitants, playing with European folklore in a way reminiscent of Morrison's novel *Sula*, where she references the Pied Piper story. When Minnie, shuffling "through these tapes," doesn't seem to find the music she is looking for, her guide Old Wife remarks that "[w]hat you looking for is in the chapel, Min, if you ain't too proud to come and join me there" (47). After this, they walk through the woods headed to the chapel: "See, I told you, Min. You'd be feeling better once we got to chapel" (62). This chapel, which Minnie "was told to [. . .] build" (53), recalls the Chapel Perilous of the Grail legend. After wandering through the woods, the knight comes across a mysterious chapel built by Queen Brangemore of Cornwall, who was later murdered by her son and buried beneath the altar. Inside the chapel, the knight questing for the Grail underwent a "test of fitness for an initiation" into the Mystery ritual: he had to confront horrific visions (Weston 183). However, Minnie's quest is not a solitary endeavor since she is not the only one who is on this maternal quest, and Bambara plays with references to the Grail, mixing them with allusions to non-Western traditions.

Opposed to the motherless landscape and connected to the characters' quest for the maternal symbolized by Minnie is the imagery of the novel: images of water, symbolizing fertility, recur often, culminating in the final storm, and references to the moon, another symbol of fertility, abound. Another maternal symbol that recurs, often linked to Velma, are cowrie shells, whose shape is reminiscent of a vagina with teeth (25–36). Palma wears the cowrie shell bracelets that Velma has given her: in the shop where she bought them, the bracelets are advertised as "MATRIARCHAL CURRENCY" and as "divination tools" (36), linking them to Oshun's maternal powers. Cowries, a potent symbol associated with Oshun, the river orisha or goddess in the Yoruba religion, relates to the power of rebirth and regeneration. This divinity is associated with water, purity, and fertility: in West African cultures, those who want children and who may suffer from infertility call on Oshun for assistance. Oshun's ceremonial colors, white and yellow, characterize the dresses of the people present at Velma's healing: "[y]ellow seemed to predominate, yellow and white [. . .] Shirts, dresses, smocks, slacks—yellow and white were as much an announcement that a healing session had been scheduled as the notice on the board" (11). The room in which Minnie performs Velma's healing is also yellow with white tiles (18). Amongst a childless and motherless world, the novel conjures up maternal symbols that, together with Minnie's ritual, unconsciously engender a maternal quest and enable a reclamation of the maternal.

Velma's desire for rain, which will finally come at the end of Minnie's ritual, manifests her desire for fertility and maternal sustenance experienced by other characters. This yearning for rain echoes a passage in *Those Bones Are Not My Child*, where Mama Lovey confronts her fears following reports of the Atlanta child murders and the temporary disappearance of her grandson, who has just returned: "the best part of her locked him in tight while she prayed for a long, hard driving, relentless rain" (569). Velma's yearning for fertility is connected to her miscarriage, which is characterized as the pivotal moment acting as catalyst for the mental breakdown that leads her to suicide: "maybe the cracking had begun years earlier when the womb had bled, when the walls had dropped away and the baby was flushed out" (94). Her "journey back from the kitchen," where she committed suicide, is compared to a traveling through the woods (34), which she must cross in order to recover the maternal otherworld represented by "that other place where the mud mothers were painting the walls of the cave and calling to her" (8).

The mud mothers are mysterious figures that repeatedly appear to Velma, trying to restore her connection to a maternal imaginary: "In the attic they came in the mirror once. Ten or more women with mud hair, storing yams in gourds and pebbles in cracked calabash. And tucking babies in hairy hides. They came like a Polaroid. Stepping out of the mouth of the cave, they tried to climb out of the speckled glass, talk to her, tell her what must be done all over again, all over again, all over again" (255). Connected to nature and repositories of a suppressed maternal knowledge, the mud mothers represent versions of mother earth goddesses that the novel explicitly links, via the references to yams and calabash, to Africa. According to Joan Relke, mother earth goddesses are mythological figures that appear in various traditions: they can be "Inana, Durga, Cybele, and Sekhmet, goddesses of Ancient Mesopotamia, India, Anatolia and Egypt" ("The Archetypal Female"). Here, as is the case for Mama Day and Mattie Michael in Naylor's novels, they represent a "healer of the soul, someone who helps other people to overcome unbearable mental but also physical pain" (Procházková 11). They perform a maternal praxis linked to life rather than death: against the childlessness plaguing the community, they cocoon babies in their hair, hiding, protecting, and nurturing them. This nourishing praxis of being is "what must be done all over again": through these figures, the text manifests a yearning for the maternal and an otherworld where its nurturing potential can be released, and new subjectivities fostered.

In another vision, the mud mothers are "on the ice building a fire, fanning the babies" to protect them from the cold (115). They are there to shelter Velma but she does not trust their maternal powers: seeing them on the ice rink, she thinks "it's too cold for them babies" (115). These ancient mothers scare Velma, who does not even want to see them and hangs "an old velvet drape over the mirror and smother[ing] them. They were not going to run her off her own place. Not the attic" (255). Velma's maternal quest is rendered necessary by her inability to read her recurring visions of the mud mothers. Refusing to draw from their ancestral source of creativity, Velma is left with no other maternal imaginary but a deadly oven gas, which supplants the cave inhabited by the mud mothers and their babies. Her attempted suicide is a consequence of her rejection of the mud mothers' ancestral powers, and the displacement of their maternal shelter with an oven.

Against a childless and motherless environment, Velma creeps into the oven attempting to regain a lost maternal space where she could feel safe again (5). Recalling Douglass's closeting, Velma's attempted suicide represents her desperate effort to reclaim a womblike space, like that inhabited by the mud mothers, in order to undo the maternal erasure enacted by the vending machines and waterless bathroom: "Maybe the act of trying to sever a vein or climbing into the oven was like going to the caves, a beginning . . ." (147–48). Hearing a melody "thickening as she was sucked into the carbon walls of the cave, then the song blending with the song of the gas" (18), Velma is drawn to the oven, which to her appears as a cave, linking it to her visions of the mud mothers. Much like the woman crawling into Minnie's lap, Velma is seeking to retrieve both childhood and motherhood at the same time. Creeping into this maternal space where she can "be sealed and inviolate," Velma attempts to regain a lost feeling of invulnerability and security: "She tried to withdraw [. . .] the self to a safe place where husband, lover, teacher, workers, no one could follow, probe. Withdraw her self and prop up a border guard to negotiate with intruders" (5). Having no other place to go to for nurturance and shelter, the oven-cave functions for Velma as a womblike space, which she hopes will provide much-needed maternal protection and give her back the child she lost. It is the same maternal space she was looking for when as a child she used to crawl underground and safeguard what bell hooks has called a "homeplace" (42) for her family: "She'd been a borderguard all her childhood, so she knew something about it. She was the one sent to the front door to stand off the landlord, the insurance man, the greengrocer, the fish peddler, to insure Mama Mae one more bit of peace. And at her godmother's it was Smitty who sent her to the front door to misdirect the posse" (5). She seeks to retrieve this maternal safe space she used to preserve in her house.

But the oven is revealed as an illusory proxy for the womb that denies mothering: through her sister's embodied response to it, the text links Velma's suicide to enforced sterility and maternal erasure. While unaware of Velma's attempted suicide, Palma's period stops abruptly when her fragmented memories and recollections implicitly reveal it. Palma surrenders "to the flood of dream fragments, premonitions, replays of conversations: 'Do you think, Palma, that suicides reincarnate more quickly than say—' [s]he was crowded off her chair. And then her period stopped abruptly" (140).

Displacing the nourishing cave of the mud mothers, the oven and its deadly song—like the closet in Douglass's *Narrative* and the womb-machine in Ellison's *Invisible Man*—erase and displace the maternal, further severing Velma from it and aiding her transformation into a ghostlike figure. In a misguided attempt to retrieve a maternal safe space, she lets the oven displace it, making herself more vulnerable to death and violence. Seeing a picture of her sister "with blood-red flowers" where she appears "childlike and vulnerable," Palma feels that something terrible happened to her since her face is "like a blur but the eyeballs [are] black and sharp as though someone had stabbed her there with a black felt pen" (139–40). Much like Priscilla's photos in *Linden Hills*,

Velma's are a sign of her gradual disappearance, which no one can interpret as such: Palma, like Fred Holt, feels an uneasiness she is not able to translate into words. Despite the menstrual blood traces Velma leaves behind or her troubling questions regarding suicide, nobody knows where she is or registers her pain. Her identity negated, she takes on the invisibility enforced by the urban infrastructure. Reflecting on her sister's endless wanderings as she works "odd hours on terminals all over the city" (142), Palma notes that "[h]er son doesn't even know where she is these days [. . .] She rarely remembers to take her pocketbook when she goes out these days. That Velma. She could be anywhere. And no I.D." (145).

In order to remake her being, Velma must embrace Minnie's maternal powers and her "pull toward life" (60). She needs to regain the ability to draw support from the "tug to come on, get up, move out" that had been "nudging her back toward life" when she nearly died in a hotel fire, and when she almost bled to death in a hospital. This pull towards life is represented by her godmother Sophie's caring and holding hands without which "she might have died an infant gasping" (271–72), and is taken over by Minnie's life-giving touch. She is the one who performs a midwifery role, assisting Velma's rebirth and remaking her subjectivity: "I'm throwing you the life line. Don't be too proud to live" (42). Through her embodied musical ritual, Minnie engages in the performance of a life-infusing maternal praxis that undoes the invisibility effected by the ghostly towns, vending machines, and waterless bathroom, converting the deadly sorrow song of the gas oven or "*hambre del alma,* the song of the starved soul" (Estés 4), into a life-affirming maternal shout, "the joyous *canto hondo,* the deep song [performed] when we do the work of soulful reclamation" (Estés 4).

A Musical Laying on of Hands

Minnie performs her ritual under the guidance of her spirit guide, Old Wife, a "teller of tales nobody much wants to hear anymore" (43). Only Minnie can detect her presence. Minnie invokes her help as she is worried that she will not be able to save Velma: "I'm gonna lose the patient too if you don't give me some directions. She's lost a lot of blood and her system's still full of gas. I just can't seem to generate the energy to bring her back and restore her" (59). Like Circe, Old Wife's age is impossible to determine as the concept does not even apply to her: "There is no age nor death in spirit" (56). She is neither dead nor alive, and even Minnie is unsure and asks her: "You dead ain't you?" She again replies: "There is no death in spirit, Min, I keep telling you" (62). Old Wife lives outside of time as "[n]othing much had changed since she passed," and her "complexion was still like mutton suet and brown gravy congealed on a plate" (51). Having assumed a spirit form, the concepts of death/life, past/present, and old/young do not apply to her and are useless in trying to make sense of her existence: linear time has ceased to exist for her. Like Aunt Cuney, she used to wear men's garments as Minnie remembers seeing her "coming to church in men's overshoes" (56). She also never combs her hair and smells "[o]f dirt and gumbo and wintergreen and nasty salves and pitch [. . .] of everything" (57). When she was alive, she was an outsider and people thought she was "crazy as a loon" and "called me a witch" (56).

She mothered Minnie and the other kids, telling them about the past and teaching them how to survive: "We used to like to hear you and Wilder talking over the old days and things like that. I know you know that or you wouldn't've been telling us kids things to do and think about and read and check out and reach for. We couldn't've grown up without you, Old Wife. None of us" (57). Against the sterile, childless world envisaged by the designers of apartment complexes, vending machines, and Gulf station bathrooms, Old Wife created an otherworld where life could be restored through maternal nurturance. Minnie now carries on this creative ability. If motherhood in the Black community is threatened to the point that mothers themselves start to seem a mere fiction, Minnie remains a tangible presence: "even Buster had said Miss Ransom was for real, and Buster didn't even say that about his own mother" (113). The maternal can become imaginable through her presence.

Mothered by Old Wife, Minnie performs a similar othermotherly role for the community and for Velma. She refers to her as a daughter, asking Old Wife: "Tell me, how do I welcome this daughter home to the world?" (44). Minnie reminds Velma of her own mother: when Minnie says 'Hold on' "the way Mama Mae would say it," Velma recalls her mother washing her hair, "leaving her bent in the sink while she went to get a washcloth to wipe the shampoo from her eyes" (14). She also refers to the entire community of Black women as daughters, musing "What happened to the daughters of the yam? Seem like they just don't know how to draw up the powers from the deep like before" (44). Feeling a deep connection with the children of the community, whom she now sees "going up in flames," Minnie is committed to save them: "I'd throw that blanket over them chirren's head like a kidnap snatching sack and throw'm on the ground and roll'm in the dirt and jump all over them to smother out the flames till fire turn'm loose and they can live. Like you say, ole gal, the chirren are our glory" (62). Having learned from Old Wife, Minnie takes part in the othermothering tradition that, as we have seen, was central to the survival of African American communities. With the rampant infrastructural deterioration of inner cities and the crack epidemic, such communal networks of care not only survived but became even more crucial: in 1980s North Philadelphia, for instance, Miss Nee performed a fundamental supporting role for the children of her community, filling her house with up to a dozen children (Collins 181).

Setting in motion a "pattern of growth" against the sterility that plagues the community, Minnie's othermothering enacts an embodied ritual of transformational rebirth. Her maternal ritual is enabled by music and touch as she lays her hands on Velma while "spinning out a song" (4). Reminiscent of Rosalie's laying on of hands in *Praisesong*, Minnie's ritual makes use of this ancient practice, which recalls the rebirthing power of hands in midwifery and consists of using this maternal touch "in a symbolical act of blessing, healing, and ordination" while bestowing some gift (Gabbin 247). Minnie presses "three fingers, warm and fragrant, against Velma's forehead, the left hand catching her in the back of her head" (6), performing a laying on of hands that she has repeatedly used: "Over the years it had become routine: She simply placed her left hand on the patient's spine and her right on the navel" (47). An act of transformative nurturance, the ritual practice of the laying on of hands "represents the transmission of a miraculous power that heals, restores, and transforms all that it touches" (Gabbin 247).

Reclaiming an embodied othermothering practice of love and nurturance, Minnie's ritual establishes sensuality and touch as crucial to the transformation of being. Much like Baby Suggs and Paul D in Morrison's *Beloved*, through her maternal praxis, Minnie attends to both bodily and spiritual needs. Grounded in an understanding of the body as connected to the soul, a central concept in many African philosophies, this relational view stands in opposition to the dualism of mind and body that is at the foundation of liberal humanist conceptions of subjectivity.[10] According to Foucault, liberal man is defined "by his freedom, or by the opposition of soul and body" (45). By contrast, as folklorist Beverly J. Robinson has observed, "metaphysical traditions belonging to an African worldview . . . [do] not separate mind and body" (410). For instance, the Akan believe that good health depends upon a harmonious coexistence of the spiritual and material: if one is ill, they concern themselves with both the physical and spiritual aspects of illness (Asante and Mazama 7).

Minnie hums and repeatedly asks the question that opens the book as if it were a chorus: "Are you sure, sweetheart, that you want to be well?" (3). Hearing the discordant music of her patient, which nobody else can register, she makes it melodious through her touch and her rhythmic tapping of her foot (48). As Velma feels "caught up, caught up in the weave of the song Minnie was humming," Minnie drawls out "her hummingsong, unconcerned that any minute she might strike the very note that could shatter Velma's bones" (4). Even when Minnie is speaking, Velma can still hear "the song somehow buzzing right on [. . .] The song running its own course up under the words, up under Velma's hospital gown, notes pressing against her skin" (4–5). Minnie's music confuses Velma, who feels she is "losing her eyes" and is not sure "whether she'd been hearing music anyway," wondering "Music? [. . .] what was this anyway, a healing or a jam session?" (114). Velma tries to "resist the buzzing bee tune coming at her," but she lets herself spin in the music, her confusion culminating in a shattering of her certainties which results in an opening up of possibilities precluded before: "Everything was off, out of whack, the relentless logic she'd lived by sprung [. . .] Anything could happen. She could roll off the stool like a ball of wax and melt right through the floor or sail out of the window" (5). Overwhelming Velma, Minnie's music manages to possess her until she feels that "the music was her own": "the music rumbled in her hands, her feet, against her behind on the bench, all around her. She was surrounded by music and had never felt more at home in the world" (226).

Through her maternal praxis, Minnie is able to transform the carceral space of the hospital, which throughout African American history has often been associated with death and state violence (Holloway 27; Nash 184), into a space for the playful reclamation of life: the Infirmary, where her healing takes place, suddenly becomes a "clean, freshly painted, quiet music room with lots of sunlight" (113) where Velma can play and be rebirthed anew. According to Reed, adult creativity, similar to childhood play, takes place in a protected "transitional psychic area" whose conditions are created by a mother figure who engages in what she terms "mothering the mind" (34). Minnie creates an alternative maternal space of play that functions as this transitional psychic area, engendering a creative remaking of subjectivities through her musical ritual and music-like speech.

Her maternal praxis aids Velma's rebirth through the power of the word or what is called, in West African philosophy, *Nommo*. As Angela Davis has observed, *Nommo* is "the magic power of the word," which actualizes the life force:

according to an African proverb, "the spirit cannot descend without song," a song that is not "rigorously differentiated from everyday speech" (6). This generative power of the word has been at the center of Black music making, in particular that of Black women: "for Blacks, their *being* depended upon a song" (qtd. in Davis 8). Minnie's ritual of the laying on of hands draws from this tradition of imbuing songs with a life-affirming spiritual power that can remake subjectivities, conjuring up a maternal creative space that can offer an alternative mode of being to that constructed by practices of racial terror.

Recalling Mama Day in Gloria Naylor's eponymous novel, Pilate in *Song*, and Aunt Cuney in *Praisesong*, Minnie, through her ritual, performs the role of spiritual mother, a figure central in African societies where they are also called diviners and are highly respected elderly women. During slavery, they performed a central role for the slave community: "On the plantation the diviner also served as medicinal healer, midwife or prophetess. Spiritual mothers also directed and guided seekers through their symbolic travels into the wilderness or world of the dead. The spirit mother guides the diseased person to the ancestors and also takes them through their past pains and alienation" (45). Minnie reimagines and performs this ancestral role, guiding Velma's mind through time so she can revisit the moments in her life that led to her crawling into an oven. Under Minnie's guidance, as Eleanor Traylor has remarked, "Velma enters a region where time melds the dead, the living, and the unborn, where the bold act of the historical is redeemed by the possible" (64).

Through Minnie's maternal ritual of music and touch, which combines the embodied practice of the laying on of hands, the ancestral art of midwifery, and the magical power of *Nommo*, Velma gets access to an otherworld where different times and places coexist: "she [Minnie] had gone off somewhere [. . .] And it seemed that the patient [Velma] was elsewhere as well" (57). Observing them, Dr. Meadows is reminded of "the catatonics he'd observed in psychiatric. The essential self gone off, the shell left behind" (57). Velma sees herself attempting suicide as if she were "in a telepathic vision with her former self who seemed to be still there in the kitchen reenacting the scene like time counted for nothing" (18). She is engulfed by memories and dreamlike visions of other times and places, some imagined, others taken from her past, which rebuild her communal and familial links. Like Avey in *Praisesong*, she feels an umbilical cord connecting her to the entire community: "The silvery tendrils that fluttered between her fingers, extending out like tiny webs of invisible thread. The strands that flowed from her to Minnie Ransom to faintly outlined witnesses by the windows" (267). Linked to the practice of midwives, Minnie's musical ritual provides an embodied language with which to nourish Velma and bring her back from the deadly oven, acting as a surrogate and deceptive maternal womb, to a new life of interconnections.

Minnie's use of music sharply contrasts with and provides a corrective to the lack of communication that plagues the community. Shuffling through tapes to find some music "to say it," Minnie remarks that "[t]hese crazy folks need some saying-it music" (47). Like Perceval, Buster and Palma are unable to ask questions crucial to their quests. Buster, seeking to find out more about the Spring Festival to write an article about it, concludes that "[h]e'd never become a good journalist. He never got what he went after. Maybe he'd just make up something" (129). Interviewing Doc Serge, the manager of the Infirmary, he does not enquire about the obscure instructions he is given: "he left without asking where Dr. Arias might be found or how to get to see The Hermit" (135). Palma, too, is unable to locate Velma because she does not ask crucial questions: "She didn't have time to ask him [her partner] any of the questions forming in her mouth: Had he seen Velma? Heard anything? Was Obie in town? Had Marcus gone by her house, were her children all right? Had there been a burglary or a fire in the apartment? [. . .] Was everything really all right? No time" (141). Like the Grail hero, Palma and Buster fail to ask crucial questions, and like the Fisher King, Velma and the community need to be healed. But Minnie's music will also transform and rebirth them, giving them a new maternal language with which to foster communal connections against the social death to which racial terror seeks to condemn them.

The widespread lack of communication is tied to a linguistic inability to understand the figurative and rhetorical aspects of language, in particular indirection and implication.[11] Recalling a dynamic we found at work in *Praisesong*, this results in an incapacity to engage in the maternal praxis of signifyin(g), defined as a "pervasive mode of language use" where the "*technique* of indirect argument, [. . .] persuasion," and "a whole complex of expressions and gestures" (qtd. in Gates 59) are fundamental. The characters need to (re)learn this complex "second language," which the novel links to Minnie's maternal praxis: this is an educational process that, as Gates has observed, usually happens during adolescence (57).

Unequipped to recognize and interpret signs and symbols, Fred and Palma feel an uneasiness they cannot translate into words. When a woman on the bus points to a flock of birds changing direction, Fred cannot read them as an ominous sign: "What was there to say about this perfectly ordinary sight?" (68). While he can only see a "bunch of birds doing what birds do," Porter "might've pointed out what there was to see, what was escaping his eye" (68). Similarly, the group of women who just got off the bus spotted "[f]lames shooting out of the chimney, but what that meant did not register" (143). Like Palma, Velma's friends are unaware that she tried to kill herself, unable to infer the implied meanings in her troubling remarks about suicide: "Do you think she was try- ing to tell you something?" (216). To them, Velma talks "in an odd way, never quite explaining what the matter was, complaining about sexual harassment on the job but not offering an example in that stand-up comic way she had—no anecdotes, just her reaction. And not saying why this should be getting to her at this late date" (139).

Such inability to interpret metaphorical meanings and understand indirec- tion corresponds to a related difficulty in employing metaphors, and expressing implications and feelings. Palma's boyfriend, Marcus, does not know how to respond to Palma's remarks about her period stopping, unable to register her preoccupation. His indifference is followed by a long list of everything he did not say (142–43). Palma, worried about her period, remarks that "[t]hat was not the way to say it. But how to explain the moony womb and the shedding of skin on schedule? [. . .] How to relay the alarm?" (141). When her friend inquires about her wellbeing, Velma "wanted to answer Ruby, wanted to say something intelligible and calm and hip and funny [. . .] But the words got caught in the grind of her back teeth" (41). The people on Fred's crowded bus lack a language with which to communicate their disparate thoughts and intuitive feelings, and thus remain silent: "No one remarked on any of this or on any of the other remarkable things each sensed but had no habit of language for, though felt often and deeply, privately. That moment of correspondence—phenomena, noumena—when the glimpse of the life script is called dream, déjà-vu, clair- voyance, intuition, hysteria, hunger, or nothing at all" (89). A prolonged silence is also Sophie Heywood's reaction after she hears about the attempted suicide of her goddaughter Velma: "it had so taken her breath away, she could get noth- ing in her throat to work" (148).

Doc Serge laments the fact that he is no longer able to decipher a "language of gesture and rhythm" (136), which he associates with the "new women" and Minnie (136). Dr. Meadows cannot understand African American vernacular language, the language Minnie employs and which, according to Hurston, is a musical language ripe with metaphors and figurative meanings ("Characteristics" 23). He thinks that Sophie "has been introduced by Doc Serge as Nadir" when in fact it is M'Dear: "You mean M'Dear? As in Maa Deeear, everybody's good ole boardinghouse grandma?" (189). He is mocked by a group of Black people, who give him a lesson in African American vernacular English: "Calling people out of their name. Didn't mama teach you nuthin? I won't embarrass you by asking you our names. My name's Thurston, as in need for a beer" (189). Dr. Meadow's incompetence and his inability to understand this second language and perform signifyin(g), as theorized by Gates, are juxtaposed with Minnie's expert employment of the Black vernacular and her playful manipulation of the English language, evident in the scene where she plays the dozens with Old Wife. But it also contrasts sharply with Bambara's proficient use of the Black vernacular, which she exhibits in the numerous seamless movements, in the novel, from standard to African American vernacular English, blending the two to the point of indistinguishability. The text practices a linguistic equality that eludes Dr. Meadow's grasp as he is not able to move freely between the two different discursive universes.

Minnie's maternal ritual offers music as a gateway to a mode of communication that can navigate smoothly between two different realms: "before you can signify you got to be able to rap" (qtd. in Gates 49). Her music can give voice to the unsaid and unsayable, reclaim the maternal, and, much as what happens in the Grail legends, restore fertility to the land and its inhabitants. Her maternal ritual of music and touch engenders a torrential rain followed by thunder, lighting, and an earthquake that shakes the community and restores fertility: "it couldn't be simply a storm with such frightening thunder as was cracking the air as if the very world were splitting apart" (245). As is the case in many religious traditions, in the novel, the storm functions as a metaphor for spiritual renewal, recalling the climatic hurricanes in Hurston's *Their Eyes* and in Naylor's *Mama Day*.[12]

This spiritual transformation affects both Velma and the entire community, enabling them not only to heal but to remake themselves through the embracement of the maternal praxis of signifyin(g). Even though confused and unable to locate the source of the thunderous sound, all the characters are touched by the transformational power of this unusual storm that heralds the descent of the spirit mother "summoned to regenerate the life of the world" (249). As Minnie finishes her ritual and the thunderstorm unleashes, dead people are seen in the streets, sons retrace their parents, and mothers prepare to deliver their babies; all this while Minnie's hands deliver Velma to new life. Fred sees

Porter wandering the streets "nonchalant about the rain, nonchalant about the fact that he was supposed to be dead" (279). In one of the many flash-forwards that characterize the last chapters of the novel, we are told that he "would remember that something happened to him, happened inside, something he knew no words for and would not attempt to describe until six years later when his son was finally able to trace him to the Resettlement Center" (279).

Nadeen reclaims the right to motherhood: "She could argue now with folks at the clinic [. . .] It was always the same—too old to do this, too young to do that. No more" (106). Witnessing Velma's rebirth, she embraces the maternal and feels a sense of connection with the two women: "Nadeen moved closer and would have moved right up to the two stools to join hands with the healer and the woman" (106). She then prepares to go into labor as "the baby, rushing from the front of her, had slammed into her back, turned and was now shifting around trying to distribute its weight. She closed her eyes and panted one two, one two" (278).

Much like Avey and Lorde, Velma is rebirthed by Minnie's maternal touch. As she claims new life, there is "[n]o need of Minnie's hands now so the healer withdraws them, drops them in her lap just as Velma, rising on steady legs, throws off the shawl that drops down on the stool a burst cocoon" (295). Minnie's withdrawal of her touch can only happen after Velma has re-embraced the maternal through music. Welcoming Minnie's transformative song, in one of her last reveries before her final rebirth, she becomes a child "under the quilts with eucalyptus, Tiger balm, honey and lemon, apple cider vinegar and hot salt" with "[h]er mother [. . .] hugging her" (225). Back to a childlike state, she reexperiences maternal care, satisfying a need that had manifested in her childhood crawling, the apparitions of the mud mothers, and her attempted suicide: "And she'd never been closer to whatever it was she'd been hunting for in drainpipes and closets and mirrors and in the woods, listening for through floorboards and doors and heat ducts" (225). Velma's "journey back from the kitchen" has led her to a maternal otherworld where she can be hugged by her mother and nurtured.

After she reexperiences this maternal care, Velma can play once again, re-claiming the sense of embodiment and kinetic orality that characterizes double Dutch. This is a form of Black girls' play that has been theorized as the fifth element of hip-hop culture—alongside DJing, rapping, graffiti, and breakdancing—constituting a communal form of playing in which girls jump the rope while keeping time through music. With the help of Minnie's song, Velma reenacts this form of play as her legs under the quilts move as if guided by her music: "Her legs were moving under the covers as if she'd been riding a bike all day long and rode still. She was discovering that peddling the bass notes can do that to your legs too, the bass vibrating through the feet [. . .] the legs riding the keyboard [. . .] She was ice-skating now, her legs moving under the quilts" (225–26). Having reclaimed the maternal and her ability to play through Minnie's ritual, she can now be rebirthed anew: she throws off the shawl that enveloped her like a cocoon to begin a new life.

As it imagines a playful maternal otherworld, *The Salt Eaters* draws, much like Minnie's ritual, from the "energy that produces all life and influences everything" carried by *Nommo* (Asante 455), partaking of "the powerful utopian function" that Davis has attributed to the blues tradition (14). Avoiding a linear plot in favor of a jazz suite and employing a rhythmical, musical, and oral language, and African American vernacular expressions, the novel performs a ritual song to summon spiritual foremothers through the life-giving power of the spoken word.[13] As has been noted, both its language and structure are suggestive of music, and in particular jazz: Eleanor W. Traylor has called the novel "a modern myth of creation told in the jazz mode" (59). Reflecting on the numerous difficulties she encountered when translating the novel into French, Anne Wicke noted Bambara's "extraordinary ability to capture the spoken word" and the musicality she was able to create through the alternation of monosyllabic words and longer ones (82–83). This resulted in sentences in which the reader could feel the music behind the words: "The raga reggae bumpidity bing zing was pouring all over Fred Holt" (34).

While jazz is an important influence in Bambara's work, her writing practice also partakes in the musical and creative energy of the then-emerging hip-hop culture, as I have argued throughout this chapter. As it mixes numerous references to various cultural traditions—from tarots, chakras, and astrology to Native American healing strategies and African-based mythologies and cultural practices—her text juxtaposes the musicality and playful creativity of her language with her descriptions of a bleak and playless landscape. With its sampling and layering of materials, her novel engages in a literary transposition of rap music, which itself, as Gates has demonstrated, forms part of a longstanding tradition of Black cultural production in which signifyin(g), or repetition with a difference, plays a crucial role: "through the hip-hop generation of musicians, formal signifying is alive and well" (Gates xxxiii). In so doing, it not only links hip hop to the praxis of signifyin(g), but it also reframes both as connected to the maternal.

The rhythmical and oral quality that characterizes Bambara's language, here as well as in her other works, recalls the speechlike patterns found in the works of Hurston and Shange, which she explicitly connects to the maternal. Echoing similar observations in Marshall's essay "From the Poets in the Kitchen," Bambara remarked that her language draws upon that "of Langston Hughes" but also "of Grandma, [. . .] of 'mama say.' Mama say don't let cha mouth get you into what," which she calls "the mother tongue" (59). This maternal language is the result of her searching for "a written language in English that can express the African American experience," for which there are no terms at this moment (58–59). As Walker argues, "no song or poem will bear my mother's name. Yet so many of the stories that I write, that we all write, are my mother's stories [. . .] I have absorbed not only the stories themselves but something of the manner in which she [my mother] spoke" (48). Echoing the function of the songs in *Iola Leroy* and *Song of Solomon,* this "mother tongue," transmitted generationally, marks "its bearers with knowledge of and from the mother" and connects "scattered kin" (Yates-Richard 486). Through her writing, Bambara attempts to recapture and ventriloquize her mother's musical speech, reclaiming maternal bonds. Much like Minnie, the novel performs this mother tongue: its musicality provides a maternal language with which to communicate what cannot be communicated within the confines of the dominant order of knowledge, rewriting Black subjectivity into being and reinscribing it into the urban landscape.

In an interview right after the publication of *The Salt Eaters,* Bambara notes how English "has been systematically stripped of the kinds of structures and the kinds of vocabularies that allow people to plug into other kinds of intelligences" (Wilentz 75). Going beyond such limitations, her maternal language makes available these "other kinds of intelligences" rooted in the ancestral maternal practices represented by Minnie's ritual. Bambara's writing replaces the brutal American grammar that makes racial terror possible with a maternal one as it seeks to find a language with which to (re)write Black subjectivities as other than ontological aporia. Against the invisibility written in the urban infrastructures through a denial of play, her text rewrites Black being into life, reclaiming Black playfulness through the musicality of its maternal language.

In the American urban landscape as well as in its cultural imaginary, there is no place for Black childhood because, as Bambara's writing underlines, there is no place where they can safely play.[14] Even when not legally proscribed, playing can result in death or incarceration for African Americans who dare exercise such a right. Black playfulness remains marked as dangerous to enforce a violent denial of play that erases Black subjectivities. Black people riding a bike can attract the attention of the police: in the predominantly white neighborhood of Eastpointe in Detroit, between 1995 and 1998, the police stopped hundreds of Black kids aged 11 to 18 on their bikes; more recently, in New Jersey, the police detained Black kids riding a bike.[15] In 2014, twelve-year-old Tamir Rice was shot dead by an officer who pictured him as a twenty-year-old adult armed with a gun rather than as a child playing with a toy gun. Jordan Davis was shot because he was playing music too loudly. Racial violence makes Black playfulness unsafe, constructing it as a site of danger in need of violent regulation. As was the case with Emmett Till, Black children are marked as threatening not only because of the color of their skin but also because of their playfulness. This is also evident in the pervasive efforts to police the expression of hip-hop culture. Constructing graffiti as a form of juvenile delinquency and a symbol of civic disorder, police authorities searched for aggressive strategies to reestablish control.

As this chapter has shown, against this racial terror, Bambara's writing taps into the resilient and playful praxes of hip-hop culture, imagining a maternal space where Black social life can be performed through playfulness.[16] While the novel's portrayal of the bleak urban landscape constructed through urbicidal-onticidal processes demonstrates the pervasiveness of racial terror, its musical language clings on to the creativity found in Bronzeville and then reclaimed by hip-hop culture. Linking it to the maternal, her text reclaims playing as an insurgent maternal practice able to remake Black subjects. Playing with language, she invites the reader to do the same as they untangle the complexity of the text. The very act of partaking in the reading of the novel, sharing, and enjoying its linguistic jokes enacts playfulness and establishes a community by choice. Even though Bambara never loses sight of the urbicidal and onticidal foundations of the ghetto, she imagines Black subjects that, while shaped by, are not totally defined by this racial violence: through their playfulness, they resist the ontological erasure that a racist society codified in the playless urban landscape. Rupturing the laws of a brutal American grammar that undoes Black being, the narrative otherworld her writing conjures up enables a playful reimagination of ontology that can offer the hope for "a new way to be in the world" (104). The maternal otherworld that Bambara's writing superimposes upon the grim urban environment highlights a resilient maternal praxis of being, without losing sight of the racial violence that made it a necessity: through her text, Bambara has created a palimpsest wherein both Bronzeville and the ghetto can be seen at the same time, one image superimposing the other as in a double exposure.

If, as Tricia Rose has argued, graffiti and rap constituted "displays of counterpresence and voice," each rewriting the city and asserting "the right to write—to inscribe one's identity on an environment [. . .] resistant to its young people of color," then Bambara's writing takes part in this process of playful reclamation of place and being, establishing it as a maternal praxis. Existing in a maternal space that engages in "a duet with reality," her text performs maternal praxis as an act of play, rewriting the city as a maternal playground against racial terror's maternal erasures. As a result, while acknowledging the deadly and violent underpinnings of the ghetto, Bambara's novel manages to rewrite a different origin story for the ghetto, one that emphasizes a creative, specifically *maternal* continuum rather than the carceral one posited by scholars such as Wacquant.

Conclusion

In her essay "The Condition of Black Life is One of Mourning" (2016), Claudia Rankine underlines the precarious status of Black motherhood:

> Years after his birth, whenever her son steps out of their home, her status as the mother of a living human being remains as precarious as ever. Added to the natural fears of every parent facing the randomness of life is this other knowledge of the ways in which institutional racism works [. . .] I asked another friend what it's like being the mother of a black son. 'The condition of black life is one of mourning,' she said bluntly. For her, mourning lived in real time inside her and her son's reality: At any moment she might lose her reason for living (145).

Writing in the wake of the 2015 Charleston church massacre, Rankine questions the utopian vision of a color-blind society, underlining the harrowing continuities between a past that is not past and a present too redolent of what are, apparently, bygone days. She highlights how Black motherhood remains affected by racial terror, observing that Black lives still "exist in a state of precariousness" in a society in which antiblackness permeates every aspect of life: it's "in the culture. It's in our laws [. . .] in our scientific experiments, in our language" (150). She equates mothering in an antiblack society to living in a condition of perpetual mourning. A similar concern animates her third collection of poems, *Plot* (2001), which voices the struggles of an expectant mother, Liv, reluctant to bring new life into an antiblack world.

Concerns about the precariousness of Black mothering are not new: Rankine's preoccupations chime in with those of Harlem Renaissance writers such as Angelina Weld Grimké. Through the abjection and co-optation of the Black maternal, in Man's dominant system of meaning, Black mothering has been and continues to be tethered to death. As Jennifer C. Nash has noted, "Black mothers in the United States have become [. . .] visible through the frame of crisis, one that insists on their spatial and temporal location in a death-world" reminiscent of the past (4).

While Nash traces how Black motherhood has been able to come into political view only through crisis, she also concedes that Black mothers "refuse to represent themselves as sites of crisis" (15). Discussing the maternal performances of Serena Williams, Michelle Obama, and Beyoncé Knowles, she argues that they reframe Black motherhood as "a locus of Black life": the maternal offers them the ability "to recast the platform from which Black mothers can speak and be heard" (131). If, from the Civil Rights era to the Black Lives Matter era, Black mothers have often become visible political subjects through their public grief, a long-standing tradition of Black women's cultural production has been equally grounded in the efforts, which Nash carefully traces in *Birthing Black Mothers* (2021), to complicate a narrative of the Black maternal as related only or mainly to loss and trauma. As this book has demonstrated, untethering the Black maternal from a death world has the potential to reframe not just the dominant narratives of the maternal but also those of the human.

Through its exploration of maternal praxis, this book has investigated the ways in which African American women's writing of the 1970s and 1980s has tried to grapple with the perpetual condition of mourning to which Black life has been condemned. It has engaged with literary representations of maternal practices that arose in response to racial terror's co-optation of mothering. I have argued that, while these texts do acknowledge the maternal as a site of crisis, they reimagine it as a potential space of life rather than death, establishing Black mothering as not only a site of suffering but also as a site for the reclamation of life. Foregrounding the precariousness of Black being, these texts have managed to rewrite an ancestral archive of maternal praxes and generate what I have termed a maternal grammar able to transform grief into a creative force, proffering an alternative to racial terror's unmaking of Black subjectivities. Through these maternal praxes, these writers have conjured up fictional otherworlds populated by Black subjects who seek to leave behind a perpetual state of mourning and remake their being, resisting the annihilation of Black life perpetuated by racial violence and refusing to be defined by it. Reimagining the Black maternal through a rewriting of an ancestral archive of maternal praxis, these narratives have engaged in a reimagination not just of the maternal but also of the human, revealing the liberatory possibilities of both.

These texts' portrayals of various maternal practices remain haunted by the violence of racial terror, challenging the claims of politicians like Reagan, who heralded the advent of a "post-racial" society. In these works, protagonists and other major characters find themselves in a social context that withholds human recognition from African Americans through the co-optation of mothering, echoing, and extending forms of disciplinary control associated with slavery. But, in response to this dehumanizing pressure, these narratives have managed to rewrite an ancestral archive of maternal praxis that can provide a maternal grammar upon which to base an otherworld where Black subjectivities can be remade.

These texts have thus interrogated the meaning and uses of maternal practice in a context of racial violence; how to grapple with "existence without Being" (Calvin 27), which, according to Afropessimist thinkers, is the status of Black subjects in an antiblack world. Following Patterson, Wilderson argues that "blackness *is* social death" since "there was never [. . .] a moment of social life" (102, original emphasis). If death is the inescapable condition of Blackness so that "one is born into social death" (103), what does mothering mean? Toni Morrison, Gloria Naylor, Paule Marshall, Audre Lorde, and Toni Cade Bambara have all asked through their narratives how maternal practice can take place despite racial terror, echoing questions articulated by writers throughout the twentieth century and anticipating those of Rankine. Unveiling the historical reciprocity between neoliberal and antebellum America, these texts tally with the pessimism of theorists like Wilderson, highlighting the continuity of structures of power and onticidal practices in a way that echoes Afropessimists' insistence on the haunting presence of slavery in the contemporary moment or what Wilderson has termed "the long durée of slavery" (166).

However, these narratives have not lost sight of the countervailing forces, never failing to find life amid death, creating an alternative maternal space or otherworld. Against Claudia's remarks at the end of *The Bluest Eye* that "[t]his soil is bad for certain kinds of flowers" (204), these texts have highlighted the practices that sought to turn a sterile soil into a "garden [. . .] magnificent with life and creativity" (Walker 408). They have shown an awareness of the ways in which Black people, "even as we experienced, recognized, and lived subjection, we did not *simply* or *only* live *in* subjection and *as* the subjected" (Sharpe 4, original italics). Echoing Walker's remarks, Sharpe goes on to note how her mother, despite racial terror, "brought beauty into that house in every way that she could; she worked at joy, and she made livable moments, spaces, and places in the midst of all that was unlivable there, in the town we lived in" (4). As McKittrick reminds us, there are "iterations of black life that cannot be contained by black death" ("Mathematics" 20). In the wake of racial terror's violent erasure of Black being, Black people insist on Black existence; "we insist black being into the wake" (Sharpe 11). Exploring "forms of social life [. . .] which emerge in the world marked by negation, but exceed it" (Hartman 62), these texts have identified the maternal as a primary locus in which and through which an insistent resistance to the imposition of nonbeing can take place. In so doing, they have not only participated in such insistence, but they have also unveiled *how* such insistence is made possible, the labor that sometimes gets relegated to the background if it is not forgotten. Focusing on the processes by which life emerges from unlivable conditions, these works have articulated a maternal praxis of being that radically refuses the invisibility to which Black lives are condemned by racial violence. They have thus revealed how maternal praxis forms part of a worldmaking artistic tradition based upon Black feminist philosophies of being.

While these texts have narrated Black intimacy with death, by finding a way back to the maternal, they have sought to free Black being from the crushing impositions of an antiblack society, suggesting that mothering can offer the redemption Afropessimists negate. Much like the flesh, as Weheliye argues in *Habeas Viscus* can be "simultaneously a tool of dehumanization and a relational vestibule to alternate ways of being" (95), in these texts, the maternal has been reclaimed as a means to reimagine the human, destabilizing its brutal grammar. Expanding Spillers's tentative vision of different "*representational* potentialities" for African Americans ("Mama's Baby" 80), these texts have reframed the Black subject's liminal position as a gateway to a maternal grammar with the capacity to conjure up an otherworld based upon a mode of being far removed from the dominant one.

The toll that racial violence exerts upon Black mothering is a recurring theme in these texts: Morrison's preoccupation with the echoes of slavery in the contemporary moment is also indexed in Naylor's work, articulating a need for a maternal practice that can reclaim the maternal links racial terror disrupts. While these maternal connections remain crucial to the establishment of a maternal otherworld where Black life can be reimagined, neither are these maternal links allowed space to flourish out of the reach of racial violence.

Marshall's *Praisesong* and Lorde's *Zami* offer a more utopian view as they attempt to conjure up Caribbean otherworlds of the mind where maternal connections can thrive seemingly undisturbed by antiblack terror. In Marshall's narrative, *homo economicus's* symbolic order is reimagined via a Pan-African semiotic that allows the performance of a maternal signifying praxis, while the reclamation of a maternal onto-epistemology through an eroticized maternal allows Lorde's text to write a new narrative of origin that reimagines the dynamics of the process of subjectivation.

Unlike Marshall and Lorde, Bambara does not let her reader escape from the harsh urban environment, the direct result of the post-World War II twin processes of suburbanization and ghettoization that have sought to ontologically annihilate Black being via a denial of play understood as maternal erasure. Nonetheless, her narrative strives to imagine the space to play denied by racial terror, constructing it as a maternal otherworld that functions as a palimpsest to superimpose upon a bleak landscape. Merging the pessimistic leanings of Morrison's ending and the more utopian-like undertones of Marshall's and Lorde's works, Bambara's text, through her playful use of a music-like maternal language, imagines a textual otherworld populated by Black subjects who refuse their subordinate status by engaging in an act of forbidden play through the reading of her novel. This is a completely different subject from the one that the ghetto's architecture attempts to produce: Bambara's novel does not accept its erasure of being as she crafts a reader that defies white control in their playful engagement with her writing, reclaiming a different kind of Black subjectivity through the performance of a maternal praxis akin to that of Minnie's.

Trying to envisage a viable alternative to a world dominated by antiblackness, where Black life remains tethered to a state of mourning and nonbeing, these works have all engaged with maternal praxis as a source of a maternal grammar with which to reimagine the processes through which Black subjects are (un)made. Rewriting ancestral maternal practices, they have attempted to undo the process of "thingification" that has sought to relegate Black people to what Fanon has termed the "zone of non-being" (7), refusing the dominant order's imposition of ontological negation. Employing different strategies, the narratives explored here have articulated an alternative maternal onto-epistemology of Black life. Offering a way to think through Afropessimism, these texts have attempted to create otherworlds where subjectivity can be rethought through a reclamation and reimagination of the maternal.

These narratives' articulation of relational, embodied, processual, fluid, and nondualistic ontologies, however limited, has expressed a dynamic alternative to the abyss of death and nonbeing to which, according to Afropessimists, Black being is condemned by racial terror. While never losing sight of the horrific consequences of racial violence, the texts analyzed here have performed a maternal praxis for a nascent ontology that can offer a new articulation of the human, in a way that Afropessimist thought often forecloses. The maternal focus of these texts has allowed a rethinking not only of the grand neoliberal narrative of colorblindness but also of the hopeless and bleak view of Afropessimism. Never capitulating either to facile optimism or to utter pessimism, they have managed to posit a relational ontology, rooted in centuries-long histories of struggle against antiblackness. Rewriting these histories, they have recast the maternal as a valid site of subject-formation while problematizing neoliberal and Afropessimist narratives.

To offer a viable alternative to these narratives, they have identified an archive of maternal practices that emerged from those condemned to the status of "living corpses." They have found in the creative reenactment of this maternal praxis a means through which the transformation into such living corpses can be undone, highlighting the performative nature of the human. Untethering Black motherhood from death, they have retrieved from this archive a maternal grammar upon which to base their narrative otherworlds where the subjectivities undone by racial terror can be reimagined. This positioning of maternal praxis as a starting point from which to rewrite an alternative ontology foregrounds the potential to transcend racial terror's philosophical underpinnings through a creative reappraisal of forgotten histories of ontological resistance that can challenge the current, racialized, and gendered ordering of the human. Exploring the maternal grammar of this ancestral archive, these texts have engaged with and confronted the "ontological crisis of blackness" (Warren, *Ontological* 131) that Afropessimists have theorized.

Afropessimist scholars like Calvin Warren contend that no progress is possible as long as we keep relying on the violent philosophy of humanism, which is founded on antiblack violence and relegates Black people to "the vacuous space of undifferentiation," rendering them as equipment without subjectivity ("Onticide" 395). Warren argues that in an antiblack world, "[b]lacks have function but not Being" (*Ontological* 90), as they are cast outside the human: "[t]he Negro is not a human, since being is not an issue for it [. . .] The condition of this permanent severing between black being and Being is what I call the 'execration of Being'" (27). Warren develops his theory "alongside and against Heidegger": "Heidegger's critique of metaphysics assists us in understanding how metaphysics engages the nothing that it despises but needs [. . .] I, however, depart from Heidegger, since black being is not human being (or Dasein) but available equipment, equipment in human form, that Heidegger does not consider because of his Eurocentric perspective" (28). In his "Introduction to Metaphysics," Martin Heidegger rearticulates the question of Being by asking *Wie steht es um das Sein?* [How is it going with Being?] and positing it as the fundamental question for philosophy, one that metaphysics obscured (1). But, as Warren underlines, what makes this project possible is the nothingness Black being embodies: "black being helps the human being re-member its relation to Being through its lack of relationality" (32).

At odds with "the genealogy of human being articulated by Heidegger," Black subjects lack Being and "inhabit *permanently* the 'zone of non-being'" resulting from an "onticidal enterprise" or "thanatology" (40, emphasis added). Borrowing this term from the philosopher Ronald Judy, Warren argues that "black being is the execration of Being because it emerges through a death sentence, through the death of African existence" (40). According to Judy, "writing the slave narrative is thus a thanatology, a writing of annihilation that applies the taxonomies of death in Reason (natural law) to enable the emergence of the self-reflexive consciousness of the Negro" (qtd. in *Ontological* 40). However, Warren continues, "If reason and humanity are the purported payoffs for a murder, then the Negro has indeed been defrauded. [. . .] Writing, reading, philosophizing, and intellectualizing have all failed as strategies to gain inclusion into human beingness" (41). According to Warren, Black being, situated outside ontology, "is not ontological": Black being constitutes an ontological aporia (31).

In common with other leading Afropessimists, Warren, in his plea to "destroy humanism and its grammar" (407), tends to leave unacknowledged the call for a new grammar of the human, wherein Black being is not an aporia, that is present in the writings of anti-colonial Black radical theorists. Even though he draws upon the work of Frantz Fanon, he seems to forget Fanon's intimation to imagine a Black humanism, which echoes Steve Biko's quest for "a more human face" (108): "We must turn over a new leaf, we must work out new concepts, and try to set afoot a new man [*sic*]" (*Wretched* 40). As Paul Gilroy reminds us, "Fanon, like Césaire actually, is a great humanist," who, like Jean Améry, is "a combative proponent of [. . .] a 'radical humanism'" ("Never Again"). Warren thus misses the potential that can be found in a reappraisal of the processes through which the human has been made and unmade, a challenge that other Black scholars have taken up.

Gilroy, spurring us towards a "planetary humanism," shares Césaire's yearning for "a humanism made to measure of the world" (*Against Race* 357) rather than to the measure of Man: "Our challenge should now be to bring even more powerful visions of planetary humanism from the future into the present and to reconnect them with democratic and cosmopolitan traditions that have been all but expunged from today's black political imaginary" (356). Gilroy foregrounds the potential to "rebuild an alternative by taking cues from the agonistic humanisms of the black Atlantic thinkers [. . .] Readings of the work of Cooper, Senghor, Hurston, James, Fanon, Césaire, Wynter etc. can be combined with the fruits of long-forgotten versions of black feminism with which those endeavors were entangled" ("Never"). While Wynter acknowledges that the omission of Black people remains constitutive of the Western tradition of humanism, she concedes the possibility of rupturing this provincial conception of humanness, urging us not to dispose of the figure of the human but to return to it otherwise.

These Black Atlantic philosophical traditions not only challenge the onto-epistemological authority of the figure of Man or, to use Wynter's term, its descriptive statement of the human. They also attempt to rewrite the figure of the human, drawing from "cosmologies that do not consider individuality, subject formation, agency, temporality, property or groupness in exclusively European terms" (Gilroy, "Never"). It is in these traditions of Afro-diasporic thought that these texts locate themselves. Understanding the human as a continual process of becoming and challenging the onto-epistemological primacy of Man through the reclamation of an ancestral archive of maternal praxis, these narratives situate themselves in the long tradition of Black humanism. Finding in the maternal a way to reimagine the human, they draw a connection between Black feminism, the decolonial practice of Wynter, and theories of Black humanism rooted in Césaire's and Gilroy's yearnings.

If "the construal of *homo oeconomicus* as human capital leaves behind not only *homo politicus*, but humanism itself" (Brown 42) so that "[t]he West has never been further from being able to live a true humanism—a humanism made to the measure of the world" (Césaire 73), the texts analyzed here creatively rewrite the human. Through a reappraisal of maternal praxis, they remake Black being while undoing *homo economicus*. They disentangle the concept of the human from the logic of private property, dominion, and freedom understood as "the function of possession," reminding us that the human is not and needs not be isomorphic to the liberal humanist subject who is supposedly free "from dependence on the wills of others" and is "the proprietor of his own person and capacities, and owes nothing to society for them" (Macpherson 3). Thus, they not only provide a way to unthink Afropessimism by reimagining Black being as other than ontological aporia. They also challenge the current turn towards posthumanism, exposing its tendency to seldom acknowledge traditions of Black and decolonial thought. As these works have shown, the human is not, and needs not be, equivalent to a liberal humanist conception of subjectivity. Rather, such a conflation, or, to use Wynter's phrase, mistaking "the map for the territory" ("No Humans" 49), was the result of the very same processes that have relegated some people to the status of "living corpses." As Wynter reminds us, the conception of the human as isomorphic to Man is merely a provincial genre:

> We have lived the millennium of Man in the last five hundred years; and as the West is inventing Man, the slave-plantation is a central part of the entire mechanism by means of which that logic is working its way out. But that logic is total now, because to be not-Man is to be not-quite-human. Yet that plot, that slave plot on which the slave grew food for his/her subsistence, carried over a millennially other conception of the human to that of Man's . . . that plot exists as a threat. It speaks to other possibilities. (qtd. in McKittrick "Mathematics" 20)

It thus remains crucial to question, as Zakiyyah Iman Jackson has done, "[w]hat and crucially *whose* conception of humanity are we moving beyond?" (215, original italics). In the "racial long durée" (qtd. in Wynter 263) of Man, how can we proclaim to be moving *beyond* the human, if, in the words of Césaire, we have "never been further from being able to live a true humanism—a humanism made to the measure of the world" (73)?[1]

Testifying the presence and resilience of radical onto-epistemologies in what Walter Benjamin has called "the tradition of the oppressed," these narratives have suggested that "we can drift in and out of humanness—and that humanness, like geography, is alterable" (McKittrick, *Demonic Grounds* 146). As Jackson, Cristin Ellis, and Weheliye have argued, posthumanist thought has not only tended to minimize the centrality of racism to the Western humanist tradition it purportedly moves beyond, but it has also often overlooked counter-discourses of the human or "other humanities" available in Black cultural and literary traditions (Weheliye 5). As a growing body of scholarship has shown, the attempt to reimagine the human and the concomitant critique of Western, bourgeoise conceptions of the human as Man are not unique to posthumanism and even precede the current critical turn. These endeavors return to a long tradition of Black theorists and artists who have interrogated the processes by which the human is made and unmade, seeking to reimagine its onto-epistemological order.

We might ask, then, what insights might these ways of living otherwise and their theoretical practices bring to debates about the (post)human? If the displacement of the Black maternal has been instrumental in the processes that created "living corpses" and the related overrepresentation of the human as Man, then the rewriting of an archive of maternal praxis performed by the narratives analyzed here opens up possibilities to reimagine the onto-epistemology of the human according to a maternal grammar. These works share Gilroy's aspiration to elaborate "new ways of understanding humanity and [. . .] new varieties of humanism," building upon "the humanizing possibilities of conviviality and care" ("Never"). They demonstrate how maternal praxis can have a transformative ontological effect, encouraging a rethinking of the human rather than its abandonment tout court. Such a rethinking can begin, they suggest, with a reassessment of the role of maternal praxis in the making and unmaking of human subjectivities. Urging a sustained engagement with Black feminist theories of the human and the maternal, they put forward Black feminist philosophies of being based upon what I have termed *maternal grammar*. In doing so, they highlight that what needs to be left behind are the processes of maternal abjection that engendered the teleological conception of the human as Man. Having begun to unveil these complex dynamics, this book hopes to spur further conversations around the co-optation of maternal praxis upon which Man's onto-epistemic order is built.

NOTES

Introduction

1. Many scholars have studied the persistence of this tradition of othermothering throughout the African Diaspora. See also Isa María Soto (123), Stanlie M. James (20), Stack (1974), and Ruth Wilson Gilmore (1999).

2. See, among others, Jane Mayer, "Addiction's Child: How a Florida Mother Needing Cash for Crack Handed Over Her Baby," *Wall Street Journal*, 10 October 1989.

1. Naming and Belated Breastfeeding

1. While the scene has sexual undertones, the erotic in the sense of a powerful creative force, as theorized by Audre Lorde, is absent.

2. This contrasts with Avey's reclamation of her name in *Praisesong for the Widow* and Lorde's renaming of herself in *Zami*. Both Avey and Lorde actively perform their renaming at the culmination of their processes of maternal recuperation. By contrast, Milkman remains passive and has not yet undergone this processual recovery of the maternal.

3. Anna Hinton focuses on Pilate's motherwork, viewing Ruth as completely abiding "by the rules of patriarchy" (59). According to Soophia Ahmad, Ruth leads a "pathetic existence" and is "immensely passive" (60).

4. In his 2018 biography of Harlem Renaissance's leader Alain Locke, Stewart recounts the story of Locke's "eccentric" wake for his mother, when he seated and dressed her "as if alive" (6). He interprets her role in his life as stifling and "dominating," highlighting his inability "to separate from his mother. Even death did not finally sever that cord" (7).

5. O'Reilly makes a similar claim arguing that, through her mothering, Sethe seeks to counteract "the commodification of African Americans under slavery and the resulting disruption of the African American motherline" (139).

6. While Wyatt and Demetrakopoulos argue that Sethe's mothering is self-effacing (476; 52), Patton underlines the selfishness that drives her consuming love (128). Mock has argued that nursing in *Beloved* is a symbol of both ownership and loving communion (120).

7. Well-known instances of this trend are the cases of Malcom X, previously Malcolm Little, who replaced his surname with an "X," and Stokely Carmichael, a prominent leader of Black nationalism, who changed his name to Kwame Ture. Since naming is "inevitably genealogical revisionism" (Benston 667), African Americans were refashioning a new, self-made identity as

free subjects and recreating a sense of heritage and communal identity, which the slave system violently negated.

8. Many scholars have studied the persistence of this tradition throughout the African Diaspora. See also Isa María Soto (123), Stanlie M. James (20), Stack (1974), and Ruth Wilson Gilmore (1999).

9. According to this myth, also central in Marshall's novel, Ibo's Landing was "the place where they bring the Ibos over in a slave ship and when they get here, they ain't like it so they all start singing and they march right down in the river to march back to Africa" (qtd. in Brown 121). According to historian Ras Michael Brown, this orally transmitted story is a central "mythical narrative in the collective imagination of African-descended communities" (121). Even though it does not contain the flying motif, the Ibo Landing story is similar to the Flying African legend as both recount the story of enslaved people who leave slavery and travel back to African through supernatural means (Walters 19).

10. In *Dialectic of Enlightenment,* Adorno and Horkheimer read Homer's epic as a "civilizing" text, bearing the traces of the conflict between enlightenment and myth. In their analysis, they treat Odysseus as a *homo economicus* figure, comparing him to Robinson Crusoe (48–49). According to them, "the *Odyssey* is already a Robinsonade" (48), and Odysseus's isolation, like Crusoe's, forces him "into a ruthless pursuit of [his] atomistic interest," embodying the principle of capitalist economy even before he makes use of any worker (48). Treating people as objects to fulfill his needs, he "lives according to the principle which originally constituted bourgeois society": radical alienation (48). Detached from his senses, he cannot "give way to [the] self-abandonment" and the self-dissolution that the Sirens' and Circe's magic can engender.

2. Human-Making Mourning

1. As Genovese has observed with respect to Jamaican slave societies, enslaved people often buried their dead in the garden, which thus not only served as a source of food but also acquired a "religious significance and contributed to the slaves' sense of familial roots:" it constituted a "social center" that provided a "a strong basis for the development of an independent spirit" (537–39).

2. Drawing on Foucault and Mignolo, in her article "Unsettling the Coloniality" Wynter shows how our present conception of the human (Western bourgeoise) is a culturally and historically specific one. Describing the different genres or modes of being human, she argues that our present one originated in the fifteenth/sixteenth century as a reaction the previous conception of the human as a religious being.

3. Holloway, however, acknowledges that Black churches were hardly immune from brutal episodes of racial terror as they remained highly "vulnerable to white hatred and resentment" because of their racial activism (156).

4. His narrative, which comprises also the voices of other enslaved people, is structured and interrupted by detailed descriptions of food received and denied, highlighting the daily deprivations of slavery. It is mainly through food that his narrative conveys the suffering of enslavement: as Kennedy has argued, "starvation, according to the narrative, is the most potent tool for creating slaves out of men" (513).

3. Performing a Pan-African Semiotic

1. As Morales-Franceschini notes, while Kristeva's theory has been popular in North Atlantic feminist studies, literary criticism, and film studies, she has not inspired many creative elaborations or debates in Caribbean or Black Atlantic criticism (512). For further critiques of the Eurocentrism and ahistoricism of Kristeva's work see Ian Almond (2007), Gayatri Chakravorty Spivak (1987), and Judith Butler (1989), among others.

2. For an in-depth discussion of the figure of Eshu, see Robin Brooks (161–83), and Susan Rogers (77–93). Eshu-Elegba or "the God without boundaries" (Falola 3) is a divine messenger central in Yoruba religion and worldview, not only in Africa but also "in related religious and cultural traditions in the African diaspora" (Borgatti 165). He can transform into other people, and is commonly regarded as the Yoruba trickster. "Large and small, powerful and gentle, high and low, swift and immobile, present and absent," he is a figure of sharp "contrasts and reversals, and apparent contradictions" (Borgatti 25).

3. As some critics have pointed out, Kristeva's semiotic cannot achieve anything more than a mere episodic relevance: see Butler 1988 (110–11), Fraser 1992 (56), Gallop (1982, 115), and Jones (1984, 60), among others.

4. Genderless and ageless, Eshu is the trickster god that rules the interpretative process: in Ifa divination, they represent plurality of meanings or indeterminacy (Gates, *The Signifying Monkey* 40). Much like their African American heir, the Signifyin(g) Monkey, they embody the ambiguities of language and "represent the figure of an oral writing" (42). As such, they evoke Kristeva's theorization of the pre-Oedipal mother, a figure that "encompasses both masculinity and femininity" and is associated with "the fluid motility" of the semiotic, troubling all fixed positions (34). Aunt Cuney is similarly described as inhabiting a realm of indeterminacy, eschewing easy categorizations relating to both age and gender.

5. It recalls Joshua Bennett's description of his grandmother's beauty salon as "refuge" and "haven," a place where "there was no such thing as death" in spite of the racial violence of the outside world: "an entire atmosphere of sounds and smells too perfect to have been engineered on planet Earth. [. . .] what we built in that place was indeed a refuge, but it was also something infinitely greater than that. It was a world on and in our own terms. A haven and a home" ("Where is Black Life Lived? A Letter Home from Joshua Bennett").

4. Erotically Rewriting Maternal Connections

1. Carbon tetrachloride, a manufactured chemical that does not occur naturally, is one of the most potent hepatotoxins. Exposure to high concentrations of it causes liver and kidney damage, and it can also lead to coma and death.

2. Marcus Rediker notes how the slave ship's "capacity to incarcerate and transport African bodies had helped to bring into existence a new Atlantic order of labor, plantations, trade, empire, and capitalism" (72).

5. Maternally Reimagining the Urban Landscape

1. In one instance of Bambara's use of humor, the healer, Minnie, and the ancestor, Old Wife, play the dozens with each other because the healing is not going well.

2. See Robert D. McFadden, "Power Failure Blacks Out New York," *New York Times*, 14 July 1977, p. A1.

3. "Child Play Is Taught to Mothers in Ghetto," *New York Times*, 1 October 1972, 98.

4. For a detailed discussion see Mollenkopf, *The Contested City*.

5. This 'plantation logic' "spacialized the complementary workings of modernity, land exploitation, and anti-Black violence" (McKittrick 951).

6. "Seeks Recreation Park for Bedford-Stuyvesant Section," *New York Amsterdam News*, 4 March 1939, 11.

7. See "McLaurin Cites Moses on Lacking Sympathy for Kids," *New York Amsterdam News*, 16 October 1965, 9.

8. See, for instance, "Ask Wagner to Drop Robert Moses," *New York Amsterdam News*, Dec 26, 1953, 25; and "Moses is Assailed on Play Situation," *New York Amsterdam News*, 22 June 1940, 8.

9. According to Warren, in an antiblack society, Black people live in a state of nonbeing (*Ontological Terror*).

10. One of the founders of such a view of human subjectivity, René Descartes, in his *Meditations*, affirms this fundamental dualism when he declares: "I recognize that if a foot or arm or any other part of the body is cut off, nothing has thereby been taken away from the mind" (120).

11. Velma's remarks about suicide refer indirectly to herself even though she phrases them in more general terms; however, her friends do not understand such indirect implications.

12. In Hurston's *Mules and Men*, Zora's initiation as a practitioner of hoodoo is similarly marked by a storm symbolism: she is given the name "Rain-Bringer," and her mentor "painted the lighting symbol down my back from my right shoulder to my left hip. This was to be my sign forever. The Great One was to speak to me in storms" (210). In *Their Eyes Were Watching God*, after the hurricane, Janie is able to find her own voice, completing her journey into womanhood and self-possession. In *Mama Day*, Cocoa embraces the maternal knowledge of Mama Day as a result of the hurricane.

13. For a further discussion of these aspects, see Cheryl A. Wall (2009, 27–44).

14. As we have seen in chapter one, there is not even place for Black manhood. As Dumas and Nelson have observed, since Black males are not recognized as humans, even manhood is not fully available (38). The adultification of Black children is "no guarantee of social or human recognition" (38). This chapter, however, focuses on the erasure of childhood and motherhood since *The Salt Eaters*, I argue, offers Minnie's fertility ritual as an antidote to this issue.

15. See the 2002 article "Biking While Black" by Elizabeth Rusch and the article "Outrage Grows After Police Confiscate Bikes from Black Teenagers and Arrest One of Them in Viral Video" published on April 20, 2021, in *Independent*.

16. However, it is important to note that hip hop culture, especially in its later phases, has also been heavily commercialized and capitalized, developing a highly contradictory relationship with dominant culture. However, a discussion of these aspects is beyond the scope of this book. For a more in-depth overview, see Tricia Rose, *Black Noise*.

Conclusion

1. Jennifer Adams and Matthew Weinstein have acknowledged that Western academics "need to look to how other knowledge systems have described concepts of being human" before laying claim to the notion of posthumanism (243).

WORKS CITED

Adams, Jennifer D., and Matthew Weinstein. "Sylvia Wynter: Science Studies and Post-humanism as Praxes of Being Human." *Cultural Studies, Critical Methodologies*, vol. 20, no. 3, 2020, pp. 235–50.

Adorno, Theodor W., and Max Horkheimer. *Dialectic of Enlightenment*. Verso, 1997.

Agamben, Giorgio. *Homo Sacer: Sovereign Power and Bare Life*. Stanford University Press, 1998.

Ahmad, Soophia. "Women Who Make a Man: Female Protagonists in Toni Morrison's *Song of Solomon*." *ATENEA*, vol. 28, no. 2, December 2008, pp. 59–73.

Alexander, Michelle. *The New Jim Crow: Mass Incarceration in the Age of Colorblindness*. Revised edition. New Press, 2012.

Alger, Horatio. *Ragged Dick: Street Life in New York with the Boot-Blacks*. Duke Classics, 2012.

Almond, Ian. *The New Orientalists: Postmodern Representations of Islam from Foucault to Baudrillard*. I.B. Tauris, 2007.

Andrews, William L. *Critical Essays on Frederick Douglass*. G.K. Hall, 1991.

Asante, Molefi Kete. *The Afrocentric Idea*. Temple University Press, 1998.

Asante, Molefi Kete, and Ama Mazama, editors. *Encyclopaedia of Black Studies*. London: Sage Publications, 2005.

Baldwin, James. *The Fire Next Time*. New York: Modern Library, 1995.

———. *Little Man, Little Man: A Story of Childhood*. Durham: Duke University Press, 2018.

Ball, Charles. *Slavery in the United States a Narrative of the Life and Adventures of Charles Ball, a Black Man, Who Lived Forty Years in Maryland, South Carolina and Georgia, as a Slave . . . Containing an Account of the Manners and Usages of the Planters and Slaveholders of the South, a Description of the Condition and Treatment of the Slaves, with Observations Upon the State of Morals Amongst the Cotton Planters, and the Perils and Sufferings of a Fugitive Slave, Who Twice Escaped from the Cotton Country*. J.W. Shugert, 1836.

Bambara, Toni Cade. *Deep Sightings and Rescue Missions*. Vintage, 1996.

———. *The Salt Eaters*. The Women's Press, 1982.

———. *The Sea Birds Are Still Alive*. Vintage, 2009.

———. *Those Bones Are Not My Child*. Pantheon, 1999.

Bambara, Toni Cade, editor. *The Black Woman: An Anthology*. Washington Square Press, 2005.

Benjamin, Walter. *Selected Writings, edited by* Michael William Jennings, Harvard University Press, 1996.

Bennett, Joshua. *Being Property Once Myself: Blackness and the End of Man*. Harvard: Harvard University Press, 2020.

———. "Where Is Black Life Lived? A Letter Home from Joshua Bennett." *Lithub*, 21 July 2020, https://lithub.com/where-is-black-life-lived/.

Benston, Kimberly W. "I Yam What I Am: Naming and Unnaming in Afro-American Literature." *African American Review*, vol. 50, no. 4, Winter 2017, pp. 667–75.

Berman, Marshall. "Among the Ruins: Flaking Paint and Bad Air." *New Internationalist*, vol. 178, 1987, pp. 7.

Bogues, Anthony. "How Much Is Your African Slave Worth?" *Differences*, vol. 31, no. 3, 2020, pp. 156–68.

Biko, Steve. *I Write What I Like*. Picador, 1987.

Bonaparte, Alicia D. "'The Satisfactory Midwife Bag': Midwifery Regulation in South Carolina, Past and Present Considerations." *Social Science History*, vol. 1–2, no. 38, Spring–Summer 2014, pp. 155–82.

"Bones of Black Children Killed in Police Bombing Used in Ivy League Anthropology Course; Remains of Those Killed in 1985 Move Bombing in Philadelphia Serve as 'Case Study' in Princeton-Backed Course." *The Guardian*, 23 April 2021, www.theguard ian.com/us-news/2021/apr/22/move-bombing-black-children-bones-philadelphia-princeton-pennsylvania.

Borgatti, Jean M. "Eshu: Yoruba God, Powers, and the Imaginative Frontiers." *International Journal of African Historical Studies*, vol. 48, 2015, pp. 165–66.

Bouson, Brooks J. *Quiet as It's Kept: Shame, Trauma, and Race in the Novels of Toni Morrison*. SUNY, 1999.

Boyce Davies, Carole, and Elaine Savory, editors. *Out of the Kumbla: Caribbean Women and Literature*. Africa World Press, 1990.

Braxton, Joanne M. "Harriet Jacobs' 'Incidents in the Life of a Slave Girl': The Re-Definition of the Slave Narrative Genre." *The Massachusetts Review*, vol 27, no. 2, 1986, pp. 379–87.

Brooks, Gwendolyn. *A Street in Bronzeville*. Harper, 1945.

Brooks, Kinitra Dechaun. *The Black Maternal*. University of North Carolina Press, 2008.

Brooks, Robin. "Manifestations of Ogun Symbolism in Paule Marshall's *Praisesong for the Widow*." *Journal of Africana Religions*, vol. 2, no. 2, 2014, 161–83.

Brown, Vincent. "Mapping a Slave Revolt: Visualizing Spatial History through the Archives of Slavery." *Social Text*, vol. 33, no. 4, 2015, 134–41.

———. "Social Death and Political Life in the Study of Slavery." *The American Historical Review*, vol. 114, no. 5, 2009, 1231–49.

Brown, Wendy. *In the Ruins of Neoliberalism: The Rise of Antidemocratic Politics in the West*. Columbia University Press, 2019.

Butler, Judith. "The Body Politics of Julia Kristeva." *Hypatia*, vol. 3, no. 3, 1988, 104–18.

———. "Performative Acts and Gender Constitution: An Essay in Phenomenology and Feminist Theory." *Theatre Journal*, vol. 40, no. 4, 1988, 519–31.

———. *Precarious Life: The Powers of Mourning and Violence*. Verso, 2004.

Camp, Stephanie M. H. *Closer to Freedom: Enslaved Women and Everyday Resistance in the Plantation South*. University of North Carolina Press, 2004.

Caro, Robert. *The Power Broker*. Vintage, 1975.

Césaire, Aimé. "Poetry and Knowledge." *Sulfur*, vol. 5, no. 5, 1982, p. 17.

"Child Play Is Taught to Mothers in Ghetto." *New York Times*, 1 October 1972, p. 98.

Christian, Barbara T. "Ritualistic Process and the Structure of Paule Marshall's *Praisesong for the Widow*." *Callaloo*, vol. 18, Spring–Summer 1983, pp. 74–84.

Coates, Ta-Nehisi. *Between the World and Me*. Spiegel & Grau, 2015.

Collins, Patricia Hill. *Black Feminist Thought*. Routledge, 2000.

Coser, Stelamaris. *Bridging the Americas: The Literature of Toni Morrison, Paule Marshall, and Gayl Jones*. Philadelphia: Temple University Press, 1994.

Davis, Angela Y. *Blues Legacies and Black Feminism: Gertrude "Ma" Rainey, Bessie Smith, and Billie Holiday*. Vintage, 1998.

Dayan, Colin. *Haiti, History, and the Gods*. University of California Press, 1998.

———. *The Law is a White Dog*. Princeton, 2011.

DeLamotte, Eugenia C. *Places of Silence, Journeys of Freedom: The Fiction of Paule Marshall*. University of Pennsylvania Press, 1998.

Dematrakopoulos, Stephanie A. "Maternal Bonds as Devourers of Women's Individuation in Toni Morrison's *Beloved*." *African American Review*, vol. 26, no. 1, 1992, pp. 51–59.

Dillon, Elizabeth Maddock. "Zombie Biopolitics." *American Quarterly*, vol. 71, no. 3, 2019, pp. 625–52.

Discourse on Colonialism. Translated by Aimé Césaire and Robin D. G. Kelley, Monthly Review Press, 2000.

Doddington, David Stefan. *Contesting Slave Masculinity in the American South*. New York: Cambridge University Press, 2018.

Doriani, Beth Maclay. "Black Womanhood in Nineteenth-Century America: Subversion and Self-Construction in Two Women's Autobiographies." *American Quarterly*, vol. 43, no. 2, 1991, pp. 199–222.

Douglass, Frederick. *Narrative of the Life of Frederick Douglass*. Oxford UP, 1999.

Drake, St. Clair, and Horace Cayton. *Black Metropolis*. University of Chicago Press, 2015.

Dubey, Madhu. *Black Women Novelists and the Nationalist Aesthetic*. Indiana University Press, 1994.

Du Bois, W. E. B. *The Souls of Black Folk*. Dover, 1994.

Dumas, Michael J., and Joseph Derrick Nelson. "(Re)Imagining Black Boyhood: Toward a Critical Framework for Educational Research." *Harvard Educational Review*, vol. 86, no. 1, 2016, pp. 27–47.

Eckard, Paula Gallant. "The Entombed Maternal in Gloria Naylor's *Linden Hills*." *Callaloo*, vol. 35, no. 3, 2012, pp. 795–809.

Ellison, Ralph. *Invisible Man*. Penguin, 1965.

Estés, Clarissa Pinkola. *Women Who Run with the Wolves*. Ballantine, 1992.

"Ex-Education Secretary William Bennett Blasted for 'Racist' Comments on Blacks and Crime. (National Report)." *Jet*, vol. 108, no. 17, 2005, p. 4.

Fabre, Genevieve. "Genealogical Archaeology or the Quest for Legacy in Toni Morrison's *Song of Solomon*." *Critical Essays on Toni Morrison*, edited by Nellie Y. McKay, G. K. Hall & Co., 1988, pp. 105–14.

Falola, Toyin, editor. *Eshu: Yoruba God, Powers and The Imaginative Frontiers*. Carolina Academic Press, 2013.

Fanon, Frantz. *The Wretched of the Earth*. Penguin Books, 1983.

Fogel, Robert William. *The Slavery Debates, 1952–1990: A Retrospective*. Louisiana State University Press, 2003.

Fogel, Robert William, and Stanley L. Engerman. *Time on the Cross: Economics of American Negro Slavery*. Little Brown, 1974.

Foucault, Michel. *Society Must Be Defended: Lectures at the Collège De France, 1975–76*. Penguin, 2004.

Fountain, John. "Fear is No Stranger in Chicago Ghetto." *New York Times*, 21 October 2001, p. A20.

Frampton, Edith. "'You Just Can't Fly On Off and Leave a Body': The Intercorporeal Breastfeeding Subject of Toni Morrison's Fiction." *Women: A Cultural Review*, vol. 16, no. 2, 2005, pp. 141–63.

Frey, Sylvia R., and Betty Wood. *Come Shouting to Zion: African American Protestantism in the American South and British Caribbean to 1830*. University of North Carolina Press, 1998.

Gaard, Greta C. "Literary Milk: Breastfeeding Across Race, Class, and Species in Contemporary US Fiction." *The Journal of Ecocriticism*, vol. 5, no. 1, 2013, pp. 1–20.

Gabbin, Joanne. "A Laying on of Hands: Black Women Writers Exploring the Roots of their Folk and Cultural Traditions." *Wild Women in the Whirlwind: Afra-American Culture and the Contemporary Literary Renaissance*, edited by Joanne Braxton and Andree McLaughlin. Rutgers University Press, 1990, pp. 246–63.

Gardner, Renee Lee. "Subverting Patriarchy with Vulnerability: Dismantling the Motherhood Mandate in Toni Morrison's *Beloved*." *Women's Studies*, vol. 45, no. 3, 2016, pp. 203–214.

Gates, Henry Louis. "Frederick Douglass's Camera Obscura: Representing the Antislave 'Clothed and in Their Own Form.'" *Critical Inquiry*, vol. 42, no. 1, 2015, pp. 31–60.

———. *The Signifying Monkey*. Oxford UP, 1989.

Genovese, Eugene D. *Roll, Jordan, Roll*. Vintage, 1976.

Gilroy, Paul. *Against Race: Imagining Political Culture Beyond the Color Line*. Harvard University Press, 2000.

———. "The Holberg Lecture: 'Never Again: Refusing Race and Salvaging the Human.'" *The Holberg Prize – University of Bergen*. May 31, 2019, https://holbergprize.org/en/holberg-lecture-never-again-refusing-race-and-salvaging-human.

Glenn, Evelyn Nakano, et al., editors. *Mothering: Ideology, Experience, and Agency*. Routledge, 1994.

Glissant, Édouard, and Betsy Wing. *Poetics of Relation*. University of Michigan Press, 1997.

Glover, Kaiama L. *Haiti Unbound: A Spiralist Challenge to the Postcolonial Canon*. Liverpool: Liverpool University Press, 2010.

Goddu, Teresa. *Gothic America*. Columbia University Press, 1997.

Goode, Keisha, and Barbara Katz Rothman. "African American Midwifery: A History and a Lament." *American Journal of Economics and Sociology*, vol. 76, no. 1, January 2017, pp. 65–94.

Hamington, Maurice. *Embodied Care: Jane Addams, Maurice Merleau-Ponty, and Feminist Ethics*. University of Illinois Press, 2010.

Hanson, Clare. "The Maternal Body." *The Cambridge Companion to the Body in Literature*, edited by David Hillman and Ulrika Maude, Cambridge UP, 2015, pp. 87–100.

Harper, Frances Ellen Watkins. *Iola Leroy, or, Shadows Uplifted*. Black Women Writers Series. Beacon Press, 1987.

Harris, Trudier. "Reconnecting Fragments: Afro-American Folk Tradition in *The Bluest Eye*." *Critical Essays on Toni Morrison*. Edited by Nellie Y. McKay, G. K. Hall & Co., 1988.

Hartman, Saidiya V. *Lose Your Mother: A Journey Along the Atlantic Slave Route*. Farrar, Straus and Giroux, 2007.

———. *Scenes of Subjection: Terror, Slavery, and Self-Making in Nineteenth-Century America*. Oxford University Press, 1997.

Harvey, David. *A Brief History of Neoliberalism*. Oxford University Press, 2005.

Hausman, Bernice L. *Mother's Milk*. Routledge, 2003.

Hayles, N. Katherine. *How We Became Posthuman: Virtual Bodies in Cybernetics, Literature, and Informatics*. University of Chicago Press, 1999.

Height, Dorothy I. *Open Wide the Freedom Gates: A Memoir*. Public Affairs, 2003.

Held, Virginia. *The Ethics of Care: Personal, Political, and Global*. Oxford University Press, 2006.

Hinds, Michael Decourcy. "The Instincts of Parenthood Become Part of Crack's Toll." *New York Times*, 17 March 1990, p. 8.

Hinton, Anna. "You've Already Got What You Need, Sugar': Southern and Maternal Identity in Toni Morrison's *Song of Solomon*." *Toni Morrison on Mothers and Motherhood*, edited by Lee Baxter and Martha Saltz, Demeter Press, 2017, pp. 53–69.

Hirsch, Marianne. *The Mother/Daughter Plot.* Indiana University Press, 1989.

———. "Knowing their Names." *New Essays on Song of Solomon,* edited by Valerie Smith, Cambridge University Press, 1995, pp. 69–92.

Holland, Sharon Patricia. *Raising the Dead: Readings of Death and (Black) Subjectivity.* Duke University Press, 2000.

Homans, Margaret. "The Woman in the Cave: Recent Feminist Fictions and the Classical Underworld." *Contemporary Literature,* vol. 29, no. 3, 1988, pp. 369–402.

Hooks, bell. *Yearning Race, Gender, and Cultural Politics.* 2nd ed., Routledge, 2015.

Horvitz, Deborah. "Nameless Ghosts: Possession and Depossession in *Beloved.*" *Studies in American Fiction,* vol. 17, 1989, pp. 157–67.

Hull, Gloria. "'What I Think She's Doing Anyhow': A Reading of Toni Cade Bambara's *The Salt Eaters.*" *Conjuring: Black Women, Fiction, and Literary Tradition,* edited by Marjorie Pryse and Hortense Spillers, Indiana University Press, 1985, pp. 216–32.

Hurston, Zora Neale. "Characteristics of Negro Expression." *Within the Circle: An Anthology of African American Literary Criticism from the Harlem Renaissance to the Present,* edited by Angelyn Mitchell, Duke University Press, 1994.

———. *Their Eyes Were Watching God.* Virago, 1986.

Irigaray, Luce. "The Bodily Encounter with the Mother." *The Irigaray Reader,* edited by Margaret Whitford, Blackwell, 1991, pp. 34–47.

Jackson, Zakiyyah Iman. "Animal: New Directions in the Theorization of Race and Posthumanism." *Feminist Studies,* vol. 39, no. 3, 2013, pp. 669–85.

———. *Becoming Human: Matter and Meaning in an Antiblack World.* New York University Press, 2020.

Jacobs, Harriet Ann. *Incidents in the Life of a Slave Girl, Written by Herself.* Edited by Jean Fagan Yellin, Harvard University Press, 2000.

Jameson, Fredric. "Imaginary and Symbolic in Lacan: Marxism, Psychoanalytic Criticism, and the Problem of the Subject." *Yale French Studies,* no. 55/56, 1977, pp. 338–95.

Jenkins, Candice M. *Private Lives, Proper Relations.* University of Minnesota Press, 2007.

Johnson, Walter. *Soul by Soul: Life inside the Antebellum Slave Market.* Harvard University Press, 1999.

Jones, Ann Rosaline. "Julia Kristeva on Femininity: The Limits of a Semiotic Politics." *Feminist Review,* vol. 18, no. 1, 1984, pp. 56–73.

Jones-Rogers, Stephanie. *They Were Her Property.* Yale University Press, 2019.

Kelley, Robin D. G. *Race Rebels: Culture, Politics, and the Black Working Class.* Free Press, 1996.

Kennedy, Dana. "Grandmothers Step in to Rear Children as Mothers Succumb to Crack Drugs: 'The Absence of a Father is Bad, but Now the Mother is Missing,' One Expert Says. Older Relatives are Forced to Care for Another Generation." *Los Angeles Times,* 30 December 1990, www.latimes.com/archives/la-xpm-1990-12-30-mn-10141-story .html.

Kennedy, Kathleen. "'We Were Not to Be Eaten but to Work': Foodways, Grief, and Fatherhood in Charles Ball's Narrative of Slavery." *Slavery & Abolition*, vol. 41, no. 3, 2020, pp. 505–27.

The Kerner Commission. *Report of the National Advisory Commission on Civil Disorders*. U.S. Government Printing Office, 1968.

King, Wilma. *Stolen Childhood: Slave Youth in Nineteenth-Century America*. Indiana University Press, 1995.

Kittay, Eva Feder. *Love's Labor: Essays on Women, Equality and Dependency*. Routledge, 2020.

Kotlowitz, Alex. *There Are No Children Here: The Story of Two Boys Growing Up in the Other America*. Anchor Books, 1992.

Kristeva, Julia. *Powers of Horror: An Essay on Abjection*. Columbia University Press, 1982.

———. *Revolution in Poetic Language*. Columbia University Press, 1984.

Lawrence, David. "Fleshly Ghost and Ghostly Flesh: The Word and the Body in *Beloved*." *Studies in American Fiction*, vol. 19, no. 2, Autumn 1991, pp. 189–201.

Lee, Valerie. *Granny Midwives and Black Women Writers: Double-Dutched Readings*. Routledge, 1996.

Le Goff, Jacques. *History and Memory*. Translated by Steven Rendall and Elizabeth Claman, Columbia University Press, 1992.

Lenormand, Marie. "Winnicott's Theory of Playing: A Reconsideration." *International Journal of Psychoanalysis*, vol. 99, no. 1, 2018, pp. 82–102.

Leverenz, David. "Frederick Douglass's Self-Refashioning." *Criticism*, vol. 29 no. 3, 1987, pp. 341–70.

Lillvis, Kristen. "Mama's Baby, Papa's Slavery? The Problem and Possibility of Mothering in Octavia E. Butler's 'Bloodchild.'" *MELUS*, vol. 93, no. 4, Winter 2014, pp. 7–22.

———. *Posthuman Blackness and the Black Female Imagination*. The University of Georgia Press, 2017.

Litoff, Judy Barrett. "Forgotten Women: American Midwives at the Turn of the Twentieth Century." *The Historian*, vol. 40, no. 2, February 1978, pp. 235–51.

Lorde, Audre. *Sister Outsider*. Crossing Press, 1984.

———. *Zami: A New Spelling of My Name*. Harper Collins, 1996.

Macpherson, C. B. *The Political Theory of Possessive Individualism: Hobbes to Locke*. Clarendon Press, 1962.

Marshall, Paule. "From the Poets in the Kitchen." *Callaloo*, vol. 24, no. 2, Spring 2001, pp. 627–33.

———. "The Mother Poets of My Art." *Caribbean Quarterly*, vol. 46, no. 3–4, Sept.–Dec. 2000, pp. 59–71.

———. *Praisesong for the Widow*. Plume, 1983.

Mayer, Jane. "Addiction's Child: How a Florida Mother Needing Cash for Crack Handed Over Her Baby—Neglect, Violence and Values Born of the Streets Shaped Wonda McNeal's Behavior—She Denies Abandoning Infant." *The Wall Street Journal*. Eastern ed., 10 October 1989, pp. 1.

Mbembe, Achille. "Necropolitics." *Public Culture,* vol. 15, no. 1, 2003, pp. 11–40.

McClintock, Anne. *Imperial Leather: Race, Gender, and Sexuality in the Colonial Contest.* Routledge, 1995.

McKittrick, Katherine. *Demonic Grounds: Black Women and the Cartographies of Struggle.* University of Minnesota Press, 2006.

———. "Mathematics Black Life." *The Black Scholar,* vol. 44, no. 2, 2014, pp. 16–28.

———. "On Plantations, Prisons, and a Black Sense of Place." *Social & Cultural Geography,* vol. 12, no. 8, 2011, pp. 947–63.

McKittrick, Katherine, editor. *Sylvia Wynter: On Being Human as Praxis.* Duke University Press, 2015.

Miller, William Ian. *The Anatomy of Disgust.* Harvard University Press, 1998.

Millington, Gareth Robert. "Right to the City (If You Want It): Marshall Berman and Urban Culture." *Journal of Urban Cultural Studies,* vol. 2, no. 1, June 2015, pp. 177–85.

Mobley, Marilyn Sanders. *Folk Roots and Mythic Wings in Sarah Orne Jewett and Toni Morrison.* Louisiana State University Press, 1991.

Mock, Michele. "Spitting Out the Seed: Ownership of Mother, Child, Breasts, Milk, and Voice in Toni Morrison's *Beloved.*" *College Literature,* vol. 23, no. 3, October 1996, pp. 117–26.

Moore, Geneva Cobb. *Maternal Metaphors of Power in African American Women's Literature: From Phillis Wheatley to Toni Morrison.* The University of South Carolina Press, 2017.

Morales-Franceschini, Eric. "Tropics of Abjection: Figures of Violence and the Afro-Caribbean Semiotic." *Journal of Postcolonial Writing,* vol. 55, no. 4, 2019, pp. 512–26.

Morrison, Toni. "A Bench by the Road: *Beloved* by Toni Morrison." *Toni Morrison: Conversations,* Edited by Carolyn C. Denard, University Press of Mississippi, 2008, pp. 44–50.

———. *The Bluest Eye.* Vintage, 1999.

———. *Playing in the Dark.* Vintage, 1992.

———. "The Site of Memory." *Mouth Full of Blood.* Penguin, 2018, pp. 233–45.

———. *Song of Solomon.* Knopf, 1987.

Murray, Stuart J. "Thanatopolitics: Reading in Agamben a Rejoinder to Biopolitical Life." *Communication and Critical/Cultural Studies,* vol. 5, no. 2, 2008, pp. 203–7.

Nash, Jennifer C. *Birthing Black Mothers.* Duke University Press, 2021.

Nayar, Pramod K. *Posthumanism.* Polity, 2014.

Naylor, Gloria. *Linden Hills.* Penguin, 1985.

———. *The Women of Brewster Place.* Penguin, 2000.

Naylor, Gloria, and Toni Morrison. "A Conversation." *The Southern Review,* vol. 21, no. 3, 1985, p. 567.

Newton, Huey P. *Revolutionary Suicide.* Writers and Readers, 1995.

Ong, Aihwa. *Neoliberalism as Exception: Mutations in Citizenship and Sovereignty.* Duke University Press, 2006.

O'Reilly, Andrea. *Toni Morrison and Motherhood.* SUNY, 2004.

"Outrage Grows After Police Confiscate Bikes from Black Teenagers and Arrest One of Them in Viral Video." Independent, 20 April, 2021, 1.

"Oust-Moses Drive On: Citizen Housing Group Asks Mayor to Drop Slum Chief." *New York Times,* 17 October 1959, p. 48.

Parks, Gordon. *Outside Looking In.* Mobile, Alabama, 1956. Speed Art Museum, Louisville, KY. *Gordon Parks Foundation,* https://www.gordonparksfoundation.org/gordon-parks/photography-archive/segregation-in-the-south-1956#5.

Patterson, Orlando. *Slavery and Social Death.* Harvard University Press, 2018.

Patton, Venetria K. "Black Subjects Re-Forming the Past through the Neo-Slave Narrative Tradition." *Modern Fiction Studies,* vol. 54, no. 4, 2008, pp. 877–83.

"President Reagan's Inaugural Speech." *Human Events,* vol. 41, no. 5, 1981, p. 8.

Prosser, Jay. *Light in the Dark Room: Photography and Loss.* University of Minnesota Press, 2004.

Ramírez, Manuela López. "Icarus and Daedalus in Toni Morrison's *Song of Solomon.*" *Journal of English Studies,* vol. 10, 2012, pp. 105–29.

Rankine, Claudia. "The Condition of Black Life is One of Mourning." *The Fire This Time: A New Generation Speaks About Race,* edited by Jesmyn Ward, Scribner, 2016.

———. *Plot.* Grove, 2001.

Rediker, Marcus. *The Slave Ship: A Human History.* John Murray, 2007.

Relke, Joan. "The Archetypal Female in Mythology and Religion: The Anima and the Mother of the Earth and Sky." *Europe's Journal of Psychology,* vol. 3, no. 1, Feb 2007, DOI: 10.5964/ejop.v3i1.389.

"Report of the National Advisory Commission on Civil Disorders." Bantam, 1968.

Rich, Adrienne. *Of Woman Born.* Norton, 1995.

Rigney, Barbara. *The Voices of Toni Morrison.* Ohio State University Press, 1991.

Roberts, Dorothy E. *Killing the Black Body: Race, Reproduction, and the Meaning of Liberty.* Vintage Books, 1999.

Robinson, Beverly J. "Faith Is the Key and Prayer Unlocks the Door: Prayer in African American Life." *The Journal of American Folklore,* vol. 110, no. 438, 1997, pp. 408–14.

Rodríguez, Gloria García. *Voices of the Enslaved in Nineteenth-Century Cuba: A Documentary History.* The University of North Carolina Press, 2011.

Rogers, Susan. "Embodying Cultural Memory in Paule Marshall's *Praisesong for the Widow.*" *African American Review,* vol. 34, no. 1, Spring 2000, pp. 77–93.

Rose, Tricia. *Black Noise.* Wesleyan University Press, 1994.

Roynon, Tessa. "Toni Morrison and Classical Tradition." *Literature Compass,* vol. 4, no. 6, 2007, pp. 1514–37.

Rusch, Elizabeth. "Biking While Black." *Mother Jones,* Sept./Oct. 2002, https://www.motherjones.com/politics/2002/09/biking-while-black/.

Rushdy, Ashraf H. A. "Daughters Signifyin(g) History: The Example of Toni Morrison's *Beloved.*" *American Literature,* vol. 64, no. 3, September 1992, pp. 567–97.

Salaam, Kalamu Ya. "Searching for the Mother Tongue: An Interview with Toni Cade Bambara." *Savoring the Salt: The Legacy of Toni Cade Bambara,* edited by Linda Janet Holmes and Cheryl A. Wall, Temple University Press, 2008, pp. 58–60.

Samatar, Sofia. "Towards a Planetary History of Afrofuturism." *Research in African Literatures,* vol. 48, no. 4, 2017, pp. 175–91.

Sandiford, Keith A. "Gothic and Intertextual Construction in *Linden Hills.*" *The Arizona Quarterly,* vol. 47, no. 3, 1991, p. 117.

———. "Paule Marshall's *Praisesong for the Widow:* The Reluctant Heiress, or Whose Life is it Anyway?" *Black American Literature Forum,* vol. 20, no. 4, Winter 1986, pp. 371–92.

Shange, Savannah. "Black Girl Ordinary: Flesh, Carcerality, and the Refusal of Ethnography." *Transforming Anthropology,* vol. 27, no. 1, 2019, pp. 3–21.

Sharpe, Christina Elizabeth. *In the Wake: On Blackness and Being.* Duke University Press, 2016.

Shaw, Stephanie J. "Mothering Under Slavery in the Antebellum South." *Mothering: Ideology, Experience, and Agency,* edited by Evelyn Nakano Glenn, et al., Routledge, 1994.

Smallwood, Stephanie E. *Saltwater Slavery: A Middle Passage from Africa to American Diaspora.* Harvard University Press, 2008.

Smith, Carissa Turner. "Women's Spiritual Geographies of the African Diaspora: Paule Marshall's *Praisesong for the Widow.*" *African American Review,* vol. 42, no. 3–4, Fall–Winter 2008, pp. 715–29.

Smith, Valerie, editor. *New Essays on Song of Solomon.* Cambridge University Press, 1995.

Spillers, Hortense J. "Interstices." *Black, White, and in Color: Essays on American Literature and Culture.* University of Chicago Press, 2003, pp. 152–76.

———. "Mama's Baby, Papa's Maybe: An American Grammar Book." *Diacritics,* vol. 17, no. 2, 1987, pp. 65–81.

Spillers, Hortense, et al. "'Whatcha Gonna Do?'-Revisiting 'Mama's Baby, Papa's Maybe: An American Grammar Book.'" *Women's Studies Quarterly,* vol. 35, no. 1/2, 2007, p. 299.

Stanford, Ann Folwell. "He Speaks for Whom?: Inscription and Reinscription of Women in *Invisible Man* and *The Salt Eaters.*" *MELUS,* vol. 18, no. 2, 1993, pp. 17–31.

Stepto, Robert. *From Behind the Veil.* University of Illinois Press, 1991.

Stewart, Jeffrey C. *The New Negro: The Life of Alain Locke.* Oxford University Press, 2018.

Stone, Rebecca. "Can the Breast Feed the Mother Too? Tracing Maternal Subjectivity in Toni Morrison's *Beloved.*" *British Journal of Psychotherapy,* vol. 31, no. 3, 2015, pp. 298–310.

Sundberg, Juanita. "Decolonizing Posthumanist Geographies." *Cultural Geographies,* vol. 21, no. 1, 2014, pp. 33–47.

Tal, Kalí. "The Unbearable Whiteness of Being: African American Critical Theory and Cyberculture." *KaliTal.com.*

Taylor, Matthew A. *Universes without Us: Posthuman Cosmologies in American Literature.* University of Minnesota Press, 2013.

Thompson, Katrina Dyonne. *Ring Shout, Wheel About: The Racial Politics of Music and Dance in North American Slavery.* University of Illinois Press, 2014.

Tompkins, Kyla Wazana. "Intersections of Race, Gender, and Sexuality: Queer of Color Critique." *The Cambridge Companion to American Gay and Lesbian Literature*, edited by Scott Herring, Cambridge University Press, 2015, pp. 173–89.

Traylor, Elizabeth W. "The Language of Salt in Toni Cade Bambara's Re/Conceived Academy." *Savoring the Salt: The Legacy of Toni Cade Bambara*, edited by Linda Janet Holmes and Cheryl A. Wall, Temple University Press, 2008, pp. 70–81.

Troester, Rosalie Riegle. "Turbulence and Tenderness: Mothers, Daughters, and 'Othermothers' in Paule Marshall's *Brown Girl, Brownstones.*" *Sage*, vol. 1, no. 2, 1984, p. 13.

Tunc, Tanfer Emin. "The Mistress, the Midwife, and the Medical Doctor: Pregnancy and Childbirth on the Plantations of the Antebellum American South, 1800–1860." *Women's History Review*, vol. 19, no. 3, 2010, pp. 395–419.

Walker, Alice. *In Search of Our Mothers' Gardens.* Phoenix, 1983.

Wall, Cheryl A. "Toni's Obligato: Bambara and the African American Literary Tradition." *Savoring the Salt: The Legacy of Toni Cade Bambara*, edited by Linda Janet Holmes and Cheryl A. Wall, Temple University Press, 2009, pp. 27–44.

Wall, Cheryl A., and Linda J. Holmes, editors. *Savoring the Salt: The Legacy of Toni Cade Bambara.* Temple University Press, 2009.

Wallace, Michele. *Black Macho and the Myth of the Superwoman.* Verso, 1990.

Walters, Wendy W. "'One of Dese Mornings, Bright and Fair,/ Take My Wings and Cleave De Air': The Legend of the Flying Africans and Diasporic Consciousness." *MELUS*, vol. 22, no. 3, 1997, pp. 3–29.

Ward, Catherine C. "Gloria Naylor's *Linden Hills*: A Modern 'Inferno.'" *Contemporary literature*, vol. 28, no.1, 1987, pp. 67–81.

Wardi, Anissa Janine. "A Laying on Hands: Toni Morrison and the Materiality of Love." *MELUS*, vol. 30, no. 3, 2005, pp. 201–18.

Warnes, Andrew. *Hunger Overcome?* The University of Georgia Press, 2004.

Warren, Calvin L. "Onticide: Afro-Pessimism, Gay Nigger #1, and Surplus Violence." *GLQ: A Journal of Lesbian and Gay Studies*, vol. 23, no. 3, 2017, pp. 391–418.

———. *Ontological Terror: Blackness, Nihilism, and Emancipation.* Duke University Press, 2018.

Weheliye, Alexander G. "'Feenin': Posthuman Voices in Contemporary Black Popular Music." *Social Text*, vol. 20, no. 2, 2002, pp. 21–47.

———. *Habeas Viscus: Racializing Assemblages, Biopolitics, and Black Feminist Theories of the Human.* Duke University Press, 2014.

Weinbaum, Alys Eve. *The Afterlife of Reproductive Slavery. Biocapitalism and Black Feminism's Philosophy of History.* Duke University Press, 2019.

"'Welfare Queen' Becomes Issue in Reagan Campaign." *New York Times,* 15 February 1976, p. 51.

West, Emily, and Erin Shearer. "Fertility Control, Shared Nurturing, and Dual Exploitation: The Lives of Enslaved Mothers in the Antebellum United States." *Women's History Review,* vol. 27, no. 6, 2018, pp. 1006–20.

West, Emily, Erin Shearer, and R. J. Knight. "Mothers' Milk: Slavery, Wet-Nursing, and Black and White Women in the Antebellum South." *Journal of Southern History,* vol. 83, no. 1, February 2017, pp. 37–68.

Weston, Jessie L. *From Ritual to Romance.* Doubleday, 1957.

Wicke, Anne. "Translating the Salt." *Savoring the Salt: The Legacy of Toni Cade Bambara,* edited by Linda Janet Holmes and Cheryl A. Wall, Temple University Press, 2008, pp. 81–87.

Wiegman, Robyn. *American Anatomies.* Duke University Press, 1995.

Wilderson, Frank B. *Afropessimism.* Liveright Publishing Corporation, 2020.

Wilentz, Gay. *Healing Narratives: Women Writers Curing Cultural Dis-Ease.* Rutgers University Press, 2000.

Wilkie, Laurie. *The Archeology of Mothering.* Routledge, 2003.

Williamson, Joel. *The Crucible of Race.* Oxford UP, 1984.

Winnicott, Donald W. *Playing and Reality.* Routledge Classics, 2005.

Wolcott, Victoria W. *Race, Riots, and Roller Coasters: The Struggle over Segregated Recreation in America.* University of Pennsylvania Press, 2012.

Womack, Ytasha L. *Afrofuturism: The World of Black Sci-Fi and Fantasy Culture.* Chicago Review Press, 2013.

Wyatt, Jean. "Giving Body to the Word: The Maternal Symbolic in Toni Morrison's *Beloved.*" *PMLA,* vol. 108, May 1993, pp. 474–88.

Wynter, Sylvia. "Beyond Miranda's Meanings: Un/Silencing the 'Demonic Ground' of Caliban's Woman." *Out of the Kumbla: Caribbean Women and Literature,* edited by Carole Boyce Davies and Elaine Savory, Africa World Press, 1990.

———. "On Disenchanting Discourse: 'Minority' Literary Criticism and Beyond." *Cultural Critique,* vol. 7, 1987, pp. 207–44.

———. "On How We Mistook the Map for the Territory, and Re-Imprisoned Ourselves in the Unbearable Wrongness of Being, of Désêtre: Black Studies Toward the Human Project." *Not Only the Master's Tools: African American Studies in Theory and Practice,* edited by Jane Anna Gordon and Lewis R. Gordon, Routledge, 2016.

———. "Unsettling the Coloniality of Being/Power/Truth/Freedom: Towards the Human, After Man, Its Overrepresentation—An Argument." *CR: The New Centennial Review,* vol. 3, no. 3, Fall 2003, pp. 257–337.

Wynter, Sylvia, and Katherine McKittrick. "Unparalleled Catastrophe for Our Species? Or, to Give Humanness a Different Future: Conversations." *Sylvia Wynter: On Being Human as Praxis,* edited by Katherine McKittrick, Duke University Press, 2015.

X, Malcolm, and Alex Haley. *The Autobiography of Malcolm X.* Penguin Books, 1968.

Yates-Richard, Meina. "'What Is Your Mother's Name?': Maternal Disavowal and the Reverberating Aesthetic of Black Women's Pain in Black Nationalist Literature." *American Literature*, vol. 88, no. 3, 2016, pp. 477–507.

Zinker, Hannah. "Mother Memory: The Maternal Figure and Memory in *Song of Solomon* and *Beloved*." *English Honors Theses*, vol. 6, 2018, pp. 1–22. https://creativemater .skidmore.edu/eng_stu_schol/6/.

INDEX

grammar, 4–7, 9, 11; of slavery, 13–18, 21–24, 26, 40–43, 46, 105–106; the maternal and, 217–218, 221–226, 229. *See also* maternal; Spillers, Hortense

griot, 74, 124, 125

Gumbs, Alexis Pauline, 34, 43

Harlem Renaissance, 220, 231n4

Harries, Trudier, 59

Hartman, Saidiya, 9, 16, 29, 43, 76; "afterlives of slavery," 46; fungibility, 97, 170; slavery and, 180–181, 223

Heidegger, Martin, 225–226

hip hop, 216. *See also* Bambara, Toni Cade; ghetto; graffiti

Hirsch, Marianne, 11, 50, 55, 57–59, 77

Holloway, Karla: *Linden Hills* and, 80–81, 85, 92–95, 106, 113, 232n3; *The Salt Eaters* and, 189, 200, 210

Homans, Margaret, 91

homeplace, 157, 206. *See also* bell hooks

Homer, 49, 68, 69, 70, 71, 232n10

Homeric quest, 49. *See also* Homer; Odysseus

homo economicus, 22, 41, 82–84, 88, 227–228

hooks, bell, 157, 206

hospital, 2; in *Invisible Man*, 17, 37, 40; maternal co-optation and, 38, 63; as carceral space 207, 210

human, 2, 4–5, 7–18, 21–25, 27–36, 38, 40–43, 46, 49, 51, 54, 56, 60–61, 65, 76–80, 84

human capital, 39, 86–87, 91, 98, 107, 227. *See also* capital accumulation

Hurston, Zora Neale, 80, 96, 213–214, 217, 227, 234n12

Ibo Landing, 49, 66, 75, 120–121, 125–126, 134, 136, 138, 157, 232n9

incarceration, 39, 170, 218. *See also* civic death; prison

infanticide, 26–27, 199

Irigaray, Luce, 159

Jackson, Zakiyyah Iman, 228

Jacobs, Harriet: loophole of retreat and, 9, 15–18; meaning of freedom and, 19–22; mothering and, 28–32, 41–42, 68, 163,

170, 176. *See also* loophole of retreat; slave narratives

jazz: funerals and, 93, 135, 136, 197, 216

Jim Crow, 191

Johnson, Walter, 86, 88

Jones-Rogers, Stephanie, 21, 23–26, 39, 79, 105–106

Judy, Ronald, 226

juke joints, 135

Kelley, Robin, 136

Kerner Commission, 194

kitchen: in *Linden Hills*, 99, 103, 109; erotic initiation in, 160, 165, 174, 176, 178, 180, 182; creativity and, 204, 211, 215, 217

Kotlowitz, Alex, 190

Kristeva, Julia, 95; semiotic and, 116–121, 123, 124, 127–128, 130, 233n3; abjection and, 132, 134, 137–139, 168, 152, 157; *chora* and, 161, 162, 164, 174; pre-Oedipal mother and, 122, 233n4

labor, 2, 35, 39, 46, 61, 88, 162; during slavery, 14, 23, 25–26, 29, 106; maternal, 27–28, 80, 106, 108, 223; "fussing" and, 62; the body and, 136; in *The Salt Eater*, 169, 197, 215

Lacan, Jacques, 161, 162

laying on of hands, 151, 152, 207, 209, 211. *See also* spirituality; touch

Leverenz, David, 18

liberal humanism, 76, 81, 84, 225–226, 228–229. *See also* Afropessimism; Black, Sylvia Wynter; *homo economicus*; humanism

Lillvis, Kristen, 56, 75

living death, 21, 28–29, 77–78, 102–103, 120, 132, 143–144, 150, 163, 225, 228–229. *See also* zombie

Logos, 117, 124, 135, 138, 138, 142, 147, 153. *See also* Kristeva, Julia; paternal; semiotic

loophole of retreat, 9; as literary Ur trope 16, 21–22; in Jacobs's narrative, 29, 30–31, 32, 42–43, 68. *See also* Jacobs, Harriet; slave narratives

Lorde, Audre, 8, 22, 36, 52, 222, 223–224; *Zami* (Audre Lorde), 155, 159, 161–183, 186, 215, 231n2; "Uses of the Erotic" (Audre Lorde), 85–87, 160, 231n1; "Poetry is Not a Luxury" (Audre Lorde), 160

lovemaking, 137, 142, 172, 177; Afrekete's, 180, 182

ludus, 185. *See also* play

malnutrition: slavery and, 102; food abundance and, 103. *See also* malnutrition; Naylor, Gloria; Warnes, Andrew

Marshall, Paule, 8, 22, 160, 175, 222; "From the Poets in the Kitchen," 174, 217; *Brown Girl, Brownstones,* 60–61; *Praisesong for the Widow,* 116–158, 163, 186, 223–224, 232n9

maternal: erasure, 1–2, 23, 29, 219; as life-giving praxis, 3–4; grammar, 4–9, 10, 13–16, 18, 24, 26, 40–41

maternal ethics of care, 20, 43, 81–84, 90–92, 107, 109, 114–116. *See also* Naylor, Gloria

maternal knowledge, 176. *See also* creativity; erotic; garden

maternal labor, 23, 25–26, 28–29, 35, 39, 106

maternal language, 166, 174, 187. *See also* signifyin(g)

maternal praxis, 14, 23, 35, 39, 50, 136, 223

maternal quest, 16–17, 19, 47, 68, 74, 123, 187, 196–197, 202–205

maternal reclamation, and the human, 4, 9; in slave narratives, 15–16, 18–20; slavery and, 23; neoliberal reason and, 32, 39, 43; in *Song of Solomon,* 48, 55, 60; mourning as, 80, 94; the semiotic and, 122, 154–155, 158, 159, 161, 163; as reclamation of the city, 180–182, 204, 207, 210, 219, 224, 227, 231n2. *See also* maternal; slave narratives

maternal reclamation of urban space, 185–188, 189–219. *See also* play; playing

maternal rewriting: of the city, 185; of Black life, 185. *See also* play; playing

maternal role, 184

maternal safe space, 156–157, 164–168, 190, 194, 206, 218. *See also* homeplace; maternal

maternal signifyin(g) praxis, 120–121, 123, 125–127, 134, 137, 148, 155–158; hip hop and, 216–217. *See also* Eshu; Gates, Henry Louis, Jr.; Signifyin(g) Monkey

maternal tags, 203

maternal violence: during slavery, 23–25, 27, 29–30, 32, 36, 39, 47; neoliberalism and, 105–106; of the symbolic order, 120–121, 166–168, 186. *See also* Jones-Rogers, Stephanie

matricide, 159, 162–163. *See also* Irigaray, Luce; maternal

Mbembe, Achille, 28, 32, 98, 143, 192

McClintock, Anne, 41, 117, 123

McKittrick, Katherine, 13–14, 30–31, 159, 201, 228, 234n5; *Demonic Grounds,* 11, "mathematics of the unliving" and, 32–33, 223, "plantation logics" and, 192

medicalization: of pregnancy and childbirth, 63

Middle Passage, 4; mourning and, 79, 101, 150, 170, 180, 182, 201

midwife, 47, 60–63, 66–68, 70–71, 78, 123, 151–152, 207, 209, 211

midwifery. *See* midwife

Mignolo, Walter, 88, 90, 232n2

Miles, Tiya, 5, 42, 83

milk, 24–26, 49, 56, 57–58

Miss Nee, 209

moon, 168, 181, 203, 213

Morales-Franceschini, Eric, 119, 143, 233n1

Morrison, Toni, 8, 11, 22, 114, 116, 222; *Jazz,* 78; *Beloved,* 54, 56, 231n5, 231n6, 114; *Song of Solomon,* 44–78; *Paradise,* 44; *Harlem Book of the Dead, The,* 48

Moses, Robert, 192–194, 201

mother, 1, 3; mother-daughter, 10, 11, 15, 17, 19; mother-machine, 23, 25, 27, 29, 31, 35–37, 41, 43, 44–47, 49, 53, 58–59, 61, 63, 69, 71–75, 77, 79, 83, 85, 197, 199, 205, 211, 215, 217

motherhood, 1, 3; slavery and, 38, 39, 41, 53, 55, 59, 65, 201–203, 225. *See also* maternal

mothering: racial terror and, 7–9, 13, 27, 29, 31, 33, 41, 43, 44–47, 49, 55, 58–59, 75–77, 79, 83, 220–221, 223; the mind, 185, 210. *See also* Perry, Ruth; playing

motherless landscape, 193, 197, 203–204, 205, 219. *See also* ghetto; motherlessness; urban environment

motherlessness, 17–19

motherwork, 11, 231n3. *See also* maternal; otherworld

mother-child bond, 10. *See also* Morrison, Toni; mother

mother-wit, 78

mourning: in *Linden Hills*, 79–80, 82–83, 90–94, 104, 110–112, 114; in *Praisesong for the Widow*, 144–145, 220–221, 224

Moynihan, Daniel Patrick: Moynihan Report and, 34–37, 43

Moynihan Report, 34–37, 43

mud mothers, 204–205, 206, 215

mural, 184, 190

music: semiotic and, 120, 133–136, 141, 145, 153–154, 157; as an alternative mode of knowledge, 174, 179; as an alternative language, 181, 186; as ritual, 196–197, 210

naming, 5–7, 44, 58, 74, 195, 231n7. *See also* renaming

Nash, Jennifer C., 1, 36, 210, 221

Naylor, Gloria, 8, 22, 51, 78; *Linden Hills*, 80–116

necropolitics, 166, 192; "Black maternal necropolitics," 39, 200

Nelson, Joseph Derrick, and Michael J. Dumas, 189

neoliberal. *See* neoliberalism; Reagan, Ronald

neoliberal America. *See* neoliberalism

neoliberal reason, 8–9, 21–22; slavery and, 33; *homo economicus* and, 40–43, 51, 61, 63, 72, 89, 98, 141; the maternal and, 83, 85, 95, 101. See also *homo economicus*; maternal; neoliberalism

neoliberalism, 8–9, 21–23; 1980s America and, 33; as a mode of reason, 33–34; Black motherhood and, 34; the human and, 40–43; maternal co-optation and, 88, 113; slavery and, 150. See also neoliberal reason

neo-slave narratives, 20. *See also* Morrison, Toni

new life. *See* rebirth

New York City, 10, 91, 121, 156–157; in *Zami*, 167–169, 171, 172, 178–179, 181; in *The Salt Eaters*, 187, 192, 194

nommo, 210–211, 216

nursing, 23–24, 44–45, 50, 53–55, 59, 71, 231n6

nurture, 6, 25–26, 36, 45–46, 67, 73–74, 113, 136, 146, 215

O'Reilly, Andrea, 11

Odysseus, 54, 68, 69, 70, 73–74, 232n10. *See also* Homer; Homeric quest

Odyssey (Homer), 68–69, 70, 232n10

Ong, Aihwa, 40

onticide, 193, 202, 225. *See also* Afropessimism; Warren, Calvin

ontological annihilation, 21, 26, 167; the Black maternal and, 1–2, 4, 14, 20, 85, 95, 167; during slavery, 5, 6, 150; neoliberalism and, 9, 37, 39, 42; of Black childhood, 188–189, 217–218; Afropessimism and, 224–226, 228. *See also* social death

ontological resistance, 7, 10, 20, 31, 110, 114, 126, 223, 225. *See also* slavery

ontological violence. *See* ontological annihilation

Oshun, 204

othermother, 12, 20, 32, 43, 47, 60–61, 64, 66–68, 70–71, 75, 78, 93; pre-Oedipal, 116, 157, 118–120, 122–123, 125–126, 128, 146, 151, 162, 170, 173, 182, 208–209, 231n1

othermothering, 12, 20, 32, 43, 61, 64, 68, 70–71, 75, 78, 93, 119–120, 126, 209, 231n1. *See also* Collins, Patricia Hill; othermother

othermother-midwife, 60, 68. *See also* midwife; othermother

otherworld, 9–11. *See also* geography; otherworldly loophole

otherworldly loophole, 9, 16, 21–22, 29–32, 42–43, 68. *See also* Jacobs, Harriet; slave narratives

oven: as maternal shelter, 205, 206, 207, 211, 212. *See also* womb

paideia, 185. *See also* play

Pan-African, 119, 122, 131, 136

Parks, Gordon, 190

partus sequitur ventrem, 5, 19, 25, 96. *See also* slavery

paternal, 58, 77, 89, 96; the semiotic and, 116–117, 134, 138, 161. *See also* Kristeva, Julia; semiotic; symbolic

Patterson, Orlando: social death, 5, 28–29, 79, 99, 222. *See also* living death; slavery

performativity, 7. *See also* Butler, Judith; maternal

Perry, Ruth, 185. *See also* mothering: the mind; playing

photography, 103–105, 190

planetary humanism, 226–227. *See also* Gilroy, Paul

plantation, 17, 22, 42, 47, 126, 150; economy, 31; order, 85, 138, 211, 228; Louisiana, 103; as a space of death, 186; the city and, 192–193; logic, 234n5

play: retrieval of, 20, 196; the urban environment and, 31, 37, 43, 184, 186–187, 192–193, 201, 224; hip hop and, 215–216; on the *Bianca Pride*, 131; maternal space and, 185, 197, 219; as a praxis, 210; children and, 188, 190. *See also* maternal space of play; playfulness; playgrounds; playing

playfulness, 132, 144–145, 184, 185, 187, 195, 216–218

playgrounds, 191, 193–194. *See also* urban amusement parks

playing: as a maternal praxis of being 184, 185; Donald Winnicott, 185; Ruth Perry, 185

posthumanism, 228, 234n1. *See also* Black humanism; humanism; Wynter, Sylvia

pregnancy, 63, 122, 134, 139–140, 165–167, 198; medicalization of, 63; Avey's, 134, 139; in *Zami*, 165–167; in *The Salt Eaters*, 198. *See also* birth

pre-Oedipal othermothers, 122. *See also* Kristeva, Julia; semiotic

prison: Jacobs's, 29; civic death and, 39–40; the house as, 68, 107; womb as, 108; enslavement and, 192; the ghetto as, 193–195, 198, 200. *See also* womb

prison industrial complex, 39. *See also* civic death; prison

Quashie, Kevin, 42

racial violence. *See* living death

Rankine, Claudia, 220, 222

rap (music), 195, 214, 215–216, 219. *See also* hip hop; play; playing

Reagan, Ronald, 33, 38, 43, 49, 199, 222; "Reagan mythology," 34; Moynihan and, 35

Reagan mythology, 34. *See also* neoliberalism; Reagan, Ronald

Reagan Revolution, 33. *See also* neoliberalism; Reagan, Ronald

Reaganomics and, 33. *See also* neoliberalism; Reagan, Ronald

rebirth: Ellison's, 3; Douglass's, 17–18; maternal displacement and, 24, 37–39, 40; in *Song of Solomon*, 55, 84, 95, 97; Willa's, 107–108, 110, 112, 121–124, 136, 147–148, 151, 157; Lorde's, 181–182; Caribbean, 183; Velma's, 187, 197, 204, 207, 209–210, 212, 215–216

recipes, 99–100, 102. *See also* malnutrition; Naylor, Gloria; Warnes, Andrew

recreational facilities, 43, 186, 188, 190–194. *See also* amusement parks; playgrounds

Rediker, Marcus, 170, 233n2

Reed, Ishmael, 112

reinvention of subjectivity. *See* rebirth

renaming, 45–46, 58–60; in *Praisesong*, 123, 154, 156; in *Zami*, 175, 179, 182, 231n2

revolutionary mothering, 111

revolutionary suicide, 111

Rhys, Jean: *Wide Sargasso Sea*, 168

Rice, Tamir, 218

Rich, Adrienne, 11

rituals, 29; midwifery, 62; mourning 80–83, 110–114; burial, 92–95, 97, 113, 187; semiotic, 118, 120, 122, 124–125, 131, 134–147, 151–157; eating and, 102; erotic, 160, of rebirth, 181; playing, 185, 196, 203–204, 207, 208–212, 216, 234n14. *See also* laying on of hands; slavery; spirituality

Roberts, Dorothy, 34, 36, 38

Roedinger, David, 92, 113

Rose, Tricia, 196, 219, 234n16

Ruddick, Sara, 11

Said, Edward, 31

sea, 90, 173, 180. *See also* Walcott, Derek

segregation, 191, 194. *See also* Jim Crow

semiotic: semiotic rituals, 118; "Afro-Caribbean semiotic," 119; Pan-African semiotic,
119. *See also* Kristeva, Julia; Marshall,
Paule; paternal

Sethe, 54, 56, 231n5, 231n6. *See also* Morrison,
Toni

Sharpe, Christina, 79–80, 222–223

Shaw, Stephanie, 24, 27

ship: Middle Passage and, 10, 79; cruise, 122,
123, 128, 130, 132, 133, 134; slavery and,
150, 170, 232n9, 233n2

signifyin(g), 116–117, 118–119, 214; the
semiotic and, 120–121, 123, 125–127, 134,
137, 148, 155–158; hip hop and, 216–217.
See also Eshu; Gates, Henry Louis, Jr.;
Marshall, Paule; Signifyin(g) Monkey

Signifyin(g) Monkey, 116, 118, 120, 125–126,
148, 157–158, 233n4. *See also* Eshu; Gates,
Henry Louis, Jr.

singing, 66, 73–74, 92–93, 120, 125, 148–149,
151, 153, 181

slave burials, 80, 84, 92–93, 94, 112–113. *See
also* ritual; slavery

slave burials, 94. *See also* funerals; rituals

slave episteme, 6, 8–9, 21–22, 23, 32. *See also*
slavery; Weinbaum, Alys Eve

slave insurrections, 84, 110. *See also* funerals

slave narratives, 16–17, 19, 20, 74, 163. *See also*
Jacobs, Harriet; Douglass, Frederick

slave rebellions, 110

slavery, 1–41, 44–61, 66, 75, 80, 88, 96–103,
105, 112, 119, 125, 199–201, 211, 222–223.
See also Atlantic slave trade; Middle Passage; slave narratives

Smallwood, Stephanie, 28, 170

Smith, Valerie, 50, 59

social death, 5–6, 28–29, 34, 39; in *Song of
Solomon*, 74; in *Linden Hills*, 79–80, 88, 99,
101–102, 107; in *Praisesong for the Widow*,
140, 154–155; in *The Salt Eaters*, 193, 196;
social life and, 222

social life, 1, 79, 80–81, 83, 93–94, 107, 114,
119, 140, 155–157; in the ghetto, 193, 195,
216, 218, 223

social world, 80, 83. *See also* social life

space: playful reclamation of, 184; for playing,
185. *See also* geography; play; playing

Spillers, Hortense, 117, 150, 152, 167, 201, 223;
grammar and, 11, 13, 16, 22–23, 42; maternal erasure and, 29, 31, 36, 96; *Mama's
Baby*, 1, 2, 4–7, 13–17, 58, 100

spiritual mother, 216, 211

spirituality, 43, 61–62, 69, 71, 74; reawakening, 76, 81, 110, 113; lovemaking and, 137;
the erotic as, 160; music and, 209, 211,
214, 216. *See also* rituals; spiritual mother

St. Clair, Drake, and Horace Cayton, 194–195,
196. *See also* Black Belt; Bronzeville;
ghetto

Stepto, Robert B., 16

storytelling: Afrofuturistic, 9; as maternal
praxis, 47, 67, 172–173; cooking and, 81;
at funerals, 93; the human and, 115, 159;
the semiotic and, 120, 126, 157. *See also*
maternal

suicide: Willa's, 109–111, 116; Velma's, 199,
204–207, 211, 213, 215, 234n11

symbolic order: of racial terror, 1–9, 13–15,
20–24, 27–28, 33–34, 36–39, 42–43,
80, 93, 106; in *Praisesong for the Widow*,
116–150, 154–155, 157–158, 244

thanatology, 226

thanatopolitics, 110

thingification, 24, 29, 41, 97, 152, 156, 224. *See
also* Césaire, Aimé

Till, Emmett, 218

Time on the Cross (Fogel and Engerman), 81,
112–113

touch, 52; Rosalie's, 123, 127, 151, 152; Minnie's, 187, 207, 209–210, 211, 214–215. *See
also* laying on of hands

Traylor, Eleanor W., 211, 216

Troester, Rosalie Riegle, 47, 60–61

Ubuntu, 82, 93, 114. *See also* Africa

underworld: of *homo economicus*, 43, 119,
134, 138, 146, 163, 178–179, 181; Odysseus
and, 70; symbolic, 121–122, 130–131, 142,
145, 168–170. See also *homo economicus*;
neoliberalism

www.ingramcontent.com/pod-product-compliance
Lightning Source LLC
Chambersburg PA
CBHW030300100426
42812CB00002B/518